LOS ANGELES—
CITY OF THE ANGELS?

There were five or six lepers clustered around the entrance to Carnaby's Pit, begging alms and exhibiting their wounds to those willing to pay for a look. An upturned Stetson on the ground before them held an assortment of coins, crumpled dollar and peso notes, and gaily colored pills. Ever since the lepers' numbers had grown too large to ignore, odd rumors had sprung up around them. Many people swore that the Committee was putting something in the water, while others suspected the Arabs. Some blamed the alien Alpha Rats, claiming they were trying to destroy the Earth with "leprosy rays" from the moon.

It was Jonny's opinion that most people were idiots . . .

Ace Science Fiction Specials edited by Terry Carr

METROPHAGE

(A Romance of the Future)

RICHARD KADREY

ACE BOOKS, NEW YORK

This book is an Ace
original edition, and
has never been previously
published.

METROPHAGE
(A Romance of the Future)

An Ace Book/published by arrangement with
the author

PRINTING HISTORY
Ace edition/February 1988

ISBN: 0-441-52813-9

Ace Books are published by The Berkley Publishing Group,
200 Madison Avenue, New York, New York 10016.
The name "ACE" and the "A" logo are
trademarks belonging to Charter Communications, Inc.
PRINTED IN THE UNITED STATES OF AMERICA

10 9 8 7 6 5 4 3 2 1

ACKNOWLEDGMENTS

I would like to thank the following people for help, intentional and otherwise, in the completion of this book: Pat Murphy, Terry Carr, Raymond Embrack, Lisa Goldstein, Rolf Hamburger, Mikey Roessner-Herman, Gustav Hasford, Marc Laidlaw, Kristi Olesen, Ruth Ramos, Avon Swofford, Cherie Wilkerson, Pamela Winfrey, the teachers and students of Clarion '78, all the past and present residents of the Moulton Alamo, and my mother, Jimi Kadrey. I am grateful to physician and author Michael Blumlein, who supplied medical and scientific information for this book. Any screw-ups in these areas are mine.

I would also like to thank Robert Fripp, Brian Eno, Throbbing Gristle, and Tangerine Dream, who supplied the soundtrack.

*This book is dedicated
to Pat, predictably, with love.*

INTRODUCTION

by Rudy Rucker

Like all of the books in the New Ace Science Fiction Specials series, *Metrophage* is a first novel that is strong and strange.

Born in 1957, Richard Kadrey is in love with surrealism. Although he's published a number of stories, he's equally well known for his dadaistic collage illustrations. *Metrophage* has the framework of a fast-paced action story, but it's also true that the book itself is a kind of collage of literature, art history, and Kadrey's own striking images of wonderful drugs and beautiful weapons.

The action takes place in a mongrelized near-future cityscape similar to the Los Angeles that one sees on the *Max Headroom* show. This sleazy, violent, drugged-out, multinational setting is as standard a backdrop for contemporary science fiction as was the spacenavy starship for the science fiction of the Fifties. But Kadrey pastes on layer after layer of sharply caught images, and the final world is something quite new.

"Flattened cans of krill, backs of discarded computer terminals, and insulation tiles from L5 shuttles filled the gaps . . . to form walkways . . ." The walls are so scumbled that gangs etch their graffiti into them with sulfuric acid. One young man, a Zombie Analytic, has his skin wired for video; he is shot and all the images in his software bubble up at once: "The arm Skid held up strobed madly: the arm of a woman, a reptile, an industrial robot; crimson spiders webbed him; amber alphanumerics scrolled up his twisted face; Brando, Lee, Bowie, Vega; his system was looping, the faces flickering by faster and faster, merging into one metafantasy face, colorless, all colors, fading at the same instant it formed." This is seriously passionate hallucination; Tristan Tzara would approve.

Is who? A surrealist, like Luis Buñuel, Salvador Dali, Max Ernst, Marcel Duchamps, William Burroughs, Mark Pauline—all of whom Kadrey happily splices into the *Metrophage* dream machine.

It's nice to see an author conscious of science fiction's ties to anarchism and surrealism. A key anarchist notion informs the machinations of *Metrophage*: the notion of the Spectacle. ". . . the Spectacle is the way the government keeps control. It sets up these mysterious and complex systems . . . , it makes . . . icons of evil. That way, it keeps us isolated and makes us feel like we don't have any control over our own lives." Here and now, the Spectacle is nuclear war, Arab terrorists, Contra aid, and AIDS. The Spectacle in *Metrophage* is much the same.

It's a familiar fact that science-fictional futures are always, at some level, about the present time in which they are actually written. Orwell's *1984* was really 1948. Asimov's *Foundation* is a 1950s America the size of a galaxy. It's also often the case that an SF novel's main character is a stand-in for the author.

Now, *Metrophage*'s hero Jonny is . . . well, a fuck-up—quite unlike the civilized, artistic Richard Kadrey with whom my wife and I dine in San Francisco now and then. Perhaps Jonny is a stage which Richard has lived through. I hope there aren't as many killings in his next book. His official biography alludes to the horror of growing up in Texas with a swarthy complexion, to intense involvements with controlled substances, and to a short stint working with a man who later became Ronald Reagan's joke writer.

Speaking of jokes, my favorite *Metrophage* laugh occurs early on: " 'They just nuked Kansas City. The Jordanian Reunification Army, a New Palestine splinter group. Said Houston's next.' The bartender shook his head. 'Those boys must really hate cows.' "

So here's *Metrophage*, a dazzling pinwheel of a book that spews out eyeball kicks on every page.

Readers who follow science fiction may wonder why I am writing this introduction instead of Terry Carr, who edited the line of Ace Science Fiction Specials both in the 1960s and in the 1980s. Terry died suddenly in the spring of 1987, after editing *Metrophage*, but before he could write the introduction. Terry Carr did a tremendous amount to keep science fiction vital, and he will be missed. May he rest in peace.

Rudy Rucker
Los Gatos, California
June, 1987

Now I lay me down to sleep
I hear the sirens in the street
All my dreams are made of chrome
I have no way to get back home

—Tom Waits

1

THE PETRIFIED CITY

A CRIP BY THE NAME of Easy Money ran the HoloWhores down at a place called Carnaby's Pit. At least he had been running them the last time Jonny Qabbala, drug dealer, ex-Committee for Public Health bounty hunter, and self-confessed loser, had paid him a visit. Jonny was hoping that Easy was still working the Pit. He had a present for him from a dead friend.

The ugly and untimely murder of Raquin, the chemist, had left an empty spot in the pit of Jonny's stomach. Not just because Raquin had been Jonny's connection (since it was a simple matter for Jonny to get his dope directly from Raquin's boss, the smuggler lord Conover), but over the year or so of their acquaintance Raquin had become, to Jonny, something close to a friend. And "close to a friend" was as much as Jonny generally allowed himself to become. It was fear of loss more than any lack of feelings on his part that kept Jonny at a distance from most of the other losers and one-percenters who crowded Los Angeles.

The moon was low in the east, a bone-white sickle. Jonny wondered, idly, if the Alpha Rats were watching Los Angeles that night. What would the extraterrestrials think, through a quarter-million miles of empty space, when they saw him put a bullet through Easy Money's brain?

Jonny caught sight of Carnaby's Pit a few blocks away, quartz prisms projecting captured atrocity videos from the Lunar Border Wars. On a flat expanse of wall above the club's entrance, a New Palestine soldier in a vacuum suit was smashing the faceplate of a Mishima Guardsman. The Guardsman's blood bubbled from his helmet, droplets boiling to hard black jewels as the soundtrack from an ancient MGM musical played in the background: "I want to be loved by you, just you, and nobody else but you . . ." The words CARNABY'S PIT periodically superimposed themselves over the scene in Kanz and Roman characters.

Jonny pushed his way through a group of Pemex-U.S. workers negotiating for rice wine at the weekend mercado that covered the street near Fountain Avenue. The air was thick with the scents of animal waste, sweat, roasting meat, and hashish. Chickens beat their wings against wire cages while legless vat-grown sheep lay docilely in the butchers' stalls, waiting for their turn on the skewers. Old women in hipils motioned Jonny over, holding up bright bolts of cloth, bootleg ROMchips, and glittering butterfly knives. Jonny kept shaking his head. "No, gracias . . . Ima ja naku . . . Nein . . ."

Handsome young Germans, six of them, all in the latest eelskin cowboy boots and silk overalls (marked with the logo of some European movie studio), lugged portable holorecorders between the stalls, making another in their endless series of World Link documentaries about the death of street culture. Those quickly made documentaries and panel discussions about the Alpha Rats (who they were, their intentions, their burden on the economy of the West) seemed to make up the bulk of the Link's broadcasts these days. Jonny swore that if he heard one more learned expert coolly discussing the logic of drug and food rationing, he was going to personally bury fifty kilos of C-4 plastique under the local Link station and make his own contribution to street culture by liberating a few acres of prime urban landscape.

At a stall near the back of the place, an old curandera was selling her evil-eye potions and a collection of malfunctioning robot sentries: cybernetic goshawks, rottweilers, and cougars, simple track-and-kill devices controlled by a tabletop microwave link. The sentries had been very popular with the nouveau riche toward the end of the previous century, but the animals' electronics and maintenance had proven to be remarkably unreliable. Eventually they passed, like much of the mercado's merchandise, down from the hills, through the rigid social strata of L.A., until they landed in the street, last stop before the junk heap.

There by the twitching, half-growling animals, the film crew set up their lights. Jonny hung around and watched them block out shots. The filmmakers infuriated him, but in their own way, Jonny knew, they were right.

The market was dying. When he had been a boy, Jonny remembered, it sprawled over a dozen square blocks. Now it barely managed to occupy two. And most of the merchandise was junk. Chromium paint flaked off the electronic components, revealing ancient rusted works. The hydroponically grown fruits and vegetables grew steadily smaller and more tasteless each season. All that seemed to keep the market going was the communally owned bank of leaking solar batteries. During the rolling brown-outs, they alone kept the tortilla ovens hot, the fluorescents flickering, the videos cranking.

"Isn't it time you kids were in bed?" Jonny asked, stepping on the toes of a lanky blond cameraman. "Sprechen sie 'parasite'?"

Huddled in the doorways of clubs and arcades, groups of fingerprint changers, nerve-tissue merchants, and brain-cell thieves regarded the crowd with hollow eyes, as if assessing their worth in cash at every moment. The gangs, too, were out in force that hot night: the Lizard Imperials (snakeskin boots and surgically split tongues), the Zombie Analytics (subcutaneous pixels offering up flickering flesh-images of dead video and rock stars), the anarchist-physician Croakers, the Yakuza Rebels, and the Gypsy Titans. Even the Naginata Sisters were out, swinging blades and drinking on the corner in front of the Iron Orchid.

As Jonny crossed Sunset, a few of the Sisters waved to him. When he waved back, a gust of wind pulled open his tunic, revealing his Futukoro automatic. The Sisters whooped and laughed at the sight of the weapon, feigning terror. A tall Sister with Maori facial tattoos crooked her finger and began blasting him with an imaginary gun.

Coming toward him from the opposite direction was a ring of massive Niku Yaro Meat Boys—uniformly ugly acromegalic giants, each easily three meters tall. In the center of the protective ring, an old Yakuza oyabun openly stared and pointed at people. It was rare enough for people to see a pureblood Japanese in the street that they stopped to stare back, until the Meat Boys cuffed them away. Jonny thought of a word then.

Gaijin. Foreigner. Alien.

That's me. I'm gaijin, Jonny thought. He could find little

comfort in the familiarity of the streets. Jonny realized that by acknowledging his desire to kill Easy Money, he had cut himself off from everybody around him. He walked more slowly. Twice he almost turned back.

A tiny nisei girl tried to sell him a peculiar local variation on sushi—refried beans and raw tuna wrapped in a corn husk—commonly known as a Salmonella Roll. Jonny declined and ducked into an alley. There, he swallowed two tabs of Desoxyn, hijacked from a Committee warehouse.

It was good stuff. Very soon, a tingling began in his fingertips and moved up his arms, filling him with a pleasantly tense, almost sexual energy. Beads of sweat broke out on his hands and face, ran down his chest. He thought of Sumi.

"I might not be back tonight," he had told her before he left the squat they shared. "Uno tareja. Got some deliveries to make," he lied. "Routine stuff."

"Then why are you taking that blunderbuss?" Sumi asked, pointing to the Futukoro pistol.

Jonny ignored her question and tried to look very interested in the process of lacing up his steel-tipped boots. Sumi terrified him. Sometimes, in his more callous moments, he considered her a slip-up, his one remaining abandonment to emotional ties. Occasionally, when he felt strong, he would admit to himself that he loved her.

"I'll be passing through the territories of a dozen gangs tonight, and then if I'm *lucky* I'll be landing in Carnaby's Pit. That's why the blunderbuss," he said. "I should be taking a Committee battalion with me."

"I bet they'd be thrilled if you called them."

"I bet you're right."

Almond-eyed Sumi stroked his hair with delicate, calloused hands. He had met her at the zendo of an old Buddhist nun. The Zen study had not stuck, but Sumi had. Her full name, Sumimasen, meant variously "thank you," "I'm sorry," and "this never ends." She had been on her own almost as long as Jonny. Along the way, she had picked up enough electronics to make her living as a Watt Snatcher: for a fee she would tap right into the government's electric lines under the city and siphon off power for her customers.

Jonny got up and Sumi put her arms around him, thrusting her belly at the pistol in his belt.

"Is that your gun or are you just happy to see me?" Sumi asked. She did a whole little act, rolling her eyes and purring in her best vamp voice. But her nervousness was obvious.

Jonny bent and kissed the base of her neck, held her long enough to reassure, then longer. He felt her tense up again, under his hands.

"I'll be back," he said.

During the last few months, Jonny had begun to worry about leaving Sumi alone. Officially, the government's power lines did not exist. All the more reason the State would like to wipe out the Watt Snatchers. All the gangs were outlaws, technically. The elements of the equation were simple: its components were the price of survival divided by the risks that survival demanded. And in an age of rationing and manufactured shortages, survival meant the black market. The gangs produced whatever the smuggler lords couldn't bring in. And the pushers sold it on the streets.

Jonny had chosen his own brand of survival when he'd walked away from the Committee for Public Health and thrown in with the pushers. It was a simple question of karma. Now he worked the black market, selling any drugs the smuggler lords could supply—antibiotics, LSD analogs, beta-endorphins, MDMA, skimming the streets on a razor-sharp high compounded of adrenaline and paranoia.

In his more philosophical moments, it seemed to Jonny that they were all engaged in nothing more than some bizarre battle of symbols. What the smuggler lords and gangs provided —food, power, and drugs—had become the ultimate symbols of control in their world. The Federales could not afford to ease up their rationing of medical treatment, access to public utilities, and food distribution. They had learned long ago how easy it was to control vast numbers of people simply by worrying them into submission, keeping them busy hustling to stay alive.

Los Angeles, as such, had ceased to exist. L.A., however —the metaphorical heart and soul of the city—was alive and kicking. An L.A. of the mind, playground of trade and commerce: the City of Night. Known in the local argot as Last Ass, Lonesome Angels, the Laughing Adder, Los Angeles existed in the rarefied state of many port cities, functioning mainly as a downloading point for a constant stream of data, foreign currency, dope, and weapons that flowed onto the continent from all over the world.

It was the worst-kept secret in the street that half the State Legislature had their fingers deep in the black market pie. Like some fragile species of hothouse orchid, the city existed only as long as it had the politicos' backing. Without that, the Committee would be on them like rabid dogs. For the moment, though, the balance was there. Merchandise flowed out and cash flowed in, blood and breath of the city.

Jonny understood all this and accepted the tightrope existence. He knew too that someday the whole thing was going to crash. It was their collective karma. Sooner or later some politico was going to get greedy, try to undercut one of the gangs or simply sell them out for a vote. And the Committee would move in. Jonny knew that this knowledge should make a difference, but it did not.

In the alley, the speed came on like an old friend, an electric hum up and down his spine. Suddenly all things were possible. The nervous glare of neon signs and halogen street lamps domed Sunset in a pulsing nimbus of come-on colors. Stepping from the alley, Jonny barely felt his boots on the pavement. Easy Money was as good as dead.

There were five or six lepers clustered around the entrance to Carnaby's Pit, begging alms and exhibiting their wounds to those willing to pay for a look. An upturned Stetson on the ground before them held an assortment of coins, crumpled dollar and peso notes, and gaily colored pills. Ever since the lepers' numbers had grown too large to ignore, odd rumors had sprung up around them. Many people swore that the Committee was putting something in the water, while others suspected the Arabs. Some blamed the Alpha Rats, claiming they were trying to destroy the Earth with "leprosy rays" from the moon. It was Jonny's opinion that most people were idiots.

One leper in a ragged spacer uniform was reciting in a low whiskey voice:

> "The streets breathe, ebb and flow like the
> seas beneath a sodden twilight eye.
> The sky appears from a maw of rooftops.

Dusk streets, dry fountains
coax the cemetery stars."

Jonny pulled a few Dapsone and tetrahydrocannabinol capsules from his pouch and dropped them into the battered Stetson. The leper who had been reciting, his head and face heavily bandaged, opened his jacket.

"Thank you, friend," the leper said through broken lips, pointing to his freshest scars.

Nodding politely, Jonny left the lepers and stepped down into the Pit.

The skyline tilted, angled steeply downward, then up, became a vertical blur of mirrored windows, skyscrapers leading to a hologram star field. Jonny was in the Pit's game parlor, separated from the bar by a dirty lotus-print curtain. Around the edges of the room, antique pinball machines beeped and rang prosaically while the air in the center of the parlor burned with the phantom light of hologram games. Crossing the parlor, Jonny was caught in a spray of hot-blue laser blasts from Sub-Orbital Commando, showered with fragments of pint-sized galaxies spinning from Vishnu and Shiva's hands. Rat-sized nudes swarmed above his head, frantically groping at each other for Fun In Zero-G.

One angry pinball player threw a glass and it shattered against the far wall. Jonny stepped back as two members of the Pit's own Meat Boys moved smoothly from opposite ends of the room to intercept the shouting man.

"Goddamit, this machine just ate my last dollar!" screamed the pinball player.

He was still screaming as the two beefy monsters grabbed an arm apiece and ushered him through the front doors. They came back alone. Jonny half expected to see them return with the guy's arms.

"Peace! Can't we have a little peace in here?" mumbled a sweating man lining up Jacqueline Kennedy in the sights of a fiberglass reproduction of a Mannlicher-Carcano rifle. It was Smokefinger, the pickpocket, fat and nervous, jacked into the Date With Destiny game by a length of pencil-thin cable extending from the game console to a 24-prong mini-plug implanted at the base of his skull. Most of the players in the room were jacked into various games by similar plugs.

Jonny's stomach fluttered at the sight. Elective surgery, he had decided years before, did not extend to having little platinum bullets permanently jammed into his skull, thank you. He could watch the World Link on a monitor, and as for the games, they seemed real enough without skull-plugs.

Smokefinger tracked the ghostly hologram of the presidential limousine as crimson numbers flickered in the metallic-blue Dallas sky, reading out his score.

Jonny leaned close to the pickpocket's ear and said, "How's it going, Smoke?" Smokefinger ignored him and continued to move the toy rifle with steady, insectlike concentration. "Hey Smoke," said Jonny, waving his fingers before Smokefinger's eyes just as the fat man pulled the trigger.

No score. "Shit," mumbled the pickpocket, still ignoring Jonny. He had aced the chauffeur.

This wasn't going to be any fun at all, Jonny decided. He pushed the release button on the plug at the back of Smokefinger's head. The wire dropped and a spring-loaded coil drew it back inside the game console.

"What the hell—" yelled Smokefinger, grabbing for his neck. He looked at Jonny dumbly as his eyes slowly refocused. In a moment, he said, "Hey Jonny, qué pasa?"

"Not much," Jonny said. "I can't believe you're still playing this game. Haven't you killed everybody in Dallas by now?"

Smokefinger shrugged. "I pop 'em, but they keep coming back." Sweat pooled on the pickpocket's glasses where the rims touched his cheeks.

Jonny smiled and looked around the room, hoping there was anyone else from whom he might get information. However, in the pastel glare of meteor showers and laser fire, none of the faces looked familiar. "You seen Easy Money around?" he asked Smokefinger. "I've got to talk to him."

"Right, talk. You and everybody else." Smokefinger looked back at the empty hologram chamber and cursed. "I almost broke my own record, you know," he said. He looked at Jonny accusingly. "No, I ain't seen Easy. Random's tending bar tonight. Maybe you should go talk to him. To tell you the truth, you're distracting me." Smokefinger never took his finger from the trigger of the fiberglass rifle. Jonny pulled some yen coins from his pocket and fed them into the machine.

"Thanks for all your help, killer," he said. But Smoke-finger did not hear him; he was already jacking in. Jonny left Smokefinger, wishing he could find peace as easily as that, and pushed his way into the bar.

Jonny always found it a little disconcerting that the main room never seemed to change. He imagined it frozen in time, like a scratched record repeating the same snatch of lyric over and over again. The usual weekend crowd of small-time smugglers, B actors, and bored prostitutes stared from the blue veil of smoke around the bar. The same tired porn played on the big screen for the benefit of those unfortunates not equipped with skull-plugs. Even the band, Taking Tiger Mountain, was blasting the same old riffs, stopping halfway through their own "Guernica Rising" when the crowd shouted them down. They switched to a desultory "Brown Sugar," a song that had been out of date long before anybody in the club had been born. Dancers undulated under the strobes and sub-sonic mood enhancers as projectors threw holograms of lunar atrocities onto their hot bodies.

In fact, the only real difference Jonny could see in the place was the darkness in the HoloWhores' bundling booths.

Jonny pushed his way through the tightly packed crowd and tried the door to Easy's control room. It was locked, and the bar far too full to force the door. He would have to wait. Feeling relief, and guilt at that relief, Jonny made his way to the bar for a drink and some questions.

Random, the bartender, was drying glasses behind a bar constructed of old automobile dashboards. Tall and thin, his skin creased like dead leaves, Random offered Jonny the same half-smile he offered everybody. Jonny ordered an Asahi dark and gin; he put a twenty on the bar. Random set down the beer and slid the bill into his pocket in one smooth motion.

The bartender inclined his head toward the dance floor. "Necrophiliacs," he said above the roar of the band. "They can't stand new music. Like it's deadly to them or something. Bunch of assholes." Random shrugged. Then he looked away, like a blind man, eyes unfocused. "They just nuked Kansas City. The Jordanian Reunification Army, a New Palestine splinter group. They called the local World Link Station. Said Houston's next," he reported. The bartender shook his head. "Those boys must really hate cows." Random had a passion for morbid news and stayed plugged into the Link's data lines constantly, relaying the most worthy bits to his customers. Jonny thought it was one of his most charming qualities.

He turned back to Jonny as if anticipating his question. "Easy split. Been gone a couple of days now. Left quick, too. Didn't touch his holo stuff."

"I don't suppose you have any idea where he went," said Jonny.

"I'm afraid he neglected to leave a forwarding address. A shame, too, so close to Thanksgiving and all."

The band's volume jumped abruptly as they broke from the song into a tense, rhythmic jam. Saint Peter, the guitarist, stood at the edge of the stage between soaring liquid-cooled stacks of Krupp-Verwandlungsinhalt speakers. Eyes squeezed shut, shoulders loose, Saint Peter pumped walls of noise, his myoelectric left hand racing like a frantic silver spider up and down the fretboard. As he played, a pattern of light glinted off the chrome hand, marking its progress through the air. Then, just as the jam reached its peak, the song died; the porn faded and the lights dimmed. "Brown-out," said Random. He casually threw a switch under the bar and the power returned. "Tell Sumi gracias for the watts," he said.

Jonny nodded. "Did you hear that Easy had another Flare Gun Party?" he asked.

"No. Who got burned?"

"Raquin."

Random raised an eyebrow in sympathy. "Sorry, man," he said. "Although I must admit I'm not entirely surprised to hear he's been up to something." He took a long hit from a hookah next to the cash register. "Looking for Easy Money seems to be the hot new game in town. Last night the crowd was so thick I had 'em line up and take numbers. Of course, Easy's not the only one who seems to have captured the public's imagination." Random smiled at Jonny. "You appear to have developed a bit of celebrity all your own."

"Me?" Jonny asked guardedly. "Who's been asking about me?"

Random shrugged. "No one I knew." The bartender winked conspiratorially. "Come on, boy-o. Whose ankles have you been nipping at?"

"I am pathetically clean," Jonny said. "Tell me about them. Anything you can remember."

Random stuck two nicotine-yellow fingers into his shirt

pocket and pulled out a glicene envelope of white powder.
"Pure as Mother Mary and twice as nice," he said, giving the
envelope a light kiss. "Interesting lads. They didn't try to pay
off in crude cash." He dropped the envelope back into his
pocket.

"Smugglers?" asked Jonny.

"Could be, only what's a smuggler lord doing shooting for
small shit like Easy Money? Or you, for that matter."

"Who knows," Jonny said. He took a long gulp of his
drink. "Maybe he's decided he's in the wrong business."

"Hell," said the bartender, "everybody in Last Ass's in the
wrong business."

Random set down the glass he had been cleaning and said,
"Weather." His eyes shifted. "Junior Senator on the Atmo-
spheric Management Committee announced they can clean up
the mess left by the Weather Wars. Says they ought to be able
to stabilize weather patterns over most of North America in
three to five years."

"Didn't they announce that same program three to five
years ago?" asked Jonny.

"At least." And with that, Random gave Jonny the other
half of the smile and moved on to other customers.

Swirling the dregs of his beer, Jonny turned and studied the
noisy crowd moving through the bar. He searched their heads
for a sign of goat horns grafted above a thin face, inset with
darting, suspicious eyes. Or arms thick with tattooed serpents,
like the stigmata of some junky god. Easy Money always
stood out in a crowd—which, Jonny supposed, was the idea.
If Easy was around, he should not be hard to spot.

Jonny had met Easy while they had both been in the em-
ploy of the smuggler lord Conover. This had been just after
Easy had made a name for himself with his first Flare Gun
Party.

The party had become something of a legend with the
pushers. It had gone like this: Easy Money, a human parasite
with the unerring ability to detect the softest, most vulnerable
part of his prey, had acquired a contract to kill the leader of
the Los Santos Atomicos gang. Beginning with a philosophy
that later became his trademark (like the hourglass on the belly
of a spider), Easy reasoned that with gang retribution being
such a swift and ugly thing, eliminating the entire gang would
be less trouble than the removal of any single member.

It was well known to those like Easy, who always kept a metaphorical ear to the ground, that the Los Santos Atomicos gang's particular vice was free-basing cocaine. Easy located their safe-house with information from a rival gang. He also found that the Los Santos Atomicos liked to buy in bulk the ether they used to treat the coke. They kept big tanks of the stuff hidden under the floor.

As he was fond of saying, from there it was easy money.

Like some stoned Prometheus, Easy brought fire to the Los Santos Atomicos in the form of a red Navy signal flare that he fired into their lab from the roof of a Catholic mission across the street. The explosion literally ripped the roof off the ether-filled building. The fireball boiled down onto many of the adjoining buildings, igniting them, too.

Besides the Los Santos Atomicos, at least a dozen other people, mainly junkies and prostitutes, died in the fires that engulfed the grimy neighborhood. And Easy Money moved up a rung in the hierarchy of the movers and shakers in their little world.

Looking back, none of it had seemed important to Jonny at the time. When he'd heard of the deaths it had seemed somehow normal, just one more senseless act in the long series of senseless acts that made up their lives. However, Raquin's death had moved events from the abstract into a personal affront. He knew Raquin. And he knew Easy had killed him. Jonny would finish Easy Money simply because nobody else would and because the little prick deserved it.

Jonny slowed his breathing, counted each intake of breath, centering himself as his roshi had taught him. Visions of horned, tattooed Easy swam before him as he hunted for that savage part of himself he had sought before whenever he'd had to kill.

But the passion was gone, seemed pointless now. The speed had been cut with something unpleasant. It was wearing off already, leaving him feeling numb and stupid. Jonny gulped down the rest of his beer and tried to get into the buzz from the liquor.

He wondered if perhaps he had figured things wrong. If the smuggler lords really were after Easy, maybe he was not needed after all. There was always work to do, money to be made. But something bothered Jonny. He could not figure out who, besides the Committee, would be looking for him. Had he trod on someone's toes in the last few days of looking for Easy? He could not remember.

The bar seemed to tip slightly as Jonny downed his second Asahi and gin. When he wiped a hand across his brow it came away cool and covered with sweat. He left the bar, pushing carelessly through a tight knot of nervous teenagers from the Valley made up to look like they had grafts and implants. Near the restroom, a Zombie Analytic flashed Jonny, in quick succession: Marilyn Monroe, Jim Morrison, and Aoki Vega. He ignored her.

Inside the restroom, Jonny splashed rusty water onto his face. The room stank of human waste, and the paper towel dispenser was empty. On the floor he found half a copy of *Twilight of the Gods*. The toilet was full of Nietzsche. Jonny dried his hands with the few remaining pages. The water made him feel a little better. However, the comedown from the speed had left him jumpy and nervous.

When Jonny left the restroom, a hand clamped on his arm.

"Jonny, how's it going?" asked a short man Jonny did not recognize. The man's smile was wide and toothy, intended to give the impression that he was a very dangerous character. He wore shades whose lenses were dichromatic holograms depicting some cavern. Where his eyes should have been were twin bottomless pits.

"That's a good way to lose some teeth or an eye," Jonny said evenly.

The little man's smile faded only slightly. He relaxed his grip on Jonny's arm, but did not release him.

"Sorry, Jonny," he said. "Look, could I buy you a drink or something?"

"No."

Jonny shook off the little man's grip and headed back to the bar to get drunk. But again, strong fingers caught him.

"Where are you going in such a hurry?" the little man asked. "Let's talk. I've got a deal for you."

Jonny jammed his elbow into the little man's midsection, spun and pressed the barrel of the Futukoro into the man's throat.

"If you ever grab me again, I will kill you. Do you understand that?" Jonny whispered.

The little man released Jonny's arm and stepped back, his

hands held in front of his chest, palms out. "It's cool," the little man said giddily. "It's cool."

Jonny pushed the man away roughly and left him chattering to himself.

He was sweating again. Jonny went back to the bar and drank cheap fishy-tasting Japanese vodka, thinking about how vile it was and how he wished he could afford the good stuff. He put the little man out of his mind. Jonny wondered if he should call Sumi, but that seemed like a bad idea. She would ask questions he did not want to answer. Eventually, his thoughts drifted to Raquin. Jonny wondered what it was like to burn to death. He remembered that someone had once told him that you would not feel anything, that the fire would consume all the oxygen and you would smother before you ever felt the flames. That seemed like small comfort. How much better was it to smother than to burn?

Jonny continued drinking straight shots of the fishy vodka until the taste disappeared altogether. Taking six of the shot glasses, he constructed a little pyramid, but Random took the glasses away and soon Jonny ran out of money. While he was fishing in his pouch for more dope, there was a slight tug on his arm. Somehow, when he turned, Jonny knew the little man would be standing there. His shades were off and he held his hands up as if to ward off a blow.

"Truce, okay? I did not grab you," the little man said. "I just tapped you on the shoulder."

Jonny nodded. "I could tell you were quick. What do you want?"

The man leaned forward anxiously.

"Look Jonny, I didn't want to tell you before—I'm working for Mister Conover. He sent me to get you. If you don't come back with me, my ass is grass."

"Sorry to hear that. Tell Mister Conover I'll get in touch with him as soon as I'm through with the deal I'm working on now."

"I can't do that. He wants you now," said the little man. Hopefully, he added, "You know that whatever it is you're working on, Mister Conover will make it worth your while to drop."

Jonny shook his head.

"No thanks; this is personal."

The little man leaned closer. "You aren't looking for Easy Money, are you?"

"What if I am?"

"Well, that's great," said the little man. "That's the job— Easy Money copped something that belongs to Mister Conover. And Mister Conover wants you to help him get it back."

Jonny nodded, took a piece of ice from someone's empty glass, and rubbed it across his forehead. "My problem, friend, is that I know Mister Conover pretty well and I know that he is a professional," Jonny said. "No offense, but why would he send a hard guy like you to get me?"

The little man looked around, apparently to make sure that nobody was eavesdropping. "This really isn't my job," he whispered.

Jonny smiled. "No shit?" he said.

"I'm more of a bookkeeper. It's just that Mister Conover's got all his muscle guys out looking for Easy Money," he said. The little man looked at Jonny gravely. "You know how it is."

"Yeah, I know how it is," said Jonny, genuinely amused.

"He told me that you always hang out at Carnaby's Pit," the little man continued. He made a face as if he had just smelled something foul. "To tell you the truth, it's a little bit much for me."

Jonny laughed. "Sometimes it's a bit much for me, too," he said.

The little man smiled—for real, this time. "Then you'll come with me?" he asked.

Jonny shrugged. "That stuff about looking for Easy, you weren't just being cute again, were you?"

"No, all that was true," he said.

"Good."

"Then you'll come?"

"I'm not sure. I hate to beat a point to death, but how do I know you work for Mister Conover?"

"Oh yeah," said the little man, brightening. He reached into his jacket pocket. "Mister Conover said to give you this."

He handed Jonny a plastic bag containing two gelatinous blue capsules. The manufacturer's markings were Swiss, the capsules NATO issue, banded with an orange warning stripe indicating myotoxins. Jonny had seen the stuff on the Committee. Frosty the Snowman. It was a necrotic, a synthetic variation on pit viper venom that killed by breaking down collagen fibers, effectively dissolving skin and muscle tissue. The NATO variation, he had heard, was constructed with certain "open" segments along its DNA chain, allowing the toxin to bind with polypeptides in the victim's collagen and replicate itself there. Rumor had it that Frosty could break down the skin and muscle tissue of seventy-kilo man in just under fourteen hours. It was not the kind of drug that many people would have access to. Jonny stuffed the bag into his pouch.

"So, I'm convinced," he said.

"Then you'll come?"

"Why not," he said. "I'm not getting anywhere here."

The little man beamed at him. Jonny thought it might be love.

"By the way, have you got a name?" Jonny asked.

"Cyrano. Bender Cyrano, like the guy in the old book, you know? Only I haven't got the nose." Cyrano laughed at his joke.

Jonny did not know what the hell Cyrano was talking about, but he smiled so as not to hurt the little man's feelings. When Cyrano extended his hand, Jonny shook it.

"Nice to meet you, Cyrano. Let's get out of here," said Jonny.

When they reached the dirty curtain, Jonny turned and took a last look at the band. They were burning through one of Saint Peter's best tunes, "Street Prince." The crowd ignored them, utterly.

Random was right, Jonny decided. A bunch of assholes.

Outside, the hot night had cooled somewhat. That usually meant that the street people would haunt Sunset Boulevard until dawn, but an uneasy silence had settled upon the street. A scrap of paper, plucked up by the wind, did a careless pirouette before being carried away. A quiet crowd had gathered across the street, watching the club. Jonny took a step back. Cyrano walked on a few steps before he noticed that Jonny was no longer there.

"What's wrong?" he asked.

Jonny had been barely six when the first of the Protein Rebellions took place. That was when the citizens of Los Angeles, inspired by uprisings in other cities, rose up and wrecked the Griffith Park Zoo in search of fresh meat. The riots were finally put down, but not until ten days of fighting

had left the city little more than an open wound. The official
body count was something like 10,000 civilian and military
dead.

The authorities, however, had not been caught entirely un-
prepared. Many in power had seen what was coming. Plans
were pushed forward, timetables scrapped, and those select
few, wealthy enough to buy entrance or powerful enough to
demand it, began their silent pilgrimages deep into the desert
to government-sponsored havens like New Hope.

The rest of the city had remained behind with the rest of
the solution. The rest of the solution, in this case, was a para-
military organization known, without apparent irony, as the
Committee for Public Health. And several armed members of
that organization were waiting for Jonny when he left Car-
naby's Pit.

Spotlights hit Jonny and Cyrano from across the street.

An adolescent, bullhorned voice called, "Do not move.
You are both under arrest."

Jonny dropped to the ground, pulling his gun. Cyrano
awkwardly wrestled a Mexican Barretta from his belt and got
off one shot before a Futukoro blast ripped into his chest. The
little man fell on Jonny, bleeding everywhere, looking horri-
fied. He clutched at the wound, as if by holding it closed he
could keep his life from slipping out. Jonny looked up in time
to see the leper in the Spacer uniform peering at him from
around the side of the bar.

Automatic weapons fire bit into the front of the Pit as the
Committee opened up. Shattered glass and concrete showered
down on Jonny as he flattened himself on the ground. From
behind, the door of the bar burst open and a phalanx of the
Pit's Meat Boys emerged, armed to the teeth. Jonny wanted
very much to disappear.

Across Sunset, the evening crowds were pinned down in
windows and doorways, watching the fire fight. Occasionally,
one or two kids wearing gang colors would make a break into
the open and run across Sunset, waving and shouting as they
reached the other side alive. A young, fat Gypsy Titan started
across behind his faster friend. It looked as if the fat boy
would make it, when a shot spun him around. He tore at the
long scarf knotted about his throat before collapsing between
two parked cars.

Jonny heard orders barked from somewhere in the dark and

the sound of scrambling feet. The Meat Boys were fanning out, covering the entrance of the Pit. No escape that way. Why the hell were the Meat Boys fighting the Committee? Jonny wondered. Must think it's some rogue gang trying to shake them down.

Jonny pressed close to the building for cover. Sounds like thunder, breaking glass, and splintering wood enclosed him. He tried to crawl behind the Meat Boys, but they were moving all over the street.

At the side of the bar, Jonny saw the leper again, giving him the finger with one diseased hand. At that instant, Jonny recognized him. Even with the bandages and the uniform, he knew the leper was Easy Money. Jonny took a shot at him, but Easy ducked behind the building.

Again the door to Carnaby's Pit burst open and Smoke-finger came running out. He was screaming what sounded like "Motherfuckers" at the top of his lungs. His right arm was a mass of wet red flesh. Running into the street, he was cut to pieces by Committee cross fire.

Jonny made a break for the alley behind the Pit. Moving quickly to a low crouch, he crawled around the perimeter of the building. He'd almost made it when he felt a terrible kick in his shoulder. Jonny's muscles turned to water.

Sometime later, he was not sure how long, Jonny awoke in the alley. He had no idea how he had gotten there.

He could still hear occasional bursts of automatic weapons fire. When he tried to stand, Jonny discovered that his whole right arm was numb.

With his left arm Jonny grabbed the rim of an overflowing dumpster and pulled himself to his feet. It took him a few seconds to find his balance, but when he did, he started running to the exit at the far end of the alley.

Somewhere along the way, a boot whipped out of the darkness and sent him sprawling.

Oh fuck, Jonny thought.

This time, he did not get up.

2

HISTORY, PAYBACK, AND AN
UNHAPPY REUNION
IN THE BELLY OF THE BEAST

THE GREATER SOUTHERN CALIFORNIA Detention facility: an
ant hill; a graveyard; a factory where souls were processed,
packaged, and delivered to what some laughingly called jus-
tice. At least, many on the inside (guards and prisoners alike)
had heard rumors to that effect. Rumors of the search for
justice. Memos were circulated about it. Petitions were signed
for it. Statues of Greek goddesses brandishing scales were
erected to it. Still, few had seen any sign of it.

The prison squatted, blank and huge, by the port in what
was left of the old warehouse district. Built on the bones of an
old liquid-natural-gas plant, it had originally been envisioned
as the location for the flagship lab of the Pentagon's notorious
genetic warfare programs in the late nineteen nineties. The
building had sat unused when the government's war plans ran
out of steam and money at the same time. It was not until
eighteen months later, with a few billion yen to back it up,
that the order had come down to pull out the half-finished labs
and begin slicing up the old storage tanks, refitting them to
form the cell walls within the new facility.

The majority of the prison's bulk was hidden, sunk deep
into the ancient pig iron waste pits. Lichen-streaked, great
solid planes of cracked concrete rose at severe angles to a flat
roof studded with sealed cooling ducts and dish antennae. A
damp ocean breeze kept the walls of the prison perpetually
glistening, the concrete stinking with a thousand dock smells:
the ozone residue of synthetic fuels, overripe fruit, rusting
machinery, dead fish.

A common joke was that the average prisoner was doing

19

five to ten while the guards were doing nine to five. They, like the prisoners, were just trying to get by. They were young men mostly, Jonny's age and a little older. Primarily recruits from the Committee for Public Health, at twenty the boys were already considered too old for street duty, burned out on the Committee's steady diet of speed and anabolic steroids.

Two years earlier, with motives as mysterious to himself as anybody else, Jonny had joined the Committee. Indifference and boredom seemed to be his main reasons. A few years as a petty thief and courier for the smugglers had left him fast on his feet and quick with a knife and pistol. Still, he remained naive enough to be surprised when it was these same criminal qualities that had helped land him a high-paying job with the Committee.

After his training, Jonny had been assigned to what was called "Perimeter Maintenance." The mechanics of the job were not too different from what he had been doing all his life—meeting with thieves, tracking down warehouses of stolen drugs and food. However, the Committee had little patience with prisoners; they had paid him a commission for each smuggler he had killed above his quota. Recruits were encouraged to compete. Body counts were posted at Committee headquarters; there were bonuses and prizes to be won at the end of each month.

Jonny had tried to make the best of it, telling himself how much better it was to be off the streets and on the side of power for a change. But killing for the Committee did not make any more sense than killing for the smugglers. Sometimes, when he was helping load bodies into transports after a raid, Jonny would see a face he recognized: a junky from the Strip, a panhandler, a street musician. More than once, in the hallucinatory haze of the synth-fuel's fumes and halogen lamps, he thought he saw his own face among the dead.

And he had grown increasingly dependent on the speed. He simply could not let go; the comedown was too awful. Without the speed he would begin to think again.

Jonny had never known self-loathing before, but there it was. He had sudden bouts of vertigo, mouth ulcers, cramps in the gun hand. He had found himself growing more sympathetic to the cause of the smugglers; at least he understood their motives. In the end it simply grew too ugly, the self-deceptions too obvious for him to continue.

The manner of his desertion, however, was more complicated. It was generally known that he had turned in his uniform, pressed and clean, and had picked up the last of his commissions. But he had never turned in his pistol. That became significant later when his immediate superior, a one-eyed brute named Cawfly, was found shot through his good eye.

And Jonny, barely twenty-one, in his inevitable search for the point of least resistance, had drifted back to the streets. No longer resisting the flow of events or pretending to chart a course through them, he existed by luck. But that was before; now it seemed even that had deserted him.

He awoke, with a small cry, to the stink of vomit and antiseptic in a damp, gray holding cell. As the sound of his cry died away, Jonny rolled onto his side, where he was distressed to find that the vomit he smelled was his own. His left hand was resting in a small pool of the stuff. His mouth burned with bile.

He lay on a bare aluminum cot frame, his head spinning, wondering where he was. Eventually, he was able to focus on the wall. GAMMA LOVES RAMON and DEZ were scratched there, and THE EXQUISITE CORPSE WILL DRINK THE NEW WINE. Much of the graffiti was in Spanish and Japanese. He was too tired to translate, but he did not need to. He already knew what it said. "Fuck you!" or "I didn't do it" or just "Let me out!" The international language of the dispossessed. He grinned; it was almost comforting. Jonny knew where he was now.

When he tried to sit up, he found that his right shoulder was wrapped in gauze and a thermoplastic carapace. For a terrible instant he panicked, but relaxed when he felt the reassuring bulge of his arm, intact under the cast.

Rubbing his injured arm, Jonny tried to figure out who had turned him. It was clearly no coincidence that the Committee had been waiting for him outside Carnaby's Pit. It was possible, he thought, that it had been a routine sweep for all pushers, but that did not seem likely. "Deep shit," he said to the empty cell. "Extremely deep shit."

He was almost asleep when the polarized glass panel on his cell door blinked to the transparent, then darkened. Jonny lay still on the aluminum frame as the cell door scraped open. He heard whispers—three or four distinct voices. Annoyance and nervousness. He kept his eyes closed. The door opened further, then closed quickly. The voices stopped. Jonny was aware of somebody standing over him.

"Is that him?" came a low, adolescent voice.

"Yeah, I think so," said a different voice.

"He's a skinny motherfucker. Look like mi pegueña hermana," came a third, huskier voice.

"That gives you ideas, man?"

"Yeah—I'm gonna cut him."

"Hey, don't—"

Jonny heard the metallic *snick* of a switchblade opening. He did not move.

"Touch him and we're dead. He's tagged, man."

"Doesn't look special."

"I seen his files. Interrogacion especial."

"Man, I'm not going to kill him," came the husky voice. "Just gonna get a knuckle or part of his ear."

"No!"

"Who's gonna stop me?"

Jonny swung one steel-tipped boot into the gut of a blond boy and the other onto the floor, screaming like a lunatic, letting his momentum carry him up and toward the door. The other boys fell back without being touched, too surprised to stop him.

He almost had the door open before they came to their senses and grabbed him. But he kept moving, biting fingers, kicking shins, not letting them get a good grip. Finally, a boy with some sort of scarring on his hands and neck caught him with a smooth uppercut of the jaw. Jonny went down on his face. The scarred boy rolled him over and dropped onto his chest, bringing the switchblade up level with Jonny's throat. The other boys crowded in behind him, grumbling and shaking their injured hands and legs. Jonny realized that the hands of the boy holding the knife were covered with sores, similar to leprosy lesions.

"You funny, man?" the boy with the knife demanded. "What's your story?"

"Fuck you, la chinga," said Jonny.

The boy sliced Jonny's cheek. "You're dead, man. I don't care who you are," he said.

"You haven't got the cojones."

"You got to stick him, now. He'll tell," said the blond boy.

Jonny twisted around and kicked the blond boy again. The boy on his chest punched his throat.

"What are you doing?" came a new voice.

The boys drew back abruptly, staring guiltily at the door. The boy with the knife stood up and glanced at his nervous accomplices, then back at the door. All Jonny could see from the floor was a pair of highly polished boots and a sleeve with lieutenant's stripes.

"I asked what you were doing," said the lieutenant.

The boy with the lesions pointed to Jonny. "He was trying to escape. We stopped him."

The lieutenant nodded. "What were you doing in this cell?"

The boy glanced at his friends for support. They would not look at him. "I told you, man. He was trying to escape," he said.

"Don't lie to me."

The boys in the back of the cell, the blond and a tall mestizo with bad teeth, stared at the floor. Jonny guessed that they were about sixteen. The boy with the knife looked to be a year or two older. The insignia on his Committee uniform indicated that he was a corporal. That explained it, then. It had all been good, clean fun. An older boy out to show his young friends a good time.

The lieutenant made a curt gesture with his hand. "Get him up," he said.

The two younger boys moved quickly. Slipping their arms under Jonny, they lifted him easily, their steroid-thickened muscles hardly straining. Then they set him gently on the cot frame and stood against the wall, trying desperately to blend with the peeling paint.

The older boy still held the knife, moving it uncertainly from hand to infected hand. The lieutenant faced him. "You're all on report," he said. "Return to your duties."

"I'm telling you, this man tried to escape," the older boy insisted.

"I understand," said the lieutenant, a flat-nosed young black who, Jonny could now see, was not much older than the boy with the scarred hands. That was how it was in the Committee. They worked mainly with teenage boys. Give them the right stimulants and guns and they would go anywhere, risk everything. Higher-ranking boys kept them in line, while desk-bound old men ran the rest of the show. It was cheap and efficient. The Committee never had to pay much in the way of retirement benefits.

"Get out of here," the lieutenant said.

"But—"

"One more word and you can explain it to the Colonel."

That shut the boy up. Reluctantly, he closed the switch-blade, tucking it into the top of his boot. While adjusting his uniform, he gave Jonny a quick, accusing glance, and fol-lowed his friends out of the cell.

"So long, guys," called Jonny. "Keep in touch." He laughed and nodded to the lieutenant. The young man's iden-tity tag read TAUSSIG. "Thanks for your help. I thought I was dog food for sure—"

"On your feet, pusher," said Lieutenant Taussig.

Jonny took a deep breath and leaned against the wall. "You mind if I catch my breath first?" he asked.

Taussig reached down to examine Jonny's face, turning it this way and that in the light. He did not look pleased.

"If anybody asks, tell them the anesthetic hadn't quite worn off and you fell on the stairs," the lieutenant said.

"Why? What do you care about those clowns?" asked Jonny.

"Just do it."

Jonny smiled. "Oh, I get it. Afraid someone'll find out you can't handle your troops?"

Taussig pulled Jonny up by his good arm. "Let's go," he said.

The lieutenant led Jonny out onto a rusted loading gantry, through a maze of small-bore piping and frozen transfer valves to the floor of the old processing plant cum prison. Vague breezes and convection currents kicked up scraps of paper, fluttering them around the pylons of fifty-foot cryogenic tanks.

The floor sloped; the air cooled. They entered a battered hydro-plunge service lift whose burnished walls reflected the harsh industrial lighting in jagged bolts and loops. As they descended, Jonny noticed that Taussig had punched a button in the Yellow Sector. Jonny was impressed. He had never received clearance to enter any of the restricted areas.

When the elevator doors opened, Taussig pushed Jonny to a jerry-rigged desk (a horizontal slab of tank cladding bolted

athwart two enormous shock-coils) and handed a sheaf of doc-
uments to a pale boy whose eyes seemed to have no pupils at
all. The pale boy motioned for a couple of prepubescent
guards to follow them, and walked Jonny and the lieutenant
down a short corridor. At the end, he unlocked a scuffed yel-
low door for them.

Inside, it was another world.

The light came from incandescent bulbs, a muted nonin-
dustrial glow. They stood in a small anteroom whose walls
Jonny was sure were real wood, not plastiform. Between two
locked doors at the far end of the room was a low table, in the
Kamakura style. On the table was a small bowl holding a
single bonsai. Jonny coughed into his fist a couple of times.
The sound was flat, swallowed up by the walls like water on
sand. Soundproofed, he thought.

Taussig walked to a door on the right of the table and leaned
over the eyepiece of a portable Haag-Streit retinal scanner. A
moment later, a buzzer sounded. Gripping the ornamental brass
handle, the lieutenant pushed the door open and motioned Jonny
inside. Taussig did not enter. When Jonny turned to look at him,
the lieutenant closed the door in his face.

"What the hell happened to you?" came a familiar, avun-
cular voice.

Jonny faced the room, seeing only a computer terminal on
the far side of a mahogany table with four matching chairs
drawn up to it. Dragons inset in some lighter wood coiled in
battle or play on the table's surface. In the dim light, Jonny
could not see the face of the man sitting on the opposite side
of the table. But that voice. It made Jonny feel a little sick.

"I thought they cleaned you up in the infirmary," the man
said. Jonny could just make out the silhouette. It gestured for
Jonny to take a seat.

"I tripped on the stairs," Jonny said. "The—uh—anes-
thetic." He sat in the chair as he was told.

Jonny could see the face now. It smiled at him. The short-
cropped hair was whiter than he remembered.

"What's the matter, Gordon? Not even a 'hello' for your
old C.O.?" The officer, Colonel Brigidio Zamora, set a small
pile of crumpled currency next to a collection of pills and
Jonny's tagged Futukoro.

"Captain Zamora—" Jonny began.

"Colonel."

"Congratulations," Jonny said. He rubbed his wounded shoulder reflexively. "Look, Colonel, you're too late. I know this room and the ride down here were supposed to mind fuck me, but you blew it. Three of your puppies broke into my cell just now and tried to slice me up. I'm exhausted and my shoulder hurts like hell." Jonny leaned his good elbow on the table. "So tell me, Colonel, what kind of deal are you prepared to offer me?"

For a moment Zamora did nothing and Jonny found himself wondering if he had chosen the wrong tactic. The Colonel, he remembered, liked to have a good time. In a moment, though, Zamora relaxed, exhaling little bursts of air from his throat. His version of laughter.

"I tell you, Gordon, you kill me," the Colonel said with good humor. "You beg for it; that's what you do. You beg people to smash you up. No wonder your life's such a mess."

"What's wrong with my life?" asked Jonny.

"Well, for starters, look where you are."

Jonny could not argue with that one.

The Colonel, Jonny noticed, had put on some weight. The jacket of his uniform now fit tight across his belly. The creases around his mouth and eyes had taken on the exaggerated depth of cheap statuary. Colonel Zamora did not seem to be aging so much as fossilizing. In his presence, Jonny was always reminded of reptiles—slow, solid beasts of ancient bloodlines, all muscles and teeth.

"Is that why I'm here?" Jonny asked. "You're a social worker now? Gonna fix my life?"

Zamora shook his head. "No, Gordon; you're going to fix mine."

"What does that mean?"

"You really have no concept, do you?" Zamora asked. He spoke slowly, as if addressing someone of less than average intelligence. "See if you can grasp this: you killed Captain Cawfly—one of my officers—and then just waltzed away. Do you know how that makes me look? And then you turn up with these smugglers—selling their drugs, giving them Committee secrets. Working for terrorists, Gordon, I mean, just how much abuse am I suppose to take?"

Jonny started to say something, then met Zamora's tired gray eyes. Thin ice.

"The way I figure it, you owe me," said the Colonel.

"I don't owe you anything," Jonny replied quickly.

That seemed to amuse Zamora. "See, you're doing it again."

Jonny looked around the room impatiently. "Look, Colonel, I had enough of this crap when I was in the Committee. That's why I took a walk."

"Oh, is that the reason?" asked the Colonel. He raised an eyebrow. "Just a case of restless youth, was it? No gestures were implied? Giving the finger to me, to the Committee?"

"I didn't even think about it."

"Well, you should have," said Zamora.

"Fuck you and your disgrace," blurted Jonny. "If you want to deal, fine. If not, charge me with something and let me call my lawyer."

For the second time, Jonny made the Colonel laugh. "You think I'm going to bother with the courts? I'm not subtle like you, Gordon. You play this my way or you're dead. That's my gesture to you."

"Bueno," said Jonny. He did not even know any lawyers, but at least he knew where he stood. His throat was dry and raw. "Can I get some water?"

"Later," said the Colonel. "First, you're going to help me out with some information."

"What could I tell you that your agents don't already know? Raquin was my connection and he's dead."

"I know all about Raquin. He worked for the Committee."

Jonny stared at the Colonel. He's baiting me, he thought. It worked, though. "That's bullshit," Jonny said.

Zamora grinned. "It's a buyer's market, Gordon."

"You offer him a deal like mine? Play or die?"

"No," said the Colonel with great satisfaction. "He came to us."

"Liar."

"Grow up, Gordon. This city is full of troglodytes who'd peddle your ass to some organ broker as soon as look at you. That's what you walked back to."

"I don't believe you," Jonny told the Colonel.

Zamora shrugged. "You can believe anything you want. It doesn't change our situation one bit. What I want from you is information about the smuggler lord Conover," said Zamora. He typed something on the computer terminal and activated the room's recording unit. "I want you to tell me about Conover and his connection to the Alpha Rats."

For a moment, relief washed through Jonny like a cleansing wave. Pointing to the pile of pills, he said, "Your fingers in the cookie jar, Colonel? Been taking home samples?"

Zamora gave Jonny a look of absolute disgust. "What are you, an animal? I'm giving you a chance to stay alive."

"How am I supposed to take a question like that seriously?" asked Jonny. "I don't know anything about Conover and I sure don't keep tabs on space pirates."

"You're a liar, Gordon," said the Colonel. "Remember? Your friend Raquin worked for me. I have videos of you with all kinds of nasty people, including Conover."

Jonny looked away from the Colonel, wondering how long he had been inside the prison. Sumi would be worried by now. All she would hear is that he'd been shot and taken away by the Committee. Sumi, he was afraid, would not survive long on her own. She did not protect herself enough; she left herself too open, was too willing to trust and be wounded. It was that inner calm that had originally attracted Jonny to her. At the moment, though, it merely chilled him.

"All right, so I know Conover," said Jonny. "I move merchandise for him. I help get his trucks through Committee checkpoints, but you know all that, right? As for this Alpha Rat thing, though, that is completely out to lunch."

"Is it? I don't think so."

"I can't give you what I don't have."

"No, but you can get it for me."

"What do you want?"

"Conover," Zamora said.

"Oh, man," said Jonny, "why don't you just ask me to bring the Alpha Rats down here too? I've got as much chance."

"You can't just waltz away from this one, Gordon," said the Colonel. "This hook-up between Conover and the Alpha Rats makes it too big."

Jonny slammed his hand down on the table top. "Will you layoff that 'Gordon' stuff? Nobody calls me that anymore."

"Don't tell me what to do, boy. I own you."

Jonny leaned back in his chair. "Just what is it between you and these spacemen?"

Colonel Zamora tilted his head back slightly, scrutinizing Jonny.

Jonny's fingers lightly traced the pattern of the dragons on the table top. In truth, he wished he had something to give Zamora. Some innocuous bit of information or rumor that might satisfy him. Jonny's head was light. He could not even think of a good lie.

Finally, the Colonel nodded. He keyed something on the computer and turned the recorder off. "All right, maybe you are that ignorant," Zamora said. "Let's try something else. Tell me anything you know about the Alpha Rats."

Jonny took a deep breath and let it out slowly. His mind was still sluggish from the drugs they had given him in the infirmary. He found it difficult to concentrate on anything but his anger, which he was eager to show, and his fear, which he was not. Jonny realized then that he was afraid of Colonel Zamora, had always been so—that his fear of Zamora had been another reason he had deserted the Committee. And that this confrontation had been, in a sense, preordained. He had cheated Zamora of something when he'd run away. Of what, Jonny was not sure, but he understood that, whatever it was, the Colonel had come to claim it.

"Well?" said Colonel Zamora.

"The Alpha Rats," Jonny said. "Yeah, I saw the newsrags. Big ships from deep space, right? They landed on the moon and smashed up all the bases, ours and New Palestine's. Flattened everything. Burned all the techs."

"And do you have any idea what was going on up there at the time?"

Jonny tried to remember. It had been a long time ago. "Some engineering. Mostly mining and genetic work, right?"

The Colonel seemed impressed. "Right, but there was something else going on, too, something more important. A war. An economic war between the New Palestine Federation and the Tokyo Alliance. The Arabs have always had the oil, the minerals, the heavy machinery. They've been mining the asteroid belt for decades in those big hydrogen scoop ships.

"But think—what does the Tokyo Alliance have? We have software and hardware, sure, but it's the really delicate items: protein-based data storage, genetics, microelectronics. That's where our strength lies, Gordon. And we lost a big piece of it.

"You can thank the Alpha Rats that you're in business. A

lot of the drugs you people sell illegally were produced on the moon or in those circumlunar labs. You need that environment, sterile conditions you can't get on Earth and, above all, weightlessness—or something close to it—to produce some of those items.

"The Arabs control over half the Earth's land mass. Africa alone will keep them supplied with raw materials for centuries. Do you see what I'm getting at?"

"Sure, the Tokyo Alliance lost its economic balls when the Alphas moved in on the moon. But I don't see what any of this has to do with me." Jonny opened his eyes wide. "Honest, officer, I was nowhere near the moon that day."

Zamora ignored him and typed something on the computer keyboard. A rectangle of glass set into the top of the table glowed. Rising from the projection plate, a three-dimensional chaos of fractal points and ice-blue connecting lines flared like a crystalline vascular system. The angles of the hologram filled in with colors—primary, then secondary. Jonny thought he recognized a desert. "Look at this," Zamora said.

Jonny leaned forward, staring hard at the miniature landscape. "What is this?" he asked. "Looks like a burned-up spring roll."

"It's a shuttle," said Zamora. "The moon bases used them to send samples back to the corporate labs on Earth. We picked that one up in the desert near Anza Borego. Up until a couple of months ago, all the Alpha Rats were doing was broadcasting a steady stream of signals to deep space; some French tech at Tokyo U thinks to the constellation Pegasus. There's a binary system there called 'Alpheratz.' That's how they got the name."

Jonny nodded. "I'm thrilled," he said.

"Anyway, a few months ago, the signals changed. The Alphas started broadcasting to Earth. No shit. To the desert southeast of here. And you know what?" asked Zamora, with more than a touch of glee. "Somebody broadcast back. Is that rich? Now, we've got some of the best data decryption software available. We've only been able to decipher bits and pieces, but what we got, Gordon, is tasty. Really tasty."

Jonny said, "All right, so I'm hooked. What was it?"

Zamora looked delighted. "A deal," he said. "A deal. Between your pal Conover and the Alpha Rats. But don't stop listening yet, because it gets better. It seems that you're involved."

"Christ," said Jonny. "You're too much." He got up and walked to the back of the room. Zamora did not seem very concerned; he just kept smiling. The door, Jonny saw, had a magnetic lock, a device the Committee was very fond of. You could blow the whole wall away and still not get one of those locks to move, he thought. He remained there, though, taking comfort in the small distance he could put between himself and the Colonel.

"Calm down, Gordon. I said you were involved. I didn't say you were a participant."

"What's the difference?"

"Willingness," said Zamora. "I tell you, boy, if I was working on a deal of this magnitude I might let you sharpen pencils; hell, I might even use you as a courier, but I sure wouldn't let you near anything important. Therefore, I'm willing to accept that you are not a conscious participant in all this."

"Thanks."

"But you've got something I want: access to Conover. If he does have a connection to the Alpha Rats, no matter what the nature of their deal, it can only end up benefiting the Arabs."

Jonny leaned against the wall, mindlessly working his fingernails between two strips of paneling. "Funny, I never pegged you for a flagwaver, Colonel."

"I'm not. This is simple economics. What they've got, we want. By the time we found that shuttle, its cargo section had been emptied," Zamora said. "Whatever the deal is, it's already in motion."

Jonny smiled at him. "You know, I don't believe a word of this."

Colonel Zamora glanced at his watch. "Well, believe this: As of right now, you have forty-eight hours to deliver Conover to me. If you do that, you and I are square. Bullshit me and maybe I'll give you back to those children upstairs. Some of them have very vivid imaginations. I imagine they'd start on your eyes."

Jonny walked back to the table, working the kinks from his legs. His hands were shaking, so he shoved the left one into his pocket. "If I go along, how soon can I get out of here?" he asked.

"Right now," said Zamora. "Do you accept my terms?"

Jonny smiled. "Colonel, I'm a happy child of the New Rising Sun. No camel jockey's gonna push me around."

Zamora narrowed his eyes at Jonny. "You should take this more seriously," he said.

"If I took this any more seriously, I'd drop dead."

"Good. Consider that your new koan, Gordon." Zamora rose, picked up a leather satchel, and pulled Jonny with him to the door. "Meditate on it. At least for the next forty-eight hours."

Colonel Zamora took a flat metallic octagon from his pocket and placed it against the magnetic lock. The door clicked open and Jonny followed him outside.

Jonny and Colonel Zamora waited in the lobby of the Yellow Sector for an elevator. Across the plant floor, a recruit with polarized corneal implants was jacked into a construction masterboard, directing a bank of plasma torches. Whacked out on alkaloid stimulants, he still managed to move a dozen torch-bearing waldoes in a smooth tidal dance, like a clockwork anemone, simultaneously slicing four sides of a gutted fission furnace.

"That's a neat trick," said Jonny.

Zamora nodded. "We have to clear away some of this old equipment. We'll be needing the space for new cells soon."

"Come on, Colonel, no one's recording us now," said Jonny. "That stuff you were saying before—you really don't buy all that space pirate crap, do you?"

Colonel Zamora sighed. "Seeing you has depressed me, Gordon. You remind me too much of the sad state of the world. Paranoia. Self-centeredness. All the symptoms of information overload. The World Link's the real enemy. Thirty years ago we didn't have the Link, plugs in our heads. We had to rely solely on videos and the newsrags. The Arabs were the enemy and we still had a chance to kick Japan and Mexico in their industrial balls. Now we've got the moon, and the Alpha Rats hanging like Damocles's sword over our heads. The Link should never have broken that story. I'm telling you, this city, this country would be a different place if they had kept all that under wraps. It's too strange to assimilate. Too alienating. That kind of information invites paranoia and destroys trust."

"It's hard to trust, Colonel," said Jonny, "when you've got something like the Committee breathing down your neck."

"Bullshit. In a sane world, our presence wouldn't cause a ripple. As a nation, we've allowed ourselves to behave like animals in a trap, gnawing off our own legs to get out."

"You wouldn't be trying to win me over by telling me this is some kind of crusade, would you?"

"Of course not," said Zamora. "That would be expecting too much of you." The Colonel pushed the elevator button again. The boy directing the waldoes aimed them at the base of the furnace, cutting at the support structure with long, smooth strokes that reminded Jonny of kendo strikes. "We're at a crossroads," said Zamora. "Do you know that? The next few years will tell the story. Whether we're going to end up another post-colonial back alley like Britain or France, or whether we're going to take back the dominance we gave up too easily. To do that, we have to get rid of the Alpha Rats. Until they're gone we can't even start on the Arabs." The Colonel smiled. "It all comes down to economics. It always does."

A few meters away, a bell rang and elevator doors slid open. Nimble Virtue, a slunk merchant and one of the least trustworthy lords in the city, stepped out. She was leaning heavily on the arm of one of her handsome young "nephews." When she spotted Jonny, she gave him a tiny bow, indicating that she had no time to talk. Then she and her young man walked down the corridor, awash in the echoes of insect clicks from the exoskeleton Nimble Virtue wore beneath her kimono. At the end of the corridor, a door hissed open for them and they were gone.

A moment later, Jonny found himself being pushed into the elevator car that Nimble Virtue had just vacated. He and Zamora rode up in silence. Jonny felt a nasty satisfaction at having caught the Colonel with his *snitches* down. The look on Nimble Virtue's face had said it all. She had sold Jonny out.

"Now, that I can believe," said Jonny. "Nimble Virtue'd sell off her grandmother's iron lung, if she thought the old lady would keep quiet about it."

"Don't let her concern you."

Jonny sniffed the air distastefully. "Sorta stank up the joint, didn't she?"

Zamora backhanded him across his injured shoulder. Something blue and hot exploded in Jonny's eyes, fragments trailing away down some bottomless cavern. He slid down the wall to the floor.

"Don't even think about going after Nimble Virtue. You haven't got the time," said Zamora.

The elevator shuddered to a halt and the doors slid open. Taussig was waiting, a small grin spreading across his face when he saw Jonny on his knees.

"Help him up," ordered Zamora.

The lieutenant pulled Jonny to his feet and walked him from the car. When they caught up with Zamora, the Colonel turned to Taussig and said, "Later, you and I are going to talk about what went on in this man's cell." Jonny had the satisfaction of seeing the blood drain from the young lieutenant's face.

Zamora led Jonny out a side exit and left him weak-kneed, standing in an oily puddle. The Colonel removed a Futukoro from his satchel and tossed it behind Jonny.

"Take that with you. Wouldn't want you getting mugged, now that you're back on duty. I'll be available to you for the next forty-eight hours, Gordon. After that, the deal's off. I'll be seeing you," said the Colonel.

The door swung in quietly, hissing as it sealed itself shut.

Jonny was alone in the alley. He drew himself up and, taking a few drunken steps forward, kicked savagely at the door's heavy, riveted face; he pounded it with his good hand.

"Like hell, you bastard!" he screamed. "You can't do this to me!" For a vertiginous second he was insane, turning in frustrated circles, splashing more filth onto his ruined jeans.

Finally, panting and lightheaded, Jonny stepped away from the unyielding door, feeling angry for such a stupid waste of energy. He should be on his way out of town.

Jonny's gaze slid down the damp walls to the thin fog at the alley's mouth. He stooped awkwardly, protecting his throbbing shoulder, and scooped up the Futukoro. He walked to the infrared scanner that monitored the alley, took aim, and blew it off its mounting. Somewhere, an alarm went off. Jonny hurried away from the place.

3

THE FLIGHT OF A
NON-EUCLIDEAN FLY

"SHIT," JONNY MUMBLED as he stepped on something soft and clinging in the doorway of the abandoned hotel. Then, "Shit" again as he recognized the accuracy of his curse. He was somewhere near Exposition Boulevard, out of breath, a few blocks from the old Lockheed rocket bunkers. Ancient booster engines and decaying nose cones displayed their brittle bones behind fences topped with razor wire.

Gingerly, Jonny scraped his soiled boot on a cracked stone step and peered from the alcove. Whoever Zamora had following him was being very cagey. Jonny still had not caught sight of the tail, but he knew the man was out there. Zamora would never let him just walk out like that.

He had exhausted himself, running for cover and for the sheer joy of running, for the momentary sense of freedom it gave him. Still, he had not been able to spot the tail and that bothered him. Even now, as he watched from the alcove, nothing on the street moved. Except for the doorway bums shifting restlessly with their chemical dreams.

The hot night had remained hot, was giving way to another hot day. Jonny's tunic clung to him like a second skin. He relaxed against the hotel and tried to regain his bearings. His shoulder had begun to throb within a few minutes of leaving the prison. He desperately wanted a drink, a snort, a smoke— anything that would transport him from the pain, the Colonel's obsessions, and the old neighborhood in which he was hiding.

Writers had been at work on the old buildings with their compressed-air cannisters of sulfuric acid, burning their messages, like grim oracles, into the very bodies of the structures.

Over the years, the fronts of the abandoned hotels and shops
had taken on the texture and feel of old candle wax. In the
alcove, Jonny ran his fingers over crumbling letters. DUCK
AND COVER. And, ALPHA RATS ARE SCARED OF
CATS.

On an impulse, Jonny pushed on the hotel door. It scraped
across a warped wooden floor and stuck, revealing a bleak
interior. Jonny took a tentative step inside.

It looked to him as if a bomb had gone off in the lobby.
The plaster meat and wooden bones of the place were visible
where sections of the wall had caved in or been torn away. An
old fashioned wrought-iron elevator lay scattered among blis-
tered Lockheed tail fins and useless landing gear.

But, as depressing as the old hotel was to look at, it was
the smell of the place that got to Jonny. The deadly stink
(ammonia, old cheese, mildew) brought tears to his eyes. But
he held his breath and pushed the lobby door closed. It took a
moment for his eyes to adjust to the darkness; then, tired and
leadfooted, his shoulders bumping into walls that appeared
from nowhere, he started up the stairs for the roof. From there
everything would be visible, and he reasoned that by leaping
from rooftop to rooftop, he could lose whoever was following
him.

He had not counted on the smell, though. At the first land-
ing, Jonny's eyes were watering; by the second, he was hav-
ing trouble breathing. Then on the third floor he abruptly ran
out of stairs. There was a door, labeled ROOF, but it was
immovable—crusted shut with age and grime. Jonny put his
boot to it, but that only brought a pitiful rain of dust from the
sagging ceiling.

Outside, he thought, and up the fire escape. Jonny entered
one of the guest rooms that opened off the corridor and headed
for a window.

Inside, the room was large and, empty of furnishings,
faintly echoed his steps. A dim rectangle of street light out-
lined the smashed innards of an old telephone-comsat uplink.
The place must have been nice once, he thought, if they could
afford to put those in the rooms. In the middle of the floor was
an upturned hubcap someone had been using to cook in.

Jonny had taken perhaps a dozen steps into the room before
the smell got to him. It was a physical presence, twisting in
his lungs like a tormented animal. His nose ran; he coughed.

Holding his arm across his face, he breathed through his mouth. If the Committee had this stuff, they could wipe out the whole city, he thought.

When Jonny reached the window, he found it swollen in place from the damp ocean air. Knowing that Zamora's tail would hear it if he broke the glass, he started back into the hotel to look for a pipe or board—something that would help him pry the window open.

A rustle of fabric from the far corner of the room. The flicker of something small and metallic.

Jonny took a step forward—and was in the air, falling, his legs knocked out from under him. He curled up as best he could and came down flat, protecting his shoulder.

"Goddamit!" he yelled as shapes closed in from the gray edges of the room.

"Get his clothes," came a voice dry and thin as wind.

"Get his shoes," came another voice.

"Get him."

A stooped figure in rags lumbered up to Jonny and began grabbing at his tunic. Jonny cried out at the sudden pressure on his bleeding shoulder, lashing out with his free arm. Pain exploded in his wrist as something sharp and wet dug into it.

Jonny kicked out blindly into the dark, noting with satisfaction a groan as his boot connected. Rolling into a crouch, he propelled himself up into the stomach of the tunic-puller. The figure staggered back, wheezing horrid breath.

Jonny leaned forward, letting his weight propel him toward the window. But he was knocked back as someone else jumped him.

"He's going to get out. He'll rat . . ."

"Little monster . . ."

"Watch his boots . . ."

At the window, he was dragged back by a swarm of dry, reptilian fingers. He screamed. Things like vises and knives, pincers and broken glass cut into his back and arms.

Christ, they're biting me, he thought.

Jonny managed to loop his leg behind the leg of one of his attackers. Then, pushing forward with all his strength, he heard a window crack and shatter. Suddenly, he and one or two others were on the fire escape. The sudden release of hands and rush of air left him lightheaded, but some animal part of his brain moved his arms and legs, pushing him up and away. No one followed.

Two flights up the fire escape, Jonny stopped to look at his attackers. They huddled below, cooing and mewing over their injured. Though it was cooler outside, the heat still broiled the streets, baking the old tenements; the whole neighborhood rippled behind waves of desert heat. Yet the mob was clothed in layer upon layer of cast-off coats, moldering lab smocks, and vacuum suits. A fat man in tattered test-pilot gear crawled onto the landing and gazed down at the street. His clothes hung from his arms in strips, little more than patches all crudely sewn or wired together. The mass of rags on his thick frame gave him an awkward bearlike appearance, but his eyes burned with a savage clarity.

Jonny was already backing up the stairs when the fat man caught sight of him. A scream welled up from the fat man's throat; he bared his yellow teeth. But not real teeth, Jonny knew, just polycarbonate implants, sharpened with care to needle points. In the thin, unreal light of the street lamps, the fat man's teeth glowed like a trap.

Piranhas, Jonny thought. A whole gang of them. It had been a stupid mistake, entering the old hotel. It reminded Jonny just how tired he was.

The abandoned hotels and apartments that fronted the warehouse district were useless to most gangs, lying just beyond the lights of Committee headquarters. That was why the Piranhas, septuagenarians mostly, for there were no Piranhas under sixty, held them. Used for target practice by the younger gangs, lied to and finally abandoned by the government, the old discards and defectives banded together to hold some piece of ground for themselves. Using the few weapons they could find, principally government-issued teeth—filed and set firmly in angry, withered jaws—they were tolerated because they consumed nothing but the leavings of others. Besides, even in Los Angeles, slaughtering old people in the streets would have been frowned on.

As Jonny watched, more Piranhas began to crawl from the hotel. The fat man started up the fire escape. He carried a sharpened pipe in his hand. Jonny started climbing, too.

He clumsily vaulted the low wall onto the roof and sprawled on his stomach. Gravel dented his cheeks. As Jonny pushed himself up, he saw a thin but steady stream of blood running from under his cast. The fat man was a few yards away. Jonny started running again.

Behind the fat man, more Piranhas appeared, running like a ragged army of the dead. They waved their pipes and broken bottles wearily—more, it seemed, to remind themselves of the connection they still had to the flesh they inhabited than to menace Jonny.

When he reached the other side of the roof, Jonny looked frantically for a way down. What he found puzzled him more.

An entire network of homemade bridges and catwalks, like some outrageous model of the neural pathways of the Piranhas' brains, crisscrossed the roofs, connecting all the buildings within a dozen blocks. Ribbed conduits, old antennae, the rusted drive shafts of decades-dead jet turbines were hammered into the surfaces of the roofs. Secured to these were lengths of rotting rope, pilfered from the docks. Flattened cans of krill, backs of discarded computer terminals, and insulation tiles from L5 shuttles filled the gaps between rough planks to form walkways over the street, a hundred feet below.

The bridges did not look all that secure, but the Piranhas were closing in. Jonny stepped onto the closest walkway and hurried across. The support ropes stretched and tightened as things cracked and shifted under his feet.

He leaped off onto the adjoining roof. The bridge strained behind him, weighed down by the gang. The fat man was still in front, holding the pipe before him. Jonny moved in circles around the roof, frantic for something to throw. He knew that if he used his gun, Zamora's man would find him and all this would have been for nothing. In the end, he decided that the situation did not cry out for subtlety. Fumbling in the folds of his tunic, he pulled out the sweat-soaked Futukoro and waved it in the face of the fat man, who pulled up short at the sight of the gun. The Piranhas bunched up behind him, growing silent.

"That's it!" Jonny shouted. "No more games. The first one who moves is meat for the others."

It was rubbish and he knew it, but it sometimes worked, as it seemed to be working now. The Piranhas, including the fat man, remained where they were. They stared at Jonny with empty, feral eyes.

Sentiment had always been Jonny's undoing. At heart, all cops are romantic slobs and ex-cops are worse. A terrible wave of sorrow overcame his fear as he backed away from the pathetic group. They were defectives, not unlike the losers and one-percenters that he knew, that he was a part of. Jonny scanned the faces of the crowd, wondering if whatever errant gene that had sent them out here to the wilds was present in his blood. He regarded them with a certain awe.

From behind, a brick fell and shattered hollowly. Jonny turned quickly, keeping the gun on the fat man. Dozens of Piranhas had crowded onto the other roofs, pipes and heavy connecting rods in their hands. Many grinned, showing sharp, stained teeth. Jonny was surrounded.

He shuffled to the edge of the roof, turning in slow circles, trying to cover himself in all directions. When Jonny reached the fire escape, the bridges were packed with Piranhas. When he stepped onto the ladder, a few were moving toward him across the roof. When he was straddling the wall, the fat man threw his pipe and screamed, charging him.

Jonny managed to duck the pipe and dropped over the edge of the wall, landing hard on the fire escape platform. He rolled onto his back and pointed his Futukoro. Too late. The Pirhanas were over him, pelting him with pipes and stones. But even under that hail of debris, Jonny could not bring himself to kill any of them. He settled for spraying three sides of the sky with bullets. The Piranhas fell back, unaware of Jonny's good intentions. With his gun straight up, Jonny squeezed off a few more rounds and clattered down the steps.

When he hit the ground, he hung in the shadows, pressing himself tight against the building, waiting for the sounds of pursuit. But there were none. Jonny breathed through his mouth, swallowing great gobs of hot, wet air.

He was in a blind alley; at the far end lay a vacant lot dotted with discarded dressing dummies and barbed-wire rolls. Jonny remained against the building, feeling it solid against his back. He checked the rounds left in his gun and carefully slid down the wall toward the alley's mouth.

He did not stand a chance.

A gleeful cry echoed from above. Jonny looked up just in time to see the junk raining down on him: pipes, bottles, jet canopies, and electronic components—all the technological refuse of the city.

He leaped and rolled, groaning at a sharp pain in his shoulder. The first wave of junk crashed behind him. The second wave caught him in the open with nowhere to hide.

Compassion vanished. Hunkering down behind a dressing dummy, he opened fire at the roof, his bullets chewing the head off a sexless stone cherub. Its companions made no comment and the Piranhas, who knew better than to stand close to the edge, just laughed at him. Jonny remained low in the dirt, cursing himself for not having blown a few of them away when he'd had the chance.

"DO NOT MOVE. STAY RIGHT WHERE YOU ARE," commanded a bland, amplified voice.

The Committee hovercar roared by suddenly, like an angry metal wasp—all sleek and deadly—its belly lights casting angry fingers of brilliance over the empty buildings. Shadows moved like a year of nightmares across deserted storefronts. Dust and grit followed from the roof into the alley, filling it with smoky phantoms. Jonny coughed, trying to clear his throat.

The clamor on the roof picked up as the Piranhas turned their anger toward the hovercar, pelting it with junk. Jonny took the opportunity to move into the street. His shadow circled him like a nervous cat, then appeared in a dozen places at once—thin and diffuse.

Crouching by a gutted lamppost, Jonny found a sewer grating and gave it a tug. By rocking it back and forth, he worked the grating loose and pulled it free. Peering down to see if the way was clear, a sudden attack of vertigo tilted the street toward the dark hole. Jonny grabbed the lamppost, fighting to keep his balance, and turned back toward the hotel.

Overhead, the hovercar was hanging in the air like a patient predator, waiting for an opening. Abruptly, a mechanical whine filled the air. Jonny squeezed his eyes shut and covered his ears as the Pacifiers kicked in.

The fighting on the roof died away as, much too late, the Piranhas realized what was happening. They stood as one, staring at the whirling pattern of lights, paralyzed and helpless.

Jonny decided that it was time to find the Croakers. He slid quietly into the sewer and pulled the grating closed.

The sewers were the lichen-slicked relics of another time, a means of concealment as old as revolution itself. The Croakers had taken to them soon after the shoot-on-sight orders had become official policy with the Committee. The

Croakers were outlaws, anarchists and physicians mainly, treating diseases that officially did not exist or could not be diagnosed without authority of the local medical boards. Their roots extended back to the early days of the century when the first doctors had gone underground, destroying the records of patients with AIDS and certain new strains of hepatitis, treating these patients (the new "untouchable" caste) in the black clinics hastily thrown together with whatever those original rebels could carry with them.

Other doctors, mostly young ones back from the Lunar Border Wars, frustrated by the impenetrable bureaucracy and government seizures of their patient records, joined them. It took only a few years for the medical community to split into two distinct camps: those doctors who remained aboveground, working with the powers that be, and those who walked away from all that, joining the other gangs of Los Angeles in constructing their own microsociety beyond the boundaries of conventional law.

Jonny had been a supplier and occasional courier to the Croakers and he liked them, despite their revolutionary proselytizing. He cringed when one of them called him "brother," but he felt a silly pride at being associated with them. That was also why he remained suspicious of them. To be otherwise would demand a response that he was not prepared to give. It implied certain ties, a common heritage, and that made him nervous.

The sewers, laced within the body of the city, were the corroded veins of a sick addict, shut down from age and abuse. The only things that moved in them were alien, looking for a way out. Jonny stood at the bottom of a ladder of steel rungs embedded in a stone wall. Knee-deep in black water, the floor sucked at his legs.

The air was thick with stagnancy; corrupt, buzzing with mosquitoes. They tickled his face, covering his eyes and hands. They stung him until he swung out blindly at the curtain of pests, fighting back an overpowering sense of his own death. But death was not it, not exactly. It was more a formless sense of great anxiety, a feeling that he had done something terribly wrong and that if he could just remember what it was and fix it, everything would be all right.

Jonny knew a little about the layout of the sewers, but he did not know the location of the Croakers' secret tunnels. Since all directions were the same in the dark, he started moving straight ahead, into a faint, sticky breeze. Very soon, Jonny realized that he was no longer moving through absolute darkness.

He could see the mosquitoes. They seemed to be crawling over a flat, two-dimensional background—a trick of the strange light that seemed to fill the tunnel. The lichen on the walls were glowing a weak green. When he ran his fingers over the damp stones of the wall, he left a black trail where the lichen peeled off. His fingers glowed with the little plants. Jonny walked on, his legs sluggish in the oozing mess of the floors.

But he was still moving without direction. Lightheaded, he lost track of the hours in the endless branches and sub-branches of the tunnels. The water rarely moved above mid-thigh, but a few times he had to turn back from tunnels when the water reached his chest and threatened to go higher.

Along the way, Jonny scratched messages on the walls. Crude serpents, ready to strike; he wrote his name in big block letters and some obscenities concerning the relationship of the Committee boys and their mothers. He drew the outline of his hands and eyes with wings.

He stumbled more as exhaustion crept into his muscles, loosening them at the joints. For a time, he walked with his eyes closed, mechanically trailing his fingers along the wall to keep his direction. Was it for hours or minutes? When Jonny opened his eyes again, he staggered back, nearly fell. "Jesus Christ," he said.

Slogans, names, and drawings were scrawled over every inch of the walls and arched ceiling of the tunnel. They screamed down at Jonny from all directions, black shimmering lightly above green. It looked like the last record of some tribe or group mind that had blasted itself, intact, onto the walls. The words seemed to hang in space around him.

LIFE WITHOUT DEAD TIMES
   SOCIETY IS A CARNIVOROUS FLOWER
I AM HERE BY THE WILL OF THE PEOPLE AND

WILL NOT LEAVE UNTIL I GET MY RAINCOAT BACK
BEAUTY MUST BE CONVULSIVE OR IT WILL NOT BE
AT ALL
     SKID THE KID WAS HERE!
SURREALISM AU SERVICE DE LA REVOLUTION

Humpbacked shadows skittered along the pipes near the
ceiling: rats, huge and dangerous. Jonny pulled his gun and
fired at them. Rats had caused him enough trouble for one
night. He watched as a couple of them skittered to a wall a
few meters ahead and squeezed into a small opening near the
floor. As each rat disappeared, its coat was illuminated for a
second by a flash of white light.

Jonny went to the wall, knelt, and pressed his face to the
crack. A steady stream of cooler air. Running his hand around
the edge of the hole, he realized that the wall was false, not
stone at all, but some sort of cast polymeric resin. Digging in
his heels, Jonny pulled at the opening. And the wall slid out a
few centimeters, stuck, then opened wider, trailing scabrous
fingers of adhesive. Light exploded into the sewer.

White and agonizingly bright, the light burned Jonny's
eyes. But he did not care. It was beautiful. He squinted into it,
trying to locate its source, but he had to turn away, finally,
when he thought he would go blind. It was several minutes
before he could look into the luminous cavern without flinch-
ing. But when he did, Jonny knew he was safe.

Still, it was a strange sight in the squalor of the sewer. The
transparent plastic bubble—clean, and brightly lit—glowed
like a dream, filling the tunnel before him. Through a haze of
condensation, Jonny could just make out the hydroponic racks
that lined the walls along both sides of the tunnel. Yagé vines
trailed onto the floor, aloe vera, psilicybe mexicana, and other
medicinals grew there in abundance. By pressing his face up
to the thick plastic membrane, Jonny could see the other end
of the tunnel where the plastic was tucked neatly around a
weathered access hatch.

Jonny stamped his right foot down sharply, at an angle, so
that the heel of his boot snapped away with a *click*. Balancing
against the bubble wall, afraid somehow of moving too far
away, he felt along the bottom of his boot until he found the
hilt of the hidden knife. The blade slid bright and clean from
his hollow sole; he rammed it into the bubble. Sliding the

blade down, he made a single, neat incision in the membrane wall. Then he pushed through the tight aperture into a warm, musky chamber that pulsed with the regular beating of a pump.

He replaced the knife and snapped the heel back on his boot. There was a smell of life and order in the tunnel that revived him. When Jonny reached the access hatch, he gripped the big metal handle and turned it; he was rewarded with a reassuring rumbling inside the walls as bolts drew back. After that, the door swung open effortlessly.

Jonny stepped into a darkened room and felt along the walls for a door. He went blind in the apex of the multiple cones of light, ghostly afterimages tracking his retinas. Someone grabbed his sleeve and pulled him forward. Jonny could just discern the outlines of Futukoros and crossbows pointed at him from beyond the light. He started to say something, but the air, which had seemed so pleasant a moment before, suddenly went bad. The room tilted back and forth, wobbling, as his vertigo returned. Then he was on his face on the floor. "Here we go again," he said.

Something moved in front of Jonny's nose. A Burnett crossbow pistol lowered and a woman—small, but well muscled, the planes of her face smooth, as if carved from cool black marble—took a step toward him. The woman's name was Ice. She knelt in front of Jonny and squinted at him. In a moment, her scowl softened to an expression of embarrassed recognition. She reached out and touched his filthy face.

"Jonny? Oh, my god," she said quietly. "We heard you'd been shot."

He smiled then, too, partly with affection and partly with surprise. He kissed her cool hand. "Not to worry," he said. "The pain stopped soon after I died."

The next few hours existed only in fragments, physical sensations. Later, Jonny remembered lying on the floor, wondering distantly if he was going to be sick. He remembered hands moving over him. Objects had taken on a fragile, crystalline quality. Things dripped into his arms through haloed tubes. Ice moved into view occasionally and tried to speak to him. But Jonny was off floating where there was no pain and no need to run. Then there was only the dark.

* * *

Jonny awoke on a futon, naked, his arms wrapped in clean bandages. He moved his hands, but only after a considerable effort of will. They slid from under cool sheets as if being manipulated from far away. He felt numb and dizzy, but somehow peaceful. He was in a little room stacked high with milky injection-molded cases and styrofoam packing modules. It did not look at all like part of a hospital.

"It's not. I'm just borrowing it," said Ice as she slid a dark arm around Jonny's chest, pulling him closer. Jonny remembered Ice's unnerving talent for verbalizing his thoughts.

"Ice," he said, rolling to face her.

"For an ex-cop, you've got big feet. You set off every alarm in the place."

Ice, Jonny, and Sumi: the three of them had formed a solid union for a time in the disintegrating city. Then suddenly Ice had disappeared, leaving only a short, lame note. Jonny recalled the first terrible days after she had gone. He and Sumi walked on razor blades. Each was aware that neither had been to blame for Ice's disappearance, yet each secretly sensed that they were the one responsible. It was days before Jonny could bear to let Sumi out of his sight. The terror of being alone overwhelmed him. Sumi had been no different. They trailed each other from room to room like absurd puppies, only dimly aware of what they were doing.

Seeing Ice now, lying next to her, Jonny ran his hands over the contours of her body. She had changed in subtle ways. There was a new, pleasant firmness to her hips and legs. And her arms were thicker, more muscular, which, Jonny was sure, pleased her. Her grin still possessed the openness that contradicted her usual detached expression. His fingers traced the old post-operative scar where she had received a black market liver.

"I didn't recognize you when you came crashing into the storeroom tonight. Then, when I heard your voice, I couldn't believe it was you," she said.

Jonny's throat was dry when he tried to speak. "I didn't know that you'd be here. That you were a Croaker," he said.

Ice nodded. "I've been here a few months now." She shrugged. "Sometimes, I'm not even sure why. Groucho recruited me. Do you know him? He's great. He plans a lot of the raids and holds the group together. I'll introduce you to-morrow. He helps keep the ghosts away."

The ghosts had been with Ice for as long as Jonny had known her. They were an image she toyed with, but he knew that to her the ghosts of memory were real.

Ice had been working as a prostitute at the Zone Deluxe when Sumi had introduced them. Before that, Ice had farmed out her body to the Boys of Tangier gang, allowing herself to be infected with specific viruses. The gang would then purchase her infected blood, which they used to produce various immunotoxins. These they sold on the street or to the smuggler lords.

While infected with a mutant strain of hepatitis, Ice's liver gave out. The Boys of Tangier gave her a new one, but when they demanded payment, Ice revealed that she was broke. The Boys sold her to the owners of the Zone Deluxe, a pair of identical albino twins who called themselves the Tundra Brothers.

Jonny called in some favors with a smuggler who special-ized in stolen corporate data and bought out the Brothers' interest in Ice with access codes for the Tokyo Stock Ex-change. It was a sweet deal all the way around. Jonny knew the Tundra Brothers were not particularly smart.

Using the codes, the Brothers made themselves rich in a week. They descended into a kind of madness then, like a tape player stuck on fast forward, spiraling on a terminal party high, manipulating stock prices. By the end of the second week, the Brothers' bank accounts rivaled the big corporate fortunes of the oldest families of Tokyo. It took another week for the Yakuza to find them. After that, the Tundra Brothers and the Zone Deluxe were relegated to that specialized branch of urban mythology embracing everything from the merely foolish to the truly insane. But Ice was out by then.

"Why did you go?" asked Jonny.

"I don't know," Ice answered quickly, as if she had antici-pated the question. She closed her eyes. "I really don't."

"Too many ghosts," said Jonny.

Ice lay down on the futon and rested her head on Jonny's chest. She opened her eyes, but would not look at him.

"I'm better here," she said. "I know who I am. There's a structure to reality." She tugged at her short, curly hair. "Things tend to stay in focus."

"Yeah, I understand," Jonny said.

He looked around the room, gnawing the inside of his cheek nervously. Among the packing material, clothes and books had been tossed at random. Ice and Jonny had been the slobs in their ménage-a-trois. Sumi was the only one who cared for a clean house. He was glad to see that, at least, that had not changed.

"We could all use a little structure," he said.

He looked back at Ice and watched her rubbing her eyes sleepily. It was at times like this when Jonny was reminded of just how small she was, of how much strength it took for her just to punch back the void each day. "I'll leave, if you want. I can sleep in the ward," he said.

"No," said Ice, looking troubled. "Please stay. How's Sumi?"

"I don't know. That's part of why I'm here. I have to get out of Los Angeles. Zamora's after me. We have to get Sumi before he finds the house in Silver Lake."

"We will," Ice said, "but not now. Tomorrow, when Groucho gets back."

Jonny nodded wearily and lay his head down on the pillow. Ice leaned over and kissed him. Opening her lips, she invited his tongue into the warmth of her mouth. His hands roamed her body, found the tail of her shirt, and slid up to cup her small breasts. They moved together for some time until, suddenly exhausted, Jonny felt his head begin to spin. But they kept their arms around each other, as if one of them might be swept away at any moment.

"You shouldn't have run off like that," Jonny said.

"I know," Ice whispered. "Now go to sleep."

He turned to her, groggily.

"We have to get Sumi."

"We will, don't worry."

Jonny rolled onto his side. He felt her arm encircle him.

"Too many ghosts," he said.

He felt her nod.

"Too many goddam ghosts."

__4__

PREMONITION OF
CIVIL WAR

DURING THE LAST few hours of night, Jonny was caught in a series of violent, fevered dreams in which he was being pursued by things he could not see. The end of each dream was the same: he would stumble or feel his legs lock like rusting machinery, leaving him stranded and helpless. Then something would grab him and he would be jolted awake by a phosphorous dream-flash that snapped his eyes open. He would lie in the dark room staring at the ceiling as vague pains stirred just behind his eyes. In a few minutes he would drift back to sleep. For a time he would float peacefully on a sea of nothingness, but then the dreams would start again.

There was a woman, all in white, running down Hollywood Boulevard, her hair and dress in flames. Long rows of chrome beetles moving over damp brickwork. A man in the back of a pedicab. Mirror shades, cheap plastic poncho. From the cab, he pointed a gun at Jonny. It was all deliriously slow. There was no sound, only the muzzle flash and the heat of impact.

"Jonny, wake up, goddamit!" called Ice. "You're gonna pull your stitches out."

Jonny awoke at the sound of her voice. Her face was right above his, thin lines of tension spreading out radially from the corners of her eyes. "Jesus, what a ride," he said, his voice hoarse with sleep. "How long have I been out?"

"Almost twenty hours," said Ice. She settled down next to him on the futon. She was wearing baggy fatigue pants and a tank top with the faded picture of some Japanese pop singer. "I was starting to get worried. You barely twitched in all that

49

time, then all of sudden you're moaning and rolling around like you're trying to hogtie a Meat Boy."

"Did it look like I made it?"

Ice smiled. "You were massacred."

"Typical," replied Jonny.

The room they were in was small. Seeing that brought back images of the previous night. He remembered the Piranhas, his trek through the sewers, Zamora's threats. His arms were still bandaged, and his right shoulder itched fiercely in a clear plastic induction cast, healing in its weak electrical field. Looking around, Jonny saw rough walls, gray limestone papered with yellowing layers of ancient subway schedules and anti-Arab propaganda. Hexagonal panels of radio-luminescent plastic lit cases of medical supplies and electronic gear stacked ceiling-high against two walls.

"No windows," Jonny said. "We're still underground."

"Give that man a cigar," said Ice. She picked up a styrofoam tray from a crate littered with drug ampules. The smell of frijoles and rice assaulted Jonny. "Breakfast, babe. Quieres?"

He groaned and pulled the sheets up over his face. "Take it away. I'll never eat again."

"Come on, you've got to get your strength back."

"Forget it. You're going to have to feed me with needles. I think something slept in my mouth."

Ice set the tray down, and Jonny reached out and took her arm, pulling her on top of him. Careful to avoid his bandages, she slid her arms under his shoulders, grinding her crotch into his. The scent of her body transported him; they were home, in their own bed in Hollywood. He could sense Sumi's presence nearby. Then a second later the hallucination was gone. Still kissing, Jonny experienced a terrific urge to bite Ice's tongue.

"You know I'm still pissed at you," he said.

"I know," said Ice.

"And I don't buy that 'I don't know why I left' crap, either."

"But I don't know why. It's all twisted around in my head." Ice sat up, pushing a few beaded corn-rows of hair from her face. "I just knew I had to move. Get away."

"From what?"

"From everything. From my life. And that meant you and Sumi."

"That's comforting."

"Part of it was living in this city. Nothing's real here. It was getting to me. Was getting to you, too."

Jonny put a hand on Ice's cheek and turned her head, forcing her to look at him. "What do you mean?"

"We were dying," she said quietly, almost whispering. "I watched you staring out the window night after night like you were working on some puzzle, trying to put it together in your mind. Sumi fiddling with her circuit boards. We were all together, but we might as well have been on different continents."

Jonny shrugged. "Let's face it, we have to keep a little detached in our work to stay sane. Sometimes that spills over. But we can fix that."

"But there's more than that," said Ice. "Have you ever heard the phrase 'the Spectacle'?"

"No."

"It's a political theory. Groucho talks about it. He's kind of our leader around here. Says the Spectacle is the way the government keeps control. It sets up these mysterious and complex systems like restrictions on medical service, the Committee; it makes the Arabs and the Alpha Rats into these conveniently evil icons. That way, it keeps us isolated and makes us feel like we don't have any control over our own lives."

"And you think the three of us got eaten up by the Spectacle?"

"Yeah," said Ice. "Do you understand what I'm saying?"

As Jonny sat up, Ice rolled off his lap and lay down beside him. "I understand it's all very easy to argue in the abstract," he said. "Talking politics is a good way to avoid what really hurts."

Ice looked at her hands, lines of tension deepening around her eyes. "I was sick," she said. "I didn't love you. I didn't love Sumi. I was hollow and dead and there was nothing inside me but dust and dry bones. I don't think you want to understand."

"That's not true." Jonny reached under her shirt and rubbed the small of her back. "We're back together; that's what counts. We'll get Sumi and work the rest of it out."

"For what it's worth, I'm sorry," Ice said.

"So am I. I wish I'd seen you needed help back at the old place."

Ice smiled guardedly, and rested her hand on his stomach. Under her fingers, Jonny became aware of the steady rhythm of his own breathing. He groped for something to say to ease the tension, but nothing came to him. "We kept your stupid Samba tapes," he offered finally. That made her laugh. Jonny broke up, too, and they lay on the futon giggling like idiots until she pulled him to her.

He bent to her breasts, pulling her shirt off over her head, finding her penny-colored nipples with his tongue. Ice arched her back, tugging off her pants and tossing them away, cupping his testicles on the return motion. She pushed Jonny onto his back, rubbing herself along the shift of his erect penis. When she lowered herself upon him, he held her for a moment, struck again by a cold déjà vu, needing to confirm for himself the reality of her presence, the flesh that held him. She gave a little grunt as he entered her; her face eased of tension for the first time since he had woken.

They moved slowly at first, drawing out each thrust (damp friction), the motion resolving itself at the moment of greatest tension, and beginning again. He came quickly, unexpectedly, and she, a moment later.

They lay there, clinging to each other damply, unwilling and unable to do anything else. Jonny traced the outline of her shoulder blades with his fingers. She closed her eyes, her feathery breath coming cool across his chest.

Later he asked, "So what do we do about getting Sumi?"

Ice sat up, wiping sweat from her eyes. "We talk to Groucho and see if he has any ideas."

"You called him your leader? I didn't think anarquistas had leaders."

"Every group has leaders," Ice said evenly. "What the Croakers shun are rulers."

"*Shun*. Jesus, you really are one of them, aren't you?"

"I really am," she said somewhat wickedly.

"What would your poor mother think?"

"My mama was a Hollywood whore and so was yours." Ice rolled off the bed onto her feet and clapped her hands. "Come on, you have to move around or you're going to get stiff."

When Jonny stood up, he caught his reflection in the alu-

minum housing of a portable CT scanner. "I look like a god-
dam mummy," he said.

"You look fine. Let's see how you walk."

Standing, Jonny found his balance shot by the combination
of long sleep and drugs. With his arm around Ice's shoulder,
he made it around the room a few times, his legs feeling
stronger with each circuit. However, he was aware that he was
not yet thinking straight. There was something he had to do.
Twenty hours sleep was a long time. How long had he wan-
dered in the sewers? "What time is it?" he asked.

"About four in the afternoon," said Ice, glancing at her
watch.

"What day?"

"Wednesday."

Jonny concentrated, trying to force the fog from his brain.
He counted backwards; the numbers stumbled by. Eventually,
the answer seemed right, or at least close enough. "Six
hours," he said.

"Six hours what?"

"In six hours, Colonel Zamora declares open season on
me."

Ice handed him a set of green nylon overalls with the
Pemex logo stenciled on the back. Under the breast pocket
was a small hole surrounded by a suggestive rust-colored
stain.

"Welcome to the club," she said.

Ice led him through three levels of absolute darkness,
through crawl spaces damp with leakage from underground
pipes, up frozen escalators and an elevator shaft where they
stood on a section of heavy wire mesh barely a half-meter
square and were lifted slowly by a retrofit electric dumb-
waiter. At the top of the shaft Jonny was engulfed in stars. A
three-hundred-and-sixty-degree panorama of open space
swung slowly around him, illuminating the tile walls with
solar flares and star fire.

He said, "I'm seeing this, right? This isn't just brain dam-
age or something?"

"Don't worry," said Ice. "Some lunatic dragged a Zeiss
projector from the planetarium and reassembled it down here.
We got it hooked to a satellite dish topside. Pulls down signals

from some old NASA probe. You know, Jonny..." Ice took
his hand and led him to the edge of a subway platform, then
down onto the tracks. "...things get a little strange here
sometimes. I mean, we're all dedicated anarquistas, but we're
also artists. Some of us more than others."

"You an artist, too?" asked Jonny.

Ice shrugged. Only where stars marked her face could
Jonny see her, her dark features blending evenly with the
black of space. "I'm not a painter or a sculptor, if that's what
you mean. Art here means more than that. It's a way of look-
ing at the world, a state of mind. I just don't want you to make
any quick judgments about these people."

"You afraid I might not like your revolution?"

"You work very hard at being cynical, I know that. But
what we're doing down here means something. It's not just
revolution we're after. It's political alchemy."

"What does that mean?"

"We're out to change the world."

Jonny scratched at his injured shoulder. "Sounds great," he
said. "Just hope I have the shoes to go with it."

As they moved beyond the star fields, they were plunged
back into darkness. Ice pulled Jonny to one side of the tracks
and said, "Don't step on any wires. Some of 'em are dum-
mies. Cables hooked up to vacuum alarms." Jonny was im-
pressed with the sureness of Ice's moves in the dark tunnels.
Whatever she had been doing with the Croakers for the last
year had revitalized her. Jonny thought back on the last
months he and Ice and Sumi had lived together. It had been
just as Ice described it. Stasis. The long, slow surrender of
emotions to habit. Things could be different now, he thought.
He reached for her shoulder in the darkness, and felt her hand
close around his. Up ahead, there was light on the tracks.

"This is it," said Ice evenly. But Jonny could see she was
trying to contain her excitement. "You're gonna love this.
We're right on the edge of the clinic."

Voices echoed around the edges of the the tunnel, blending
to become a single voice whispering in a language Jonny
could not understand. As they approached the light the sound
deepened and was joined by the astringent smell of disinfec-
tants. Jonny followed Ice up a short flight of particle board
stairs to the flat expanse of a subway platform. A group of
Croakers, techs, by the look of them, were lounging, smoking

and talking, on a stack of brushed aluminum packing cases. A couple of the women waved to Ice from their perch.

"Recognize the place? It's the old financial district metro line," Ice said.

"I've seen photos. But I thought the Committee dynamited these tunnels during the Protein Rebellion."

"They closed off the ends and a lot of the service tunnels, but squatters were living down here for years."

Jonny followed Ice through a maze of maintenance shops sectioned off with ruined vending machines and lozenges of graffiti-covered fiberglass. Croaker techs bent over fiber optic bundles and circuit boards in a jumble of disassembled diagnostic devices (Haag-Streit electron microscopes, magnetic resonance imagers, a video micrographer) nodding and shouting polyglot advice. Further on, Ice led him through a workshop where rusting M-16's and AK-47's were retooled and fitted with computer-aided sighting mechanisms. There was a surgery, cool lights glinting off delicate instruments. Silent children stood to the side of one table, studying a man's open abdomen through an enormous Fresnel lens. A legless woman surgeon, suspended in a harness from a webwork of runners attached to the ceiling, described the tying off of an artery in rapid-fire Spanish. Older children translated into English and Japanese for the younger ones. "We're also a teaching hospital," said Ice. She nodded gravely toward the children. "If things don't work out, they'll be the next generation of Croakers."

Jonny leaned against a wall covered in stylized biomorphic landscapes of L.A., done in watery browns and grays. "This is really ... impressive," he said. Someone had painted the Capital Records building to resemble the bleached skeleton of some prehistoric whale. The HOLLYWOOD sign, all driftwood and jellyfish. He shook his head numbly.

"The place is quiet now," said Ice. "Rumor has it that the Committee's gearing up for a big push. We've been getting almost double our usual patient load."

"How do you get them down here?"

"Same way you got here: through the sewers. Most people make a less spectacular entrance, though."

"I sure hope so," said Jonny. He rubbed his sore shoulder, wondering if he could score some endorphins. "Tell me, you getting many leprosy cases down here? I'm moving Dapsone and Rifampin like cotton candy at the circus."

Ice crooked a finger at Jonny and led him through a poured concrete arch studded with vacuum tubes and plastic children's toys. At the end of a short service corridor they entered a lab. Inside, Ice keyed in a number sequence on a Zijin Chinese PC hooked to a bank of video monitors. Three screens lit up with multicolored snow, which gradually dissipated when Ice punched the monitor housing with the side of her fist. On one screen, a couple of Croakers in vacuumsuits were taking blood from a woman's arm. Fingering the PC's joystick, Jonny moved the picture in tighter on the woman's face. There were marks there, seamless and discolored lepromatous lesions. Another screen showed the same room from a different angle. There were about a dozen other people, smoking and reading on cots. All had lesions similar to the first woman's.

Jonny let out a long breath. "What's with the quarantine?" he asked.

Ice entered another code on the Zijin and more monitors lit up. "It seemed like a good idea. Most of the lepers we've seen have been carrying a weird new strain of the disease. It seems to be viral."

Jonny squinted slightly at the monitors. On one screen, a Croaker was moving from cot to cot, using a scalpel to scrape tissue samples from each leper's arm, while a second Croaker took the samples and sealed them in a plastic case marked with an orange biohazard trefoil. "Viral leprosy? Never heard of it," Jonny said.

"Neither had we," said Ice. She pointed to a monitor where amber alphanumerics scrolled up a line at a time. "We cross-checked all our exam data with the Merck software and came up empty. The symptoms match all the known strains of leprosy— skin macules, epidermal tumors, lesions of the peripheral nerves, loss of feeling in the limbs—but the little bugger that causes it is some kind of mutant-voodoo patch job. It's also killing people."

"How?" asked Jonny.

"Secondary infection. In the latter stages, patients tend to develop high fevers and brain lesions. The pathology could be meningitis. There it is," said Ice. She nodded to a screen at the upper right.

Jonny looked up. The monitor displayed a time-lapse video

micrograph of the leprosy virus, surrounded by numbers and biodata graphs. As he watched, the virus inserted its genetic material into the nucleus of a cell. Within seconds, the virus was cloning itself, filling the cell with ghostly larvae until the walls burst, scattering parasites into the bloodstream. The virus's shape, the polyhedral head, cylindrical sheath, and jointed fibers that attached it to the cell wall, reminded Jonny of pictures he had seen of twentieth-century lunar landing modules. But the proportions of this module were all wrong.

"Jesus, the head on that thing's huge," he said. "But it's a bacteriophage. "Why's it attacking a blood cell instead of bacterium?"

"That's what everybody asks," replied a different voice. Jonny turned and saw a boy wearing the body portion of a vacuumsuit. In one hand, the boy carried the suit's head covering, in the other, a small case marked with a biohazard sticker. "Ice, you teasing the guests again?" he asked. The boy's face was luminously white, his head hairless and smooth. Jonny recognized the look. He was a Zombie Analytic.

As the Zombie shed the rest of his protective gear, depositing it in a gray metal hamper, Ice went to him and kissed him lightly on the lips. She looked back and said, "Jonny, meet Skid the Kid."

The Kid held out one thin, white hand to Jonny and they shook. Closer now, Jonny could see that the boy was no more than sixteen, and thin to the point of anorexia. He wore a tight see-through shirt and black drawstring pants. The archetypal Zombie, Jonny thought. However, there were dark patches on the boy's scalp and hands where the subcutaneous pixels had burned out or been destroyed. He obviously had not had any serious maintenance in months.

"Actually, we've met already," Skid said. "I was in the stomping party that found you in the greenhouse."

"Yeah? Those must be your footprints on the back of my skull."

Skid laughed. "Wouldn't be at all surprised." Over his features, he flashed a boxer's face, sweaty and bruised. "Croakers rule, okay! Eat the dead! Totally badass." A second later, his own face was back. "'Course, I also helped carry you up to the clinic, so maybe it all balances out, right?"

Jonny smiled. "Sure. Someday if I have to beat on you, I'll drive you to the farmacia. No problem." He was put-off by the Kid. It was almost a cellular thing. Most Zombie Analytics Jonny had known had worked too hard at being ingratiating, going straight for the hard sell. No doubt it was some habit left over from their early days in the flesh trade. And it was not helped by the fact that it cost each Zombie a small fortune to maintain their electronics. Still, knowing the time and expense they took to have their skin dermatoned off and underlayed with pixel strips, Jonny found it difficult to work up much sympathy.

But Skid the Kid kept on smiling. "Ice tells me you used to be a cop."

"No," said Jonny. "I was in the Committee for Public Health. Completely different organization."

"What's the difference?"

"The Committee knows what they're doing. And cops can't call in an air strike."

Skid the Kid laughed again, and clapped his hands in delight.

"What's a Zombie doing working with the Croakers? You moonlighting or something?" asked Jonny.

"There's lots of Zombies down here," Ice cut in. "We've got Naginata Sisters on security and the Bosozukos help with vehicle maintenance. The Funky Gurus pretty much run the armory on their own. We're a mongrel group. Everybody's welcome."

Jonny nodded curtly. He sensed a setup. "Sounds great. Think I'll pass, though."

"We weren't trying to recruit you," said Ice quickly. But she frowned so fiercely, Jonny could tell she was lying. And probably disappointed.

Hoping to steer things back to neutral ground, he said, "So tell me more about this virus."

Ice sighed. "Not much more to tell. We don't know what the hell it is or where it came from. If we catch the infection early, we can slow it down with interferon or interlukin IV. But the virus mutates in a few days, and we're back where we started." She opened and closed her hands in frustration. "We're just a clinic, you know? We patch people up and send 'em home. We're not set up to do goddam research."

Skid leaned back against the computer console, fingers busy in his breast pocket. He pulled out a crumpled pack of Beedees, broke off the filter and lit one up. The burning-rope smell of cheap Indian tobacco filled the room. "We've got scouts out, keeping tabs on how the military handles things. Also, we're watching traffic in and out of New Hope. Figure those assholes'll have access to any new vaccines before they hit the street."

"Sounds reasonable," said Jonny. He watched the monitors over Skid's shoulder. They were cycling through a programed surveillance routine, displaying a series of grainy views of the Croakers' underground lair. The greenhouse, with its newly patched bubble. Machine shops. A young mestizo girl leading a group of patients to the surface. The surgery. The children. "Listen, I'm sorry if I'm a little jumpy," Jonny said. "Truth is, I'm hurting and nervous and probably still a little punch drunk. You guys—this setup—it's a lot to take in at once, you know?"

"You have a talent for pissing people off," said Ice. But it was a small reproof, pouting and indulgent. "You'll be all right though, officer."

"Definitely all right. I sense star quality here," Skid said. He puffed at the Beedee and smiled broadly. "You gonna want to see Groucho?"

"Yeah, is he back yet?" asked Ice.

"About an hour ago."

"Aces," Ice replied. She draped an arm across Jonny's shoulders. "Looks like you get an audience with the most wanted man in California."

"Sounds like fun," said Jonny.

"He is."

Skid the Kid raised his eyebrows. "Yeah, like the riddle of the Sphinx."

Jonny followed Ice and Skid past empty and subterranean shop fronts. Each deserted glass facade presented him with a different and more bizarre tableau. He remembered that Ice had said they were all artists down here. He supposed that had something to do with the strange windows. Behind one, an animated hologram, something like a mandala or a printed circuit, showed men and women experiencing all fifty-eight versions of the Tantric afterlife. Another seemed to hold a shooting gallery. A vacuum-suited mannequin was mounted on a revolving wheel of fortune, animal and machine fetishes dangling from its arms and neck. Jonny's legs shook with the subsonic rumbling of traffic overhead. He thought of ghost trains moving through the metro tunnels on endless runs, the passengers turning to dust as they held on to the overhead straps. His reflection in a window startled him, and he hurried to catch up with the others.

"Nice architecture you got down here," Jonny said. "I dig the style. Early Nervous Breakdown, right?"

They walked through an empty lobby, behind a semicircular wall of frosted glass, into the old metro line security complex. Ice knocked on a door of cheap oak veneer and ushered Jonny through. The smell of sandalwood incense was strong. The room (actually two rooms; Jonny could see where the sheet rock had been cut away, leaving a ragged white fringe) was large and mostly empty. It contained an electronic wall map of the metro system, a small lacquered shrine to Shakyamuni, some cheap reproductions of surrealist artwork, and a slight, dark-skinned man with the smooth musculature of a dancer.

A blur of gray metal sliced the air above the man's head. When he opened his hand, the chain end of a kusairagama flew, curling itself snakelike around a bare wall beam. Then, fluid and savage, he started forward, twisting, kicking, and feinting, until he ripped the sickle portion of the weapon across the beam at eye level. He stepped back and exhaled once. Then he turned and grinned, acknowledging Jonny and the others for the first time.

"I see our guest has returned from the dead," he said, unwrapping the chain from the scarred beam. Jonny noticed that the other beams bore similar scars. "You look good in Croaker banderas, Jonny. 'Course, you better not let la Migra see you dressed like that. They'll have your ass over the border and chained to some Tijuana work gang faster than you can say 'green card.'"

Tossing the kusairagama aside, he crossed the room with the same liquid grace he had displayed while on the attack. His eyes were small and dark, but quick, missing nothing. He wore his hair slicked back, chollo-style, and had crosshatched tattoos extending from his shoulders to his wrists, the mark of a particular Iban warrior-priest class. A gold earring, a caduceus, dangled from his left lobe. As he shook Jonny's hand, he said, "The name's Groucho, by the way. Please come in."

The anarchist went to a foam-rubber mattress set in a corner of the room, and pulled on a black mesh T-shirt. On a cheap plastic folding table lay a crumbling volume of Rimbaud. Near it was an old-fashioned metronome with a photo of an eye clipped to the pendulum. Jonny wondered if it was some kind of joke.

"Do you like our setup?" asked Groucho. "I'm sure these two have been keeping you busy. That's good. Boredom and lack of purpose are the chief problems of our age. Don't you agree, Jonny?"

Jonny, who was still trying to figure out the metronome joke, was caught off guard. "What? Oh yeah, sure. Boredom and getting shot in the head."

Groucho brought over a couple of canvas chairs and sat down, smiling in a manner that Jonny found unsettling. The anarchist possessed a certain relaxed grace, an unaffected air, that was riveting. It was impossible to take your eyes off him.

"But violence is the choice we've made, isn't it?" Groucho said. "We accept the uncertainties; our lives revolve around them. As Croakers, we don't kill because we want to. As a Buddhist, it goes against all my principles. But the act of ridding ourselves of the Committee brings death with it. That's why we run these clinics. It's partly revolution, but, frankly, it's part penance, too. When you take life, you are also obligated to try and save it." He shrugged. "And speaking of payback, please accept my thanks for blowing away that pig, Lieutenant Cawfly." This last bit Groucho spoke with venom.

"Did somebody buy a billboard about that or something?" Jonny asked. He shook his head. "I was a lot younger then. I don't even know if I'd do it now. But I can tell you it wasn't for anybody's liberation but my own."

"Independent thought and action are essential for a good anarchist," said Groucho.

Jonny slammed his fist onto the table. "Don't call me that! I'm no anarquista and I wouldn't have come here if I thought I was going to get campaign speeches."

Jonny looked at Ice hoping for support, but she was reading Rimbaud over Skid's shoulder. Abandoning me to the lions, Jonny thought.

Groucho leaned forward, pointing his finger at Jonny. "No monkeys are soldiers, all monkeys are mischievous, ergo

Some mischievous creatures are not soldiers," he said. "Jonny, you're a dealer—you help to undermine a corrupt system. You subvert it and that is a basic function of a revolutionary."

The anarchist's grin widened and he held up his hands to indicate that he knew he was moving too fast. Lightly, he rose from his chair and went to a battered desk, where he pulled a bottle of red wine from a file drawer. The sight of the liquor made Jonny groan. His thought was that he would like to have the whole thing for himself, to leave these people and their strange art, their talk of politics and death, and get lost in the sweet oblivion of ethanol madness. On the other hand, his stomach turned to acid mush at the mere thought of alcohol. While he tried to sort out which impulse was stronger, his psychic desires or his physical needs, he gazed at the art reproductions above his head.

When Groucho returned, he said, "Do you like the surrealists? They were a remarkable twentieth-century art movement. The first artists to genuinely comprehend the modern age. They applied principles of both psychology and physics to their work, attempting to unite the conscious and unconscious in a single gesture. But more than that, they were the ultimate revolutionaries, questioning everything that was known or knowable."

To Jonny, the Ernsts and the Dalis could have been snapshots from an only slightly depraved tour book of Los Angeles. The empty architecture that Groucho identified as Chirico's standard made him think of crumbling freeway overpasses and stretches of Hollywood in those few hours after sunset, before the gangs took possession of them for the night. The Tanguy reproductions reminded him of the mural of Los Angeles on the train platform. Someone had copied his style very accurately.

Groucho passed around fluted, black champagne glasses, then opened the bottle and poured wine for all. The anarchist raised his glass as in a toast, but he did not drink. Instead, he went back to his chair, his eyes distant. Jonny felt relief when Ice sat beside him on the thin foam mattress.

"Forgive me if I seem to be pushing things," said Groucho. "I know about your run-in with Zamora. In fact, I may know more about old Pere Ubu's motives than you. How did you escape?"

"I didn't. Zamora let me go," Jonny replied, sniffing the tart wine. His stomach won the battle over his brain. He set the glass down beside his foot.

"Yes, that makes sense in light of everything else." Groucho nodded, off somewhere.

"In light of what?"

The anarchist frowned, rolling the crystal glass between his palms. "Things are afoot, Jonny. I don't know the specifics yet. There are layers that are still hidden to me. Did you know that we've been trying to contact you, but couldn't because there was a tail on you for the last few weeks?"

"I had no idea."

"I thought not. Then old Ubu catches you and releases you a few hours later. Nimble Virtue turned you, by the way."

"I know. I saw her at the detention center."

Ice chuckled. "I hope you shook that bitch up. She's playing finger for Zamora, sucking up to the old bastard. Got Easy Money working for her now, too."

"The slime leading the slime," said Jonny.

"Exactly," said Groucho. Over the anarchist's shoulder, Skid flashed Nimble Virtue's ravaged face. He stuck a finger up his nose, making a great production out of examining what he found there. He pulled his ears, rolled his eyes back in his sockets. A very un-Zombie thing to do. Jonny laughed in spite of himself.

"I understand that Easy Money's sticky fingers have gotten him in deep shit with Conover," Groucho said. "Did you hear that the Colonel is getting political heat from Sacramento about the smuggler lords? I believe he's getting set for a big move against them. There's talk that the Army's trying to get it together and take the moon back from the Alpha Rats. And somewhere in the middle of all this, you fit in, Jonny. Your name is all over town. Someone even mentioned Arabs."

Jonny rubbed at his sore shoulder. To Groucho, he said, "Look, if this is some simple trick to get me to join your army, you can forget it. The Colonel picked me up because he's trying to queer some deal of Conover's."

Groucho sipped his wine. He stared at the floor. "I doubt that. If anything, Zamora's trying to angle himself in for a piece of the action. That's why his move against the lords is so important. Not only will it satisfy the politicians, but if it succeeds, it will force the lords to deal with him directly. And that's what we're waiting for—when Zamora makes his move, so do we. An all-out attack on the Committee."

Jonny nodded. Something prickled along his spine as he realized that the anarchist was completely sincere. Jonny smiled and shivered at the same time. He thought of war.

"Why exactly did you come here?" asked Groucho.

"I need to get out of town," Jonny said. "You've just said I'm being watched. That means I can't use any of my normal contacts. I heard that the Croakers have some smuggling routes that'll get me out to the desert."

Groucho smiled and opened his hands. "I'd love to help you, Jonny. You're center stage in fat Ubu's carnival. Whatever we can do to trip him up is fine by me."

"There's one more thing," Jonny said. "I have to get Sumi, the woman I live with. I won't leave the city without her."

"That might be more difficult," said Groucho. He ran a finger around the rim of his glass, producing a clear, high, ringing tone. "The Committee must know where you live by now."

"I don't think so. If they did, why would they pay Nimble Virtue to tip them that I was at the Pit? Wouldn't it be better to surprise me at home?"

"Not necessarily," said Ice. "They probably assumed we'd boobytrapped the apartment, so you'd be easier to pick off in the street."

Jonny looked at Groucho. "Your mind is made up?" asked the anarchist.

"I won't go without her."

"Your loyalty's commendable. Ice, what do you think?"

"Sumi means a lot to me, too, Groucho," Ice said. "I don't like the idea of leaving her out there alone. She's not equipped to deal with that kind of craziness."

Ice sat with her legs bent. Jonny looped an arm around one of her knees. It was just like old times. The two of them taking care of Sumi. That was assuming, he reminded himself, that Sumi was all right. That no one had gotten to her yet. "What's your answer?" Jonny asked.

Groucho leaned back in his plastic folding chair, pointed to the wall over Jonny's head. "You see those photos, Jonny?" he asked quietly. "The one on the right is from the uprising in Paris, nineteen sixty-eight. The other is the Spanish war against the fascists, in thirty-seven. Yet here we are, over a

hundred years later, in a mad city in a sick century fighting
exactly the same battles they fought. Isolated, alienated,
bored, and drugged beyond caring. We're the trained dogs of
the Spectacle. Zamora whistles, and we jump through his
hoops. The Committee is the Spectacle's ultimate tool. It's
devoured our lives, all art, our dignity. But existence is not
predicated on the whim of politicians." The anarchist took a
sip of wine. "A hundred and fifty years ago the surrealists
proclaimed themselves the revolt of the spirit. The spark in the
wind, seeking the powder keg." The anarchist nodded in satis-
faction. "So, we'll get your friend and we'll get you out of
town and, with any luck at all, we'll humiliate fat King Ubu in
the process. How does that sound?"

Jonny smiled at the anarchist; he just could not resist.
"Yeah, but what if you get caught?"

Ice began to recite, and Skid joined in:

> "Well, then, rent me a tomb,
> whitewashed and outlined in cement—
> far, far underground."

Jonny frowned and fingered the musty volume of poetry.
"Rimbaud, right? Terrific. By the way, where'd that wine go?"

5

THE RESCUE OF SUMIMASEN _____

An ACID RAIN, the sins of the fathers, blew down hard and cold, etching obscure messages into the faces of the graceless old buildings. A few blocks to the south, beyond the fifty-story torus housing Lockheed's business offices, carbon arcs burned a pure white nimbus of light into the fat, menacing clouds. Pemex-U.S. was out there somewhere, Jonny knew. Exxon; Krupp International. And Sony—a flat black silicon sphere, almost invisible at night, like a hole punched in the sky. Wilshire Boulevard.

Hushed evening crowds hurried by. Businessmen, anonymous in their Gucci snakeskin goggles and respirators. Groups of giggling teenage girls in matching state school ponchos. A stoned young boy, shirtless chest aglow with bioluminescent tattoos, kicked up wings of water on a skateboard. When Ice reached Jonny's side, the boy circled once in the street, gave them the finger, and took off. Ice laughed once. "Don't say it," said Jonny. She laughed again.

"I didn't have to, doll. It's plain as day. That's your lean-and-hungry youth that just skated by."

Jonny shook his head. "I was never that skinny," he said. A great knot of tension was uncoiling in his chest. He kicked at some weeds sprouting through a crack in the pavement. Outside again, in the street, a cold wind blowing stinking sulfur rain. There was a siren fading somewhere, far off. He was home. It felt great.

"Where to?" he asked.

Ice nodded up the street; she started that way and Jonny followed. He could see Groucho and Skid a few meters ahead.

They had left the old subway terminal perhaps twenty minutes before. Jonny had been surprised at how easily they had reached the surface, cutting through sewers and abandoned underground shopping malls full of rotting acoustical tiles and dismembered mannequins. They had emerged in the back of a heavy-equipment warehouse surrounded by the smell of rust and slow leaking cannisters of toluene. Jonny had been the first one out the door. The first one into the rain. Ice had given him a belted Army raincoat before they had left the clinic. Now, walking with her, he used one hand to hold the collar of the coat closed; he kept the other hand in his pocket, around the textured plastic grip of his Futukoro. Three extra clips clicked against each other in his pocket.

Across from a storage yard full of PVC piping, Groucho and Skid were in animated conversation with an albino. Jonny followed Ice through the flooded street, over to where the men were talking. The albino was seated sideways in the cab of an armored Mercedes van, a squat, double-axled monstrosity with thick wire mesh bolted over the windows and grubby scales of titanium alloy welded to the body. Jonny thought the vehicle looked something like the chimeric offspring of a half-track and a rhinoceros. He was admiring its extraordinary and single-minded ugliness when Groucho called him over.

"Jonny, I want you to meet our driver, Man Ray. He runs with the Funky Gurus," said the anarchist.

Man Ray, the albino, gave Jonny a slight nod and Jonny responded in kind. Then he added a quick upward movement with two fingers of his right hand, drawing the fingers across his lips horizontally, running through a rapid series of similar gestures—a terse street distillation of Amerslan and gang recognition codes. Obviously surprised, Man Ray gave him the answering gesture. Jonny knew the Gurus well. They were all insane, he had decided years before, but pleasantly so. They called themselves combat artists, insisted on fighting with weapons of their own devising. Their greatest pleasure came in staging absurd and bloody raids on rival gangs. There was always a theme; sometimes it was eating utensils, sometimes patterns of light and color. For the Gurus, style always counted more than the damage done, but the damage was usually considerable.

Man Ray wore what appeared to be homemade polypyrrole body armor, cut kendo-style, and red high-top sneakers. A gold obi around his waist was studded with throwing darts, shurikens, and other small glittering things Jonny did not recognize. Like many of the Gurus, Man Ray was not a true albino; his features were Negroid, but his face was burned the palest of pinks, shading to yellow behind his ears. Traditionally, the Gurus were recruited from workers at the Daimyo Corporation's hellish zero-G foundries orbiting the moon. Constant exposure to low-level radiation often burned out the melanin-producing cells in the workers' skin.

"Thanks for the wheels," Jonny said. "I owe you."

Man Ray smiled. He had no teeth, just stained porcelain implants running along his upper and lower jaws, like twin walls. "You don't owe me nothin'. Blood's my muse. Flesh is my canvas," Man Ray said. "I wouldn't miss a run." He looked at Jonny, grinning slyly. "Groucho here's been telling me how you're a great appreciator of art, a true fan of beauty. Here—" he said, plucking something from his sash. "This is new."

Jonny accepted the object, turning it over in his hands. It was a perfect silver rose, about half the size of a natural one, its edges rimmed with hot gold from the sodium street lights. Man Ray pointed to the storage yard. "Over the top," he said.

Jonny looked at him once, glanced at Ice. He shrugged and threw the rose over the collapsing hurricane fence that surrounded the pipes.

There was silence, then a rush of air; the street was lit by an explosion of white flame that leapt ten meters into the air. In seconds, the blaze became a shaft of churning light, burning down to a sizzling white mass of flame and molten piping. Jonny turned to Man Ray, who said, "Les fleurs du mal."

"Fuck that," said Jonny. "That was a phosphorous grenade."

"Everybody's a critic," Man Ray told Groucho. The Croaker stepped into the passenger side of the van, Skid behind him. Jonny got into the back, hunkering down next to Ice. Man Ray gunned the van's big methanol engine and turned north onto La Cienega toward Hollywood.

The Funky Guru thumbed on a shortwave scanner, tuned to the Committee's frequencies, and plugged in a sound chip. The metallic voice of Committee dispatchers was overlaid with music—Taking Tiger Mountain doing an up-tempo

version of "Saint James Infirmary," Saint Peter taking the lead
vocals.

> "I went down to Saint James Infirmary.
> All was still as night.
> My gal was on the table,
> stretched out so pale, so white.
> I went to Saint James Infirmary—"

As the van rumbled across Beverly Boulevard, Jonny was
suddenly aware of being very cold. He shivered against the
jellied glycerin padding of the walls of the van, clenching his
teeth to keep them from chattering. His right shoulder was
almost numb; before leaving the clinic, Ice had placed a xylo-
caine transdermal patch under the induction cast. The Com-
mittee's last wave of raids had left endorphins in short supply,
she had explained. Now she was staring out one of the van's
armored windows, frowning to herself.

"Your optimism's contagious," Jonny told her.

Ice gave him a weak smile and asked, "What're you going
to do when we get Sumi?"

"I thought you understood that," he said. "Gonna get the
hell out of here. Groucho said he'd check his contacts in the
south. Maybe head down to Mexico. Why?"

Ice wiped away a small island of fog her breath had left on
the window. They passed a truck unloading a cargo of black
market meat. Boneless pig heads hung limply from the back,
like masks from some awful theater. "What if Sumi doesn't
want to leave?" she asked.

"That's her decision," Jonny said. "She can do what she
wants." His voice was harder than he had intended. The possi-
bility that Sumi might choose to stay behind had not occurred
to him. He did not want to battle with Ice for Sumi's loyalty.
He had, after all, stayed with her when Ice took off. But Ice
and Sumi had been lovers on and off before Jonny had known
either of them. No comfort there.

"You won't stay?" Ice asked.

"I can't."

"Why not?"

"Because the Colonel wants to use my balls for an ash-
tray," Jonny replied. "Because Easy Money knows I'm look-
ing for him and that means he's looking for me. And because I

don't believe any of this *anarquista* wet dream bullshit. Nothing changes—it never does. One bunch loses power, another comes in. So what? There's new faces to hate, new guns to run from. But nothing real ever changes."

"Maybe we can help that," she said.

"We're talking about the Committee here," Jonny said. "They'll eat your faces off. When we get Sumi, I'm gone."

"I wish you wouldn't."

"What do you want from me?"

Ice fixed Jonny with a look that he could not quite read. Anger, frustration, fear, they were all there.

"What?" he repeated.

"You never make it easy, do you?" she said. "Maybe I just want us all to be together again. The three of us."

Why does she have to bring this up now, Jonny wondered. He had been thinking along similar lines all along, the three of them together again. But with Zamora and Easy Money gunning for him, it seemed impossible. Ice, he knew, would not see it that way. Her love came in broader strokes, great passions, grand gestures. That's why she's a good Croaker, he thought. That's why she ran away. "I want the same thing you do," he whispered. "But not here."

"I can't leave," said Ice.

"I can't stay." They were on Sunset now, rolling past crowds hanging around the bars and theaters. A restaurant shaped like Kukulcan's pyramid at Chichen Itza, outlined in bright neon. Jonny's face grew hot. "Don't ask me to prove myself, okay? I'm not the one who took the big walk," he said.

Almost without sound, Ice moved to the front of the van. She sat on the floor behind Groucho. Jonny tried to look out the window, but found himself watching Ice's reflection as she rocked with the gentle motion of the van. He felt alone, hardly human—he could have been an insect observing the Croakers and the lone Guru from the ceiling. Jonny was about to speak when Ice pointed at something and said, "Pull over there."

Man Ray turned up a side street near the World Link substation, shielding the van from Sunset behind a stand of towering date palms. The Guru killed the engine, reached up and flicked on an overhead light.

Groucho turned to Jonny, his face soft and ghostly in the dim light. "Let's make this fast," he said.

Jonny nodded. "We're going in the back way."

Man Ray duck-walked past Jonny to the rear of the van and removed one of the side panels, jellied glycerine rolling in sluggish waves. From a storage area, he removed a Medusa, something like an electrified cat o' nine tails, and some smaller gear, pistols and bolos, which he handed to the Croakers. Over the Guru's shoulder, Jonny could see a whole rack of colorful and oddly outfitted weapons. "See anything you like?" Man Ray asked.

"I'm fine," said Jonny.

Man Ray looked disappointed. "You got this bad prosaic streak, you know?"

The rain had given way to wind-driven mist. Ice moved ahead of them in a loping trot, Skid doggedly at her side. Jonny did not try to catch up, preferring to let her cope with the ghosts in her own way.

Twisted winds whipped the mist into tiny vortices in the lee of an enormous tented structure. One hundred meters high and covering almost sixty square blocks, a perverse relic, it was the single remaining pavilion from the Los Angeles-Tokyo Exposition, held to celebrate the one hundreth anniversary of the transistor.

It was a series of tents, really, two hundred and eighty of them, each half an acre of teflon-coated fiberglass, all mildewed and leaking badly. Beneath the tents were three life-size thermoplast and concrete reconstructions that had comprised the Golden Age of Hollywood Pavilion: Robin Hood's castle, sporting a peeling metallic caricature that might once have resembled Errol Flynn; the Emerald City from *The Wizard of Oz*, and the Babylonian temple from D. W. Griffith's *Intolerance*. Jonny lived in the last of these reconstructions, as did two thousand other people.

At a service port near the bottom of a support pylon, Jonny pried a ten-key pad away from its housing. Sumi had set the pad there loosely, with a gummy brown adhesive, after instructing him how to short out the locking mechanism. With a *thunk*, the port slid open and the five of them entered, quickly climbing up a spiral staircase to a slimy platform at the top. Jonny shorted out a second pad, and a moment later they were out on the translucent surface of the tent itself.

Jonny motioned for them to spread out, to keep the tent fabric from sagging under their weight. Above their heads,

suspended in slings and plastic bubbles, were the lost tribes of
Los Angeles.

Any permanent or semi-permanent structure in the city was
an invitation to squatters. In the years since its construction,
the Hollywood Pavilion had served as home to thousands of
local down-and-outers, illegals from Mexico and Jamaica, in-
dentured workers from Thailand and the Ukraine. A few of
those one-percenters, the ones who had found the life below
too confining or too desperate, had moved to the open spaces
above the tents themselves, wandering like nomads across the
billowing fiberglass dunes. Years later, tribes hunted, whole
societies had sprung up with their own customs and lan-
guages. Jonny watched Man Ray and Skid taking it all in,
eyeing the delicate habitats with a combination of fascination
and nervousness. Groucho waved happily to the fleeting fig-
ures shadowing them along the cables. On the dripping wires
were hung tribal banners, crude Catholic shrines, prayer flags
marked with curious symbols resembling Mayan, Nepalese,
and parts of schematic diagrams, cabalistic cries for help di-
rected at any god or gods who might be listening.

Jonny felt in control here. He was gripped by a strange
combination of tension and elation. His mind raced. He found
himself staring at the moon as it appeared from behind a cloud
bank. He thought of the Alpha Rats. Again, he wondered if
somewhere on that airless surface they were watching all this,
noting it for some future inquiry. He had the sudden urge to
meet them, to somehow explain things to them. At that same
moment, he thought of Sumi down below, unaware of his and
Ice's presence. His senses expanded outward until they en-
compassed the whole of the saddle-backed landscape. This is
right, he thought; it was good to be moving again. He felt as if
he had regained some lost part of himself.

He broke ranks and scrambled to the crest of a corner dune.
Its peak was a circular anchorage, open to the structure below.
Quickly, he uncoiled lengths of nylon rope attached to the
cement anchor and let them drop. Ice caught up with him,
releasing other lines. She still would not look at him, but
Jonny knew she was feeling a high similar to his. Climbing
clumsily in his cast, he made it over the rim and dropped with
Ice to a ledge beside a Babylonian elephant deity, its chicken-
wire frame visible through the cracked concrete. The others
dropped down a moment later. A tangle of echoing voices

from below made it impossible to hear; Jonny signed for them to follow him inside.

They moved through a series of packed gray rooms, dusty storage areas for the concession stands that had filled the pavilion during the expo. They entered a clearing; around them, half-empty crates trailed shreds of Taiwanese gun catalogs (improvised packing material) to rows of ceiling-high shelves crowded with miniature cowboy and samurai figures, still new in their plastic wrappers. Skid picked up souvenirs as he walked along: Hollywood Boulevard sealed in a water-filled lucite bubble; when he shook it, plastic snow settled over the buildings; paper jackets emblazoned with the Rising Sun; candy in the shape of silicon chips. Except for a layer of dust, most of the merchandise seemed to have changed very little over the years. Wall-sized holograms of Uncle Sam and Disney characters, dreams figures of an extinct culture, were carefully sealed in bubble pack and duct tape, waiting for their owners to return from other errands.

They came to a flight of stairs. Jonny led them down a couple of levels, then up one, careful to keep to the deserted areas of the structure. They saw yellow signs in a dozen languages warning them not to smoke, pointing out fire exits, and giving long and detailed explanations of local hygiene laws.

From below drifted the smell of bodies pressed close together, cooking fires, mildew, and something else—the almost metallic scent of nervous action. Strange insect odors of commerce, shady deals, strictly off-the-record meetings. They came upon a young girl kneeling in the corridor, bathed in the blue light of an ancient portable television, tying off with a hachimaka. When she saw them, the girl gathered up her works and took off. She left the television, which was slowly rolling a dead channel of snow.

At the junction of four corridors, Ice signed for Jonny to take the rear entrance of the apartment, while she took Skid and Groucho to check out the front. Jonny gave her the acknowledging sign and, with Man Ray, started down the corridor to his right. Halfway down, they entered a room of immense, asbestos-wrapped standing pipes.

"Help me get this up," whispered Jonny, indicating a textured metal plate in the floor. "We're right above the apartment."

The two of them stooped, worked their fingers under the plate and lifted it free. Jonny went feet-first into the hole, kicking out the plastic louvers of a false ventilating duct, and dropped to the floor of the apartment. A moment later he heard Man Ray hit the floor behind him.

The room was dark, the air dead and hot; it clung to Jonny, bitter with the fumes of charred synthetics.

A mass of broken furniture lay scattered across the floor, blistered seat backs and pressboard chair legs forming the ribs of some skinned animal. Small appliances seemed to have been thrown into a pile and methodically smashed. Jonny had trouble identifying individual objects—he could make out a coffee grinder and a small microwave oven; the rest of it was unrecognizable, beaten beyond recognition. Someone had placed duct tape over the room's only window. To hide what they were doing, he thought. The tape was peeling off now, the pavilion's floods cutting the far wall into neat diagonal segments, alternating bands of light and dark. Pills and disk-ettes crunched beneath their feet, giving off a sour reek of spoiled hormonal extracts; an Indian throw rug was gummy with half-dissolved capsules of vasopressin and prolactin. There did not seem to be much in the room that was not burned or broken.

They followed a trail of books and Sumi's gutted electronic gear (fused circuits glowing like raw opals) down the hall to the bedroom. In the small chamber, the arson smell was stronger. Man Ray thumbed on a small squeeze light attached to his obi. The bed had been torched. Shredded clothes were scattered over the floor, and Freon slurred the wall from a refrigeration unit, now slag, that Jonny had hidden to store perishable drugs and the occasional black market kidney or lung for a client.

A scraping. From the living room.

Both men had their weapons up and out, Jonny leaning into the hall, anxious for something to shoot. In the far room, Ice and the others were silently surveying the wreckage on the floor.

"Back here," Jonny called.

They came back, huddling dumbly in the doorway. Ice performed a slow motion sleepwalk through the bedroom, stopping occasionally to finger a piece of clothing, a crushed circuit board, vials of pills. Man Ray's light fixed her in a wedge of sudden color. She turned to Jonny. "Her tool belt is gone," Ice said.

"That's good," said Groucho hopefully. "Then there's a chance Sumi got away."

Jonny leaned against the wall, sliding down into a crouch. "And maybe they just took it with them for evidence. Prove she's a Watt Snatcher."

From the corner of his eye, Jonny saw Skid shifting his weight nervously from foot to foot. "Maybe we shouldn't stay here," said the Kid quietly.

Ice stood up, holding a small prayer wheel; its half-melted copper cap squeaked as she spun it. "Either way, Sumi's long gone," she said. "Turn off that damned light."

Man Ray put the squeeze light back on his sash. Jonny remained on his haunches; Ice kicked her way through the clothes and half-melted lumps of cheap plastic furniture, and nudged him with her boot. "Looks like it's just you and me for now, cowboy," she said.

Jonny looked up at her. "I'm going to kill someone for this, you know."

Ice nodded, smiled. "Well, don't forget to leave something for me," she said.

"This is payback from Zamora," said Jonny.

Groucho cleared his throat. "I think Skid was right a moment ago," he said. "Perhaps we ought to leave. If Pere Ubu's involved, he may have left sentries behind."

Jonny pulled himself from the floor, looking the room over one more time, pressing the image in his brain for later, when he might need the anger. "Okay," he said, "we came in the back, we go out the front. Good crowds for cover."

They left the apartment. Skid abandoned his coat and walked point in his Zombie gear: an innocent hustler in search of the night's mark. They saw no Committee boys on the way out.

The main courtyard of the Babylonian temple was stifling in the overheated illumination coming from tiered ranks of klieg lamps. Dozens of made-up, costumed extras milled around, Valley kids mostly, speaking in hushed cathedral tones. The movie set reminded Jonny of something—an immense surgery, the light giving people and objects a look of startling precision and sterility.

"Okay kids, Ms. Vega's going to make her walk in a minute," came a man's flat nasal voice from a P.A. "What we need here is lots of clapping and cheering. But no whistling. You want to whistle, go see kick-boxing."

This brought shrill waves of high-pitched whistling from the temple's squatters who were massed just behind a police line around the set. The extras were costumed in cleaned-up Hollywood versions of squatter gear, much too clean and well-fed, thought Jonny.

"Very funny. Get to your positions, kids."

Jonny and the others joined the general flow of the crowd, threading their way through the back of the set, following a line of dancers in sequined parodies of Lunar Commando vacuum-suits. Jonny was not particularly surprised by the presence of the film crew; it was not the first time he and the other squatters had been forced from their digs by some local production company. Aoki Vega was one of the Link's most popular musical-porn stars. The irony of the situation, Jonny thought, was that the Link was going to turn around and sell the broadcast of Vega's performance to the same squatters they had displaced, presenting them with an expensive and glittering souvenir of their powerlessness.

The dancers Jonny and the others were following seemed to be headed to a partitioned area at the far end of the pavilion near a semicircle of honeywagons and generator trucks. Skid was walking on his toes, trying to see over the line of extras waiting to cheer the star. A bank of stadium-sized video projectors displayed views of the set from several different angles.

As he pushed his way through the extras, Jonny became aware of a certain unnerving sameness about them, as if they had all been weaned from the same shallow gene pool. Caucasian faces were blandly orientalized; nisei kids snapping their fingers to unheard pop tunes, their hair bleached and skin darkened with biologics to some bizarre ideal of southern California chic. They could have been from anywhere, nowhere. A gag postcard about sex appeal and beaches.

"I know you. You're the producer, right?" said someone nearby.

Jonny turned to her. She wore a loose jacket of woven

aluminum filament, plated gold. Her face held the same assembly-line features as the others. Only her eyes were memorable. She wore diffraction grating contacts; her eyes were spiraling rainbows.

"We met at Marty's party in Laurel Canyon," she said brightly. "You're Mister Radoslav, right?"

It was obvious to Jonny that the woman was stoned. She might as easily have thought he was the Pope. Jonny, still moving, glanced over at the police line, then fixed her with the most radiant smile he could muster. "Please keep your voice down," he said. "No one's supposed to know I'm here." He put his arm around Skid. "This is my associate, Mister Kidd."

"My pleasure," the woman said, extending a bronzed hand. She and Skid shook, the Kid mumbling an incoherent pleasantry.

"Tell me, is there somewhere we can go and talk, Ms.—?" Jonny began.

"Viebecke," she said. "But everybody calls me Becky."

"Becky, of course. Is there anywhere we can speak privately, Becky? Perhaps discuss an audition?"

"Sure," she said. "The extras' trailer is probably empty now." The look she gave Jonny was infused with such hunger and lust that, for a moment, he considered cutting right then and there and taking his chances with the police.

Something glided by. Jonny looked up. A long, articulated arm supporting a German video-cam was hovering a few meters overhead; a half-dozen lenses rotated, pulling to focus on them. His face and Skid's were splashed across the dozen enormous video screens. "The trailer sounds fine," he said.

Ice and the others were waiting beside a two-story boom crane that reminded him of an orange praying mantis. He introduced the others to Becky, who clung to his arm, looking disappointed when she saw Ice. Then she smiled, the Hollywood optimism bubbling forth.

"Oh wow, are you guys actors, too?" she crooned.

"How'd you guess?" asked Ice, flashing her teeth.

"We're casting a new feature right now," said Jonny. "Looking for fresh, interesting faces."

Becky giggled and led them to a group of trailers behind the honeywagon. The chemical smells of processed fish and beef analogs permeated the place. Becky went inside before them, holding up a hand to indicate that they should wait there. The sound of raised voices came from beyond the door. Jonny looked at Ice. She shook her head slowly.

A moment later, a young woman came storming out of the trailer. She resembled Becky so strongly that for an instant Jonny thought it was the actress in a new set of clothes. But the new woman just glared at them and stalked off. "You can come in now," Becky called from the doorway. They went inside.

The trailer was long and narrow, smelling faintly of perfume and sweat, with rows of lighted mirrors on one side, benches and hooks heavy with clothes on the other. Sun lamps and video monitors were crowded at opposite ends of the room. Jonny and the others went immediately to the clothes and started pawing through them. Becky perched on a table by the mirrors, holding her head rigid, favoring them with her best side.

"What are you guys doing?" she asked at last.

"Costumes," said Jonny. "Gotta know what's in with the 'in' crowd, right?"

Becky lit a joint, puffed, and rose from her perch, trying to keep up a merry front. Man Ray found a hound's-tooth overcoat that fit over his body armor; Ice put on a white toreador jacket, trimmed with gold beads. When Becky laid a hand on Jonny's arm she was radiating nervousness, but her face remained a smiling mask. Looking at her, Jonny felt an obscure sorrow. He wondered if she had any other facial expressions buried somewhere under all that bargain-basement surgery.

"Is there anything you want to ask me?" she purred.

"Yeah—there much security down at this end of the set?"

Becky looked at him blankly, like a deranged puppy. She screamed, "Hey! You aren't the producer!"

"We're criminals," said Jonny. "Desperate, armed criminals."

Becky fell back drunkenly and cowered in a far corner of the trailer, whimpering and mumbling "Oh wow" like a mantra.

They had their new clothes on in a few seconds (Groucho in a Mexican Air Force jacket studded with medals, Skid in a black leather jumpsuit and Chinese revivalist Mao cap) and started out the door. Jonny went to Becky to attempt a quick apology. She was still in the corner, struck dumb with drugs

and fear, and when she thrust a chair at him, he could not tell
if she wanted to give it to him or hit him with it. He just
backed away slowly saying, "I'm sorry, Becky. But it's our
asses."

Outside, the P.A. was blaring, "Okay kids, let's really hear
it."

They moved to the very back of the set, smiling at the
techs, just another group of extras waiting for their call, and
started out between two grinding generator rigs. Behind them
they heard the trailer door burst open and a shrill, hysterical
voice. "He's not the producer! He's just a goddam thief!"

Security moved in quickly on the screaming actress. By the
Babylon set, music started, drowning out Becky's voice.
Someone called out for them to stop. But Jonny and the rest
were running then, out of the pavilion and across the wet
street.

Near the van, Jonny sneaked a look over his shoulder and
saw a couple of overweight film company rent-a-cops in pur-
suit. He almost laughed. Spinning on the balls of his feet, he
brought his Futukoro up level with the rent-a-cops' heaving
chests. The nearest one saw him, momentarily misplaced his
center of gravity, and went down in a puddle like an over-
stuffed sack. His partner did a little tap dance, hands thrust
over his head, and started back toward the bright lights of the
pavilion.

Jonny ran on to the van, arriving there just in time to see
Skid hit the street under the hulked black back of a uniform.
Ice went down on top of them. The bright flicker of her knife
blade, and she and Skid were up. Groucho caught another
uniform, whipping his bolo like a garrote, pinning the uni-
form's upraised arm to his throat before dispatching him with
a kick to the solar plexus. Very weird for rent-a-cops, thought
Jonny. A couple of Futukoro rounds slammed into the scarred
armor on the side of the van. Very fucking weird.

One of the uniforms scrambled by, illuminated by the
flickering green fluorescence of a street lamp. "Oh shit,"
Jonny said.

He ducked and ran, hoping the Committee boys had not
spotted him. Man Ray was already behind the wheel of the
van, gunning the engine. Ice and Groucho had their guns out,
and were giving Jonny covering fire. The three jumped in the

back. Skid, however, remained outside in maniacal pursuit of the Committee boy who had attacked him.

Man Ray ground the van into gear, accelerating past the Kid. Jonny held onto one of Groucho's arms as the Croaker leaned out the back. He snared the Kid and they dragged him by his sleeves for a block or so before Ice got hold of his collar and pulled him inside.

A hovercar skimmed down low over the van, burning lights, manic shadows; hot fists of turbine wash forced them back from the door. Man Ray jammed through the gears. He took two corners, nearly overturning the van on one, but the hovercar just hung there. Then it suddenly veered off to the left.

It seemed for a moment that they had lost it, but it dropped down a few feet in front of them, barely skimming over the puddles. Man Ray stood on the brakes, sending the van wiggling down the street like a speared fish. When he regained control, the Guru ran them through a parking lot off Vine and out onto Melrose.

Gripping the doorframe, Jonny and the others shot at the turbine vanes on the underside of the hovercar with Man Ray's custom ammo. Pink and silver spheres impacted the polycarbonate surface; blue firework dragons pawed at the landing gear, before being sucked up through the intake ports. Skid pushed past them and threw some of Man Ray's roses, knife-fashion, at the low flying car. They exploded behind the van, blistering asphalt and palm trees.

"Let there be light!" yelled Man Ray. He cranked up the shortwave scanner, making adjustments to his own broadcasting unit. "Listen'a that dumb fuck," he said. "Thinks he's calling us in. I got that boy jammed so hard, surprised he knows which end holds the mike."

The hovercar let loose then with a burst of automatic weapons fire that hammered down on the roof of the van like a phosphorescent avalanche, blue sparks dancing around the edges of the door. Jonny and the others fell back. Man Ray steered them onto Wilshire Boulevard, dodging slow-moving low riders and pedicabs.

Jonny leaned up to the driver seat. "How far are we from the underground?" he yelled.

"Almost there," Man Ray said. He had slipped on a high-domed crash helmet.

"Can we take more of that fire?"

The Guru grinned through high-impact plastic. "Don't insult me."

The glass donut of Lockheed's office tower was glowing just a few blocks ahead. The Guru steered the van onto a side street, trying to lose their tail before heading for the clinic. The hovercar hung implacably above them.

"We're really eating it," Man Ray said. "There's no major turn-offs and the underground's just ahead. Any suggestions?"

"I got one," said Ice. She pulled one of the Croakers' Kalashnikov rifles, retrofit with an M-79 grenade launcher, from the weapons bin. The van was running fast down a side street between long rows of grimed and decaying old geodesic greenhouses, some forgotten experiment in urban self-sufficiency.

Wind tearing at her jacket, Ice sighted in on the hovercar, tracking the subtle, massive glide of the machine as it positioned itself for another attack. When she did not fire, Jonny was tempted to pull her away from the door. Then, just as he was reaching for her, she pulled the trigger, sending the burning M-79 bolt at the aft section of the car. The explosion, when the shell hit, blew out windows in one old greenhouse dome, peppering the van with dead vegetation and fragments of glass.

Black smoke and guttering light above them. The hovercar tried to rise, but its remaining engine clipped a transformer tower, flipping the car onto its back. It hung there for a moment, as if undecided what to do. Finally, in what looked like an attempt to right itself, it slammed through a greenhouse roof, emerging from the far side in flames.

"Brace yourselves!" screamed Man Ray. He wrenched the steering wheel left, sending the van broadside into the hovercar just as it skidded to the ground in front of them.

The first thing Jonny was aware of was the constant blaring of a horn; then came shadows, flickering over his eyelids in frozen microsecond silhouettes; then a thick wetness on his face, across his chest and arms. He opened his eyes. Glycerine. It was everywhere, thick puddles massing on the floor and slopping out the back, ruptured padding going limp on the walls. He crawled to the open door and dropped a couple of unexpected feet to the pavement. The vehicle was resting at a severe angle, its rear wheels spinning in the air.

He walked on some stranger's legs; they refused to work together. Around the side of the van he found the mangled hovercar, a skeletal mass of crumpled alloys and scorched plastic, two feeble red lights rotating out of synch; the fuselage had twisted itself thoroughly into the undercarriage of the van, merging with it. Symbiotic junk.

A sleeve grazed his face, electric jolt sending Jonny down to his knees. Man Ray danced past him, his Medusa out and swinging over his head. Charged lashes flowered sparks as they touched, gilding the air above the Guru's head with spinning galaxies, ghostly landscapes of exploding stars, playing cards, cometary butterflies. He was easily holding three Committee boys at bay. There was an enormous stained-porcelain smile plastered across his face. Even groggy, Jonny could read it: total fulfillment. Man Ray was in his element, writing sonnets with his weapons; the image of the artist at work.

The Guru froze and held out his arms, crystal geckos skittering from his sleeves. Light-footed, quick-tongued, they leaped to the ground at the Committee boys' feet, exploding into billowing, lavender clouds of CS gas. Jonny fell back on the van, coughing, eyes filling with tears, and saw Man Ray emerge from the cloud a moment later. Somewhere along the way, the Guru had slipped on a respirator under his kendo helmet. A Committee boy grabbed him and was jolted off by the electrical charge of the polypyrrole armor.

Then someone was pulling Jonny away, around to the back of the ruined van. It was Skid, blood ruining the white perfection of his teeth, rimming his lips. The hand he used to hold Jonny was glowing, pixels throbbing nervously, but offering no image. He was shouting something.

"We're fucked! They've blown it! We're on our own, man!"

The Kid started to pull again, but Jonny shifted his weight and held him in place. "What are you talking about? Where's Ice?"

The Kid pointed with his gun. "Pinned down with Groucho. It's the Committee, man. They've blown the clinic!"

Jonny pushed the Kid aside and ran between the rows of greenhouses. A block away, he could see a dozen of the Committee's meat wagons forming an armored barrier around the warehouse he and the others had left earlier that evening. Force men were leading a few cuffed Croakers to the wagons. There were bodies, Committee boys and anarchists, lying in the floodlit parking lot. Ice and Groucho were there, pinned down in an alley off to the right, meters apart, unable to reach the cover of the greenhouses.

"See? We're fucked!" Skid shrilled. "They found the clinic!"

Jonny watched as Ice and Groucho tried to make a run for it, shooting into the air to cover each other. The Committee boys laughed at them from the roof, cat-and-mousing them, letting them get a few meters out, then forcing them back against the warehouse under a curtain of bullets.

"If we lay down some fire on that roof, they could make it," Jonny told Skid. "Watch them. I need a weapon." He crawled away, then sprinted to the van.

Weapons and ammunition were scattered on the ground behind the van's open door. Some of Man Ray's clockwork constructions had been activated; they crawled absently off into the shadows, where they popped and flared. The Guru was nowhere in sight. Jonny grabbed a Futukoro and, as he fished for a clip in the glycerine flooded bin, paused for a moment to take a couple of deep, even breaths. His hands were shaking. He closed his eyes, tried to will himself calm. Nothing but ruins, he thought. Seeing Ice pinned down had snapped something inside him. He thought of Sumi. He could not lose them both in one night.

A high-pitched animal scream. Jonny ran back to the warehouse in time to see Skid zigzagging into the open, his pixels wild, a slight figure crawling with pastel geometrics and snapping death's heads. As the Kid ran, he shot wildly at the roof of the adjoining warehouse, forcing the Committee boys back. Ice, Jonny realized, had been caught between the buildings, unable to get out of the line of fire. Now, under Skid's cover, she made it to a greenhouse on the far side, Groucho right on her heels. They turned to give the Kid covering fire, but he seemed confused; unwilling to be pinned at the warehouse wall as they had been, he sprinted back toward Jonny.

He got about ten meters when a shot caught him from behind, punching a wet hole in his chest. The Kid spun around stiffly, firing the last of his clip into the pavement. "Skid!" Ice

screamed. The Kid was on his back, half-conscious, crawling
with snakes and phosphenes. A file dump, Jonny realized. All
the images in his software were bubbling up at once, out of
control. The arm Skid held up strobed madly: the arm of a
woman, a reptile, an industrial robot; crimson spiders webbed
him; amber alphanumerics scrolled up his twisted face;
Brando, Lee, Bowie, Vega; his system was looping, the faces
flickering by faster and faster, merging into one metafantasy
face, colorless, all colors, fading at the same instant it formed.
Skid sat up, looked around wildly, and laughed. A single
bright flash of binary, and he slumped to the ground. The Kid
lay still and dark.

By the meat wagons, a loudspeaker clicked on: "MY
GOD, IS THAT YOU, GORDON? NICE TO SEE YOU,
ASSHOLE. WHAT HAPPENED TO OUR DEAL?" came
Zamora's voice. "YOU FUCKED ME, GORDON, BUT I
DIDN'T THINK YOU WERE STUPID. I CUT YOU LOOSE
AND YOU RUN RIGHT INTO THE ARMS OF TERROR-
ISTS, FOR CHRISSAKE."

It was a game, Jonny knew. Could the Colonel make him
mad enough to do something stupid? Jonny tried to force the
sound of Colonel Zamora's voice from his brain; he conjured
up visions of clawing the man's eyes out with his hands, but
he stayed in the shadows, shaking, hating himself, and biting
his lip until he drew blood.

"I'M GOING TO ROAST YOU, KID. ONE OF YOUR
BITCHES IS MINE ALREADY. THEY LOVE FRESH
CUNT AT THE WEAPONS LAB, YOU KNOW. THEY'LL
HAVE HER INCUBATING SPINAL WORMS. EVER SEEN
THOSE THINGS? ALL THEY EAT IS NERVE TISSUE,
AND THEY DON'T STOP TILL IT'S ALL GONE. . . ."

Before Jonny knew what he was doing, he was flat on his
belly, screaming, firing the Futukoro, filling the air above the
meat wagons with dragons, burning comets, screeching har-
pies. He knocked out the P.A. with the first volley, and took
out some of the floodlights. Something occurred to him then,
and he was up, scrambling back to the van. Some of Man
Ray's toys were back there, he remembered. What a nice sur-
prise they would be for the Colonel.

But he never got there.

Two dark-suited men intercepted him as he was stepping
into the vehicle. Instinctively, Jonny brought his boot up into

one man's armpit, paralyzing the arm. But it was not enough. His whole system hummed, crying out for blood. Jonny grabbed a handful of the first man's face and pushed him into the second. They both went down, and Jonny was on them, bringing his boots down heel-first, aiming for the throat. He missed the first man, corrected his aim for the second and knocked out some of his teeth. Jonny's fun was cut short, however, when an arm clamped across his face, and something cold and stinging touched his throat. As his body went limp, some neutral part of his brain noted that he had been stuck with a neural scrambler. The effect was a strange one, since Jonny's mind continued to function perfectly, but with the pyramidal tracks of his brain jammed, his body had suddenly been reduced to so much useless meat. He was aware of the two men carrying him for some distance. He hoped they would not let him swallow his tongue.

When they removed the scrambler, Jonny found himself on the filthy floor of an underground garage. A stretched Cadillac limousine, the rear end huge under twin sweeping tailfins, was parked nearby. His tongue seem to be intact. The car door swung open, and a familiar florid scent of clove cigarettes billowed out. Then the ugliest man Jonny had ever seen smiled out at him.

"Please don't be angry, Jonny. Your friends are gone. Some of their compatriots picked them up a few moments ago," said Mister Conover, the smuggler lord. "Aside from that, it's been my sad experience that people who are ready to die for a cause all too often end up doing just that." He grinned apologetically, showing horrid yellow teeth. "There are far too many of them out there for you to do any good, you know. You'll just get yourself killed."

"Killed?" said Jonny. He laughed. "Wouldn't that be a joke on everybody."

6

THE EXQUISITE CORPSE

MISTER CONOVER, relaxed and smiling, was sporting that season's newest suit style from Milan. (High-waisted pants, shoulder pads in the jacket, all woven from Russian silk. There was a Cyrillic character on each of the gold buttons. In all, the suit violated a dozen U.S. trade embargoes against pro-Arab countries.) He was the most powerful smuggler lord in Los Angeles, single-handedly controlling most of the drug traffic in and out of Southern California.

Many of the other lords were working small, furtive drug deals of their own, deals designed to boost their cash flow and their self-esteem, and while they were technically cutting into Conover's action, he did not mind. Allowing the other lords to have their little deals helped to keep them happy and in line. And that, Conover knew, was a form of power he could not buy or do without.

Rumor had it that Mr. Conover's influence reached far beyond the limits of Los Angeles, into the governor's mansion, and the offices of the multinationals in Osaka and Mexico City. Part of this was due to an elaborate kickback scheme he had reputedly concocted with several pharmaceutical firms decades before, a scheme having to do with the scuttling of artificial-intelligence-controlled cargo blimps and tankers, allowing the companies to collect on the insurance and then returning the vessels with new names and computer logs, while he kept the cargo. However, a portion of his influence had simply to do with his age. He had been born in the previous century, making him older than most of the corporations and politicos he was dealing with. Through the years, he had become a link to a golden age when the foundations for the power structure of their world had been laid, a sort of icon to commerce and stability.

Mr. Conover was also a Greenies addict. Originally marketed in the late nineteen nineties as a longevity drug, Greenies had later been found to be responsible for a whole range of bizarre side effects. However, these effects manifested themselves only after decades of use, and by then it was usually too late—the drug had already bonded with and reinscribed large segments of the addict's DNA. To stop taking the drug would have killed Conover. The drug's street name derived from its peculiar tendency to slow the oxidation of blood in the user's system, giving the addict's skin a brittle, greenish-blue quality.

The final irony was that Greenies turned out to be an exceptionally effective life extender. Thus, the user could look forward to decades (centuries?) of addiction and slow physical disintegration. No one really knew how old Mr. Conover was, but what he had become was obvious to all.

Conover's small grayish-green skull of a head bobbed between narrow shoulders set above a thick torso. His nose was little more than a mass of jagged scar tissue surrounded by livid clusters of red tumors. He puffed constantly at gold-tipped Sherman clove cigarettes that he held in a long mother-of-pearl holder, an affectation which, like his clothes, was another symptom of his compulsion to accentuate his own ugliness. When he smiled, which was often, his thin lips stretched back from a stained jumble of teeth. His appearance always gave Jonny the feeling that he was in conversation with a well-dressed corpse.

The Cadillac moved swiftly along an all-but-abandoned stretch of freeway. Sand was blowing in off the desert, carried to the city on the backs of freak Santa Ana winds. Carbon arcs mounted on the roof threw the cracked roadbed into stark relief, made the sand look like static on a video screen. Jonny looked out the double-glazed windows, but there was not much to see. They were driving through hills northwest of the city, on the edge of the German industrial sector, a bleak dead zone of strip mining equipment and half-finished bunkers housing the Krupp Corporation's experimental tokamak. The leached hills depressed Jonny, reminded him of a painting by Max Ernst that Groucho had shown him: *Europe After the*

Rain. The landscape brought back uneasy memories of evenings on the Committee shooting speed with Krupp's young shock *truppen.* The Germans did not have Meat Boys; instead, it was common for young recruits to display their machismo by replacing their limbs with unfeeling myoelectric prostheses. Johnny had the patchy, drunken memory of a laughing boy holding a cigarette lighter to his fingertips until they melted and dripped away, revealing the silicon sensors and black alloy mesh beneath.

Jonny relaxed on the soft leather seat in the rear of the limousine. Seated next to him, Conover pulled out an ornate silver cigarette case and offered him a smoke. Jonny accepted the cigarette and a light, pulling the harsh, sweet clove smoke deep into his lungs and letting it trickle out through his nose.

It had been months since he'd last smoked a cigarette (Sumi had guilted him into stopping when a Croaker working out of the back of a taqueria told him he had a shadow on one lung), but his past seemed to be catching up with him at such a rate that Jonny figured he might as well get into the spirit of it. He coughed wearily as the smoke caught in his throat. Resting his head on the seatback, he watched the road slide by. Conover's chauffeur, a heavyset ex-Guardia Nacional man, was skull-plugged into a radar/navigational unit in the dashboard, following a trail of military sensors under the roadbed. Conover was one of the few men in the city Jonny trusted, certainly the only lord. For the moment, he felt safe. Conover leaned over and spoke to him quietly.

"You seem to have brought down the wrath of God, old son. Or at least you pissed off Zamora, which amounts to the same thing. What in the world can you have done?"

Jonny ran a hand through his hair. "I wish I knew," he said. "Maybe I'd feel like I deserved all this special attention."

"Much as he'd like to, the Colonel does not stage raids just for fun. He must have had some reason for singling you out." Conover put a hand on Jonny's arm. "No offense, you're a charming boy, but—"

"The man's insane. He thinks you and I are playing footsie with the Alpha Rats," Jonny said. "I suppose that's assuming they have feet. I don't know. This whole thing's crazier by the minute."

"The Alpha Rats," Conover said, half as a question, half a reply. He smoked his pastel Sherman, laughed mildly. "The

Colonel never ceases to amaze me. Did he happen to mention what, specifically, you and I were doing with the Alpha Rats?"

"No. He just said we'd had contact and that we're into some kind of deal," Jonny explained. He gave up and ground out the cigarette in an ashtray gouged from a crystal lump of Amazon quartz. His throat burned.

"And that's all he said?" Conover asked.

"Yeah." Jonny hesitated before saying anything about Zamora's demand that he turn Conover. Just saying the words, Jonny felt, implied a kind of betrayal. But how will it look, he wondered, if I don't say anything and he finds out? "Zamora's really got the hots for you," he said. "He cut me loose and told me I had to deliver you in forty-eight hours or—"

"—Or we get the little scene back at the warehouses. Tell me, did Easy Money ever come up in your talk?"

"I don't think so."

"Take a moment. I want you to be sure. Did Colonel Zamora mention Easy Money?"

"No, never."

"You didn't seem so sure a moment ago."

"Well, I wasn't then; I'm sure now," said Jonny. He looked at the smuggler lord.

"Good," said Conover, nodding in satisfaction. "Forgive me for being insistent, but it's important that I get to Easy before the Committee. He's made off with something of mine and I do not want Zamora involved, on any level, with its recovery."

"For what it's worth, Groucho the Croaker said Easy's gone to work for Nimble Virtue."

Conover reached forward and picked up a bottle of tequila from a well-stocked traveling bar set into the seatback before them. Next to the bar was an array of sleek, matte-black Japanese electronic gear; Jonny recognized a Sony compound analyzer, a cellular videophone and a voice-activated PC. Conover poured a shot of tequila into a glass and handed it to Jonny.

"I'd heard about Nimble Virtue," said Conover. "In fact, I've been trying to set up a meet with her, but the witch is on the run. Paranoid, that woman is. My sources say she might have a pied a terre in Little Tokyo, but only time will tell." Jonny finished his tequila and Conover refilled his glass.

"Right now, though, why don't you relax and tell me, from the beginning, everything that went on with you and Zamora. Take your time, we have a bit of a drive ahead of us."

Jonny took a gulp of the liquor, bracing himself with its cool heat. He was not wild about the idea of reliving that night, but he had known it was coming, ever since the smuggler lord had picked him up. Conover, meanwhile, was using a tiny spoon to scoop a fine white powder from a glass vial he pulled from the back of the bar. That done, he cut the pile into several neat lines with a gold, single-edged razor blade.

As the lord snorted up a couple of the lines, Jonny began to talk, telling Conover everything he could remember, from the moment Zamora had picked him up until he had found himself alone behind the prison, confused and outraged. It was painful; all that had happened since came crashing down on him. Ice was gone. Sumi was gone. Skid was dead. He even found Groucho's absence disturbing.

When he finished, Conover had him run through the whole thing again, focusing on Zamora's theories about their connection to the Alpha Rats. After going through it a second time, Jonny was drained.

Conover patted his arm, and nodded. "A very good job, Jonny. Thank you," he said. "You look like you could use a break."

"I could use a new life. But what about Zamora and the Alpha Rats?"

Conover handed the tube he had used to snort the coke to Jonny. "It all sounds fascinating. I never would have suspected the Colonel of having an imagination. It almost makes me wish it were true. Without you to pull out of the fire, Jonny, my life would be unbearable. Don't let anybody try and sell you on immortality. There simply isn't enough of interest to make it worthwhile. Do your time and get it over with; that's the best way. It's not polite to be the last one to leave a party."

Jonny snorted up the white lines and asked, "Then there's nothing to all this spaceman stuff?"

Conover shook his head, his eyes fixed miles and centuries away. "No, nothing," he replied. Then he said something else; Jonny thought it might be: "Empty."

Jonny found himself beginning to feel a certain odd sympathy for the smuggler lord. For all his power, Conover had trapped himself in the decomposing body of a junky fop through a single miscalculation—his urgent will to live. On the other hand, Mr. Conover was no fool. Had it really been a mistake? Jonny wondered. Or was it a stage in some other, infinitely more complex and subtle plan that Jonny and the rest, condemned to a pitiful handful of years, could not see? If the smuggler lord was working on something else, Jonny hoped it was very big. The price of it seemed high.

Conover lit another in his constant stream of cigarettes. Tossing the match out the window, he let in a sudden blast of hot air and dust. His mood seemed to have grown lighter.

"I hope you don't mind, but I have a little side trip to make before we can go home. Just some business, you understand. I have a boat coming in from the south with some goodies on board: pituitary extracts, frozen retinas, a few kilos of cocaine. We wouldn't want to be late and give our neighbors the impression that we keep a sloppy shop, eh?" He laughed, amused by his own rambling. "Besides, I believe these boys are going to try and burn me. And I wouldn't miss that for the world."

"Yeah? What would you do for the world?" Jonny asked, feeling pleasantly numb and reckless, buzzing on the coke. Objects in the car had taken on a warm internal glow.

Conover looked at him, not without affection. "Only a lunatic would want to run this dump," he said. "I'm content to farm my small bit and be done with it. L.A. has been a very good investment for me, in money and time."

"I always wondered why you didn't move into someplace like New Hope. I mean, those people have got to have some expensive habits."

Conover raised his ruined eyebrows. "More than you could know," he said. "But New Hope is a ghost town. The corruption there is a closed system. The same families have been running drugs and data through there for generations. Old families, very powerful. We're talking here about the Yakuza and the Panteras de Aureo. The families connected to the multinationals have their own internal organizations to keep their people happy and restful. There's no freedom in that sort of setup. Little potential for growth." He carefully ground out his cigarette and placed another in his mother-of-pearl holder. "Besides, like Lucifer in the poem, I much prefer to rule in Hell than serve in Heaven."

Jonny grinned up at him. "I thought you said you didn't want to run this dump."

"It's all semantics. You can't buy Heaven, either."

Outside, the sand had let up. Heat lightning crackled silently across the horizon. Inside the Cadillac, they had passed into what Jonny had come to think of as a pocket of silence, one of those odd conjunctions of time and place where conversation vanished of its own accord; at those moments, Jonny believed, all words became dangerous and banal. He had come to attach a certain sacredness to the silence. All things were at rest. It was a ritual from boyhood, no different from stepping around cracks so that he would not break his mother's back. Meaningless, he knew, but when the feeling passed, he missed it, and in trying to force it back he came up instead with the twin images of Ice and Sumi.

"Hey Mister Conover, anything in this stuff we're picking up have to do with the new strain of leprosy?"

"No," said the smuggler lord. "Why do you ask?"

"I just figured you might be looking around for something. It's getting pretty bad in some neighborhoods."

"Have you seen this so-called epidemic yourself?" asked Conover. "You know how these things can get blown out of proportion. AIDS and Hepatitis E have left people very susceptible to rumors of a new plague. Then the Link gets hold of the talk, and broadcasts it right into people's skulls, reinforcing their belief in their own delusions. Couldn't this plague just be some mass psychogenic reaction?"

"Yeah, I've seen it. The Croakers have a roomful of lepers quarantined. Say this new strain is viral and that it kills," said Jonny. "We're not talking about a few hysterical wackos here. The whole city's in trouble."

"Calm down, son," said Mister Conover, laying a hand on Jonny's arm. "Remind me not to give you stimulants in the future." He smiled. "Actually, I do know this new strain is real. Looks like a phage, but attacks the wrong kind of cells, right? I was just trying to get an untainted perspective. As I said, all I hear are rumors. Like in East L.A. they've taken to burning their dead. That neighborhoods are beginning to seal themselves off. The social effects of the disease are certainly real enough. Tell me, have the Croakers had any success in isolating reverse transcriptase from the virus samples?"

"You think it's a retro-virus?"

"AIDS was. And that little fellow practically had the medical community reading Ouija boards before they got anywhere."

"What about going after it with a general virus-killer like ribovirin or amantadine?" asked Jonny.

The smuggler lord shook his head. "That's been tried," he said. "Amantadine seems to have some preventive applications, but if you're already infected, it's useless."

"You know about this new strain, don't you, Mister Conover?"

"It's my job."

"You don't seem too concerned."

"Personally? No. The Greenies took care of that long ago. I doubt my blood would be very appetizing to these little bastards." He rocked with some internal laughter. "I haven't had a cold in over forty years."

"Then you don't know any treatments we could get hold of for the new strain?"

"No one is even sure how it's transmitted," Conover said. "And without the disease vector, curing a few individuals isn't going to stop an epidemic."

Seated beside the driver in the front of the car, a hawk-nosed man with an oily pompadour turned to face the back. One of his eyes was blackened, and his upper lip was swollen badly, drawing it downward and giving him a childish, sullen look. Jonny recognized the man as the one whose teeth he had loosened with his boots earlier that evening. The man appeared to be slightly embarrassed. He would not look at Jonny.

"'Scuse me, Mister Conover, but I read un transmissor en la auto," he said.

"Jonny, my boy, you wouldn't be wired for sound, would you?" asked the smuggler lord.

Jonny looked at him. "Hey, you know me, Mister Conover."

Conover nodded and turned to the front. "What do you say, Ricos? You sure your little gadget's reading correctly?"

"Si, no question. The maricon es the only new baggage 'round here. I'm not reading nothin' till he get in."

"Friend, if you can read at all I'd be surprised," said Jonny.

Ricos made a quick grab for Jonny, but Conover shoved the man back in his seat. "That's enough, children. Jonny, could somebody have planted something on you?"

"No," Jonny said. "Those Committee boys never got near me and these clothes are Croaker cast-offs. They'd have no reason to tail me to their own hideout." He looked at Ricos, pointed to his skull. "Tu tene un tornillo flojo."

Conover puffed thoughtfully at his cigarette, leaned forward and touched the driver's shoulder. "Pull over up ahead," he said. "Ricos, bring your remote. Come on, Jonny."

The car stopped near an old dumpsite for a mining operation that had flattened the surrounding hills. Conover slipped on a white Panama hat as he led Jonny out and around to the back of the Cadillac. Cottony tracers of gas clung to gummy, bitter-smelling waste pits. The smuggler lord pointed to Jonny with his cigarette holder. "Find it," he said to Ricos.

Ricos moved very close to Jonny and began moving a small electromagnetic device over Jonny's clothing, tracing the outline of his body. Jonny glanced over at Conover and wondered what was going through the smuggler lord's mind, but it was impossible to read that face. He concentrated, instead, on affecting a look of extreme uninterest as Rico studiously moved the device around his crotch.

"Ai!" Ricos yelled. He held the box to Jonny's bandaged shoulder. "Got you, maricon."

Jonny looked at the man and then at the box in his hand. "Jesus," said Jonny miserably. "Oh, fucking hell—"

"Jonny?" said Conover.

He slumped against the back of the car, Ricos standing over him delightedly. It took several seconds for the image to assemble itself; it appeared to him much the way he imagined visuals formed through skull-plugs: an out-of-focus mass of phosphenes settling slowly, like a reverse tornado, around a central spiral. In truth, he did not want to understand it, but in admitting that, he gave the thought form and terrible substance.

"Zamora did this," Jonny said. The image was clear. The prison infirmary had fixed him up nicely, and all their doctors were Committee recruits: bloodless and faceless, company men all the way. It was obvious. He had led the Committee to the Croakers. Right to Ice's room. Now he was leading them to Conover. "Oh, fucking hell—"

"What is it, Jonny?" asked Conover.

Jonny's hand moved involuntarily to his cast. "I got shot earlier," he said. "I got shot and Zamora had them wire me. It's in my goddam shoulder."

Conover approached him, shaking his head sympathetically. "I'm truly sorry, son. It's an awful thing to have done," he murmured. "We'll have to cut it out, of course. You can't go around beeping the rest of your life."

Jonny laughed when he thought about it. Zamora could not let him off that easily. The insult had been there all along; all that had been required was for him to recognize it. There was, Jonny had to admit, even a kind of twisted beauty to it.

Conover called the driver out and spoke to him for some time in quiet Spanish. When they parted, the driver opened the trunk and unrolled a cloth-bound set of surgical instruments. He helped Jonny off with his coat and pulled back the top of the Pemex jumpsuit. When he removed Jonny's cast and xylocaine patch, he did it with such sureness that Jonny was sure the man had been a medic at some time.

Jonny felt a cool punch of compressed air on his arm as the driver injected him with something from a pressurized syringe. Seconds later, Jonny was flying. The driver set him on the rear fender and hooked a small work light to the inside of the trunk lid. Before Conover retreated inside the car, Jonny heard him say, "When you find it, bring it to me."

The driver held out a small device that looked like an old-fashioned tattoo needle, but which Jonny recognized as an Akasaka laser scalpel. In Spanish, the driver told Jonny to concentrate on the hanging light.

He did not feel a thing.

Later, when the car was moving and Jonny was sacked out on the back seat, still high on whatever they'd shot him with, he heard voices in the midst of conversation. His shoulder ached with each heartbeat. But he seemed to recall that his shoulder always hurt, didn't it? Eventually, he recognized Conover's voice.

"We each do our bit as best we can, of course. Zamora is a vicious, greedy prick, but a sterling leader of men. I've seen him pull many strange stunts in my time. However, I have never before known him to betray a sense of humor." He glanced at Jonny. "Have you?"

Jonny just rolled away and fell asleep. "I'd like to go home now," he said, but nobody heard him.

A dark, sour-smelling harbor glittering oily rainbows amidst sluggish waves. Men talking in a circle some distance off, a litter of shapes around their feet; another painting came to him, Tanguy this time. Sharks—the bleached carcasses of dead sharks, stripped of their flesh by birds and their jaws by souvenir hunters, strewn across the sand like some hallucinatory crop ready for harvest. Down the beach, a roofless merry-go-round, half-collapsed, dangling a string of bloated wooden horses into the dirty water. The flares of gas jets miles away.

Jonny rubbed grit from his eyes and tried to focus on the circle of men outside on the beach. He had no idea how long he or they had been here. He was very thirsty.

From what Jonny could see, only two men were doing all the talking. One was Conover, who was easy to spot, towering above the rest, the glowing dot of his cigarette tracing erratic patterns in the air. Behind Conover stood Ricos, scowling into the ocean wind, his pompadour flailing around his ears like a dying animal.

The man Conover was talking to was considerably shorter, but very broad, wearing the white dress uniform of a Mexican naval officer. A jet foil with the name *Corpus Christi* painted on the bow floated a few meters out in the harbor, rolling gently with the surf. Two small Zodiac crafts were beached nearby, one overloaded with sealed metal containers. The identification numbers on the *Corpus Christi* indicated that the ship was from the Gobernacion fleet stationed in San Diego, but she was running no lights, and the flag on her mast was Venezuelan, not Mexican. When the moon broke through the heavy cloud layer, Jonny got a good look at her crew, spread out in a semicircle around the Zodiacs. About half wore naval uniforms; the others were dressed variously in jeans and leathers, pale gringos and dreadlocked blacks numerous among the crew.

That's it then, Jonny thought. They're pirates.

Picking up the tequila from Conover's traveling bar, Jonny took a drink. The pirate captain pointed back to his ship and shouted something. Warmed by the tequila, Jonny's thoughts drifted back to his own time as a dealer.

Jonny had always picked up a buzz when he was pushing or setting up a meet that was wholly divorced from the rest of his life. Part of it was the thrill an ex-Committee boy felt at having gone over to the "other side." Another part of it had something to do with vague notions of changing the world, but he attributed this to youthful folly, regarding it as a consequence of spending too much time sober. Groucho's casual remark equating Jonny's dealing and revolutionary politics had disturbed him. It saddled him with responsibilities he had no intention of trying to fulfill. The world (at least Los Angeles, which was all he knew of the world), as Jonny perceived it, was little more than the natural battle of competing organisms, like the virus he had seen on the micrograph at the Croakers' clinic. Each viral unit was incomplete until it had taken over a living cell and used that organism to replicate itself, and the one-percenters and gangs of the city followed the virus's pattern. Inertia swept them along in a perpetual hustle, moving in time to the endless rhythm of commerce; most knew nothing else. And, as was the way of nature, the stronger viruses ate the weaker. The strongest viruses were the Committee, the lords, and the multinationals, forces that were overwhelming and, in the end, incomprehensible to Jonny.

Did the Croakers really believe they could change a world run by Zamora or Nimble Virtue? Even Conover was just a businessman who had his own reasons for being there. And Groucho was too damned small to play Atlas, Jonny thought.

He wondered where Ice was at that moment. He felt certain she was all right; she seemed to have a talent for staying alive. In his mind, however, Sumi had become one with the ruined apartment. If Zamora really had her, she was lost. Jonny loved both women, but he felt he owed them something more than that.

The door opposite Jonny opened and Conover leaned in. Salt mist sparkled on the smuggler lord's shoulders and the wide brim of his hat. He smiled at Jonny. "How are you feeling?" he asked. "We'll be through here in just a few minutes. These boys are playing it to the last row. Hand me that box by your feet, will you?"

Jonny looked at the floor of the Cadillac and found a small, black-laquered box with brass fittings in the shape of lotus petals. His head spun as he picked the box up. Conover smiled as he took it. "Thanks, son. Sit tight. Have a drink," he said.

Watching the smuggler lord cross the colorless sand, Jonny was overcome by a sudden and overwhelming sense of loss, as if he were adrift in some vast and infinite ocean with no land in sight. He had the strong urge to bail out right there, to run from the car and to keep running. But for some reason he stayed. If he drifted long enough, he thought, a landfall was bound to appear. Besides, he was drugged silly. Where would I go if I ran? he wondered. On the beach, the pirates were smoking and passing a bottle. Jonny raised his tequila to them and decided to remain in the car. Drifting, he knew, was what he was best at.

Outside, the pirate captain was nodding as Conover ceremoniously handed him the small box. The pirate opened it for a moment, waved briskly to a couple of men by the Zodiacs. They made their way through the sand slowly with several containers, setting them a few meters from Conover and Ricos. That done, they retreated quickly from the smuggler lord's presence. Jonny caught a quick movement of one pirate's hand. He had crossed himself, Catholic-fashion.

Ricos flicked open a butterfly knife and slit the metal strips that bound the top of one container. Reaching inside, he pulled out a white brick wrapped in heavy plastic and handed it to Conover. Jonny looked around the car, wondering where Conover's chauffeur had gone. When he looked back at the beach, the pirates were moving out, pushing their Zodiacs into the surf. The moon lit, briefly, the rubber floats that flanked each craft, like twin torpedoes wrapped in skin. Ricos carried the metal containers back to the Cadillac, stacking them by the rear bumper as Conover got in.

Jonny nodded at the brick. "Real cocaine?" he asked.

"Theoretically."

"That's an awful lot."

"You would think so, wouldn't you?" The smuggler lord pushed some bottles out of the way and set the brick on the traveling bar. With his thumbnail he gouged a hole in the plastic. He touched the finger to his tongue and grunted, motioning for Jonny to have a taste. Wetting the end of his middle finger, Jonny touched it to the pile. "What's wrong?" he asked, putting the finger gingerly to his tongue.

"You tell me," said Conover as he spooned a small portion of the powder into a test tube half filled with a clear fluid. Swirling the mixture together, the smuggler lord fastened the test tube into the twin metal receptacles on the front of the compound analyzer. He punched a switch and a beam of pale laser light lit up the sample from the inside.

Jonny found the taste of the powder to be odd: alkaloid bitterness, with a sweet aftertaste. There was a thickness and a graininess that was wrong.

"Feel anything?" asked Conover.

"Nothing," said Jonny. "They've cut the hell out of it."

Conover said "Show" to the PC and the terminal's screen lit up with the rainbow bar that was a spectrographic readout of the contents of the test tube. A list of chemicals and percentages to five decimal places was displayed on one side of the screen. The smuggler lord snorted and snatched up the brick, spilling white grains onto the seat.

"Good God," Conover said. "Milk powder, sugar, and probably baking soda. Christ, you could bake a cake with this stuff. It's been cut, recut, and cut again. These lads have probably been selling my drugs to freelancers all the way up the coast and filling in the weight with whatever was at hand." He shook his head sadly. "These people think because they have that gunboat they're immune." He tossed the brick onto the bar.

Something occurred to Jonny then. "You gave it to them, didn't you?" he said.

"Gave them what, dear boy?"

"The transmitter. You put it in the box with the money, didn't you?"

Conover smiled, removed a cigarette from his case, and lit it. After bringing the last two boxes to the car, Ricos got in the front seat.

"I consider it a fair exchange. Loaded money for loaded coke," he said, chuckling. "The hormones and the retinas?" he asked. Ricos shook his head.

"*Paralizados*. Look like they break the seal and go poking inside. Es all spoiled."

The smuggler lord nodded. "Let this be a lesson to you, Jonny: there are always going to be assholes. Wherever you go, whatever you do, you have to be on guard. If you're not, the fools and the tiny minds of this world will drag you right down into the gutter with them."

Jonny leaned back in the seat and felt a slight tingling begin on the end of this tongue. It was not much, though. "You think Zamora will go after them?" he asked.

"Why not? That was a nice piece of hardware we dug out of your shoulder. Hitachi, military issue. VHF for short-range monitoring and neutrino broadcasting for long-range. The Colonel has no way of knowing you're not international. He thinks you're buying dope from moon men, remember?"

Jonny made a face at that. "This whole setup was very . . . professional of you."

Conover looked at him curiously, one hand toying with the rip in the white brick. "You find my methods uncouth? Maybe you'd be happier if the Colonel followed us back to my place. That would end the party pretty quickly, wouldn't it?"

"Let's say I'm a little disillusioned, how's that? I mean, I was kind of under the impression that the people running dope were on our side, you know?" Jonny bit the end of his tongue to see if it was numb yet. It was not. "Pretty stupid, right? You don't have to explain it to me. I know how the song goes: It's all economics. It always is."

The smuggler lord picked up the brick and held it before Jonny. "'Get place and wealth, if possible with grace; if not, by any means get wealth and place.' Alexander Pope. It's the algebra of need, son. As long as the need exists, somebody is going to service it and take advantage of it, like those gentlemen from the *Corpus Christi*. They understood, or did until they got greedy. It's mother's milk—consumerism—the Big Teat. The trouble with you, Jonny, is that you're in business, but you're not a businessman."

Conover opened his door and turned the white brick upside down, dumping its contents into the sand. "In business, sometimes you've got to take a loss in order to make a gain."

"I'll try to remember that," said Jonny.

"It would do you well."

Ricos shivered in the front seat. Conover found a bottle of aguardiente and poured him a glass. Soon the driver returned, wearing a dun-colored windbreaker and heavy pair of night-vision goggles. He was carrying a shoulder-held Arab mini-gun, its twelve massive barrels running with condensed mist.

Conover explained that the man had been hiding in the dunes
some distance away waiting for the jetfoil to pull out. After
the driver stowed the gun in the trunk (scattering the ruined
hormones and retinas on the beach for the gulls) Conover gave
him a drink and told him to take them home.

7

THE MACHINE GUN IN A
STATE OF GRACE

THEY DROVE IN SILENCE. Jonny dozed in the back, waking every few minutes when the Cadillac would hit a patch of broken concrete, causing the car to shake violently. Then he would look out the window and see hillsides covered with brightly colored fabric or a group of chrome palm trees constructed from stolen jet engines and lengths of industrial piping. A gift from the Croakers, he thought, giving the finger to the world. Closer to the city were squatter camps, long walls of corrugated tin and dismantled billboards. Jonny could make out a word here, a face there. A woman's eye. FLY. EAT. The curve of a hip. LOVE.

Just outside Hollywood, they turned off the ruined freeway and drove through an old suburban sector before starting a steep climb into the hills.

The driver switched off the carbon arcs on the roof and skull-plugged into an infrared array set into the car's headlight housings. The only light visible to Jonny was the pale green mercury vapor glow of the suburbs and the jittery firefly of Conover's cigarette.

They passed through tunnels of rotted concrete where fungus padded the walls. Even with the air conditioner on full blast, there was a strong smell of decomposing vegetation. Outlines of burned-out cars down the embankment, overgrown with weeds. As they gained altitude, the road grew narrower and more hazardous. They passed the ruins of the ancient Hollywoodland development, the New Hope of its day. The well-heeled residents had tried to seal themselves off, Jonny remembered, but it hadn't worked. They had brought all their madness with them, into the hills. And when it had all come crashing down around their ears, no one had been surprised. The rot had set in before the first foundation had been laid.

The car slowed, finally, and came to a stop. Looking out the window, Jonny could see nothing but rocky hills and the ribbon of leaf-cluttered road curving off into the distance. The driver punched a code into a key pad on the dashboard (paranoid reflexes had Jonny leaning on the seatback, memorizing the digits as he read them out of the corner of his eye). Then portions of the hillside, perfect squares of stone and grass, began to wink out. Jonny realized that he was looking at a hologram.

After about a dozen of these segments had disappeared, Jonny could see a paved driveway leading off the main road. The driver turned them onto this new road, and the hologram hillside reappeared behind them. A large cat, a cougar or jaguar ("Sentry robot," Conover said), paced the car as they passed a thick stand of madrone and scrubby manzanita. There were men up there, too. Jonny caught a glint of rifles slung over camouflaged shoulders.

"Our security is quite tight up here," said Conover. "The whole hill is wired. Motion detectors, infrared, and image intensifiers. We have quick-release neurotoxins microcapsules buried on the blind side of the hill. Those men you saw? They're carrying shoulder-fired rail guns. Models that small are very new. Very expensive. They can push a one-hundred-gram polycarbonate projectile at a thousand kilometers an hour. It's like having a small mountain dropped on you." He lit another cigarette, and from his inside jacket pocket took a black silicon card. There were gold filaments on the card's face, forming a bar code. "You need this, too. We run a magnetic scan on every vehicle that comes through here. If the system doesn't read the right code, it sets off every alarm in the place."

"You expecting the Army?" asked Jonny.

"I expect nothing," replied Conover. "I anticipate everything."

Around an out-of-place bamboo grove, they came upon Conover's mansion, stars hazy through the hologram dome. Jonny's first thought was that the main building of the estate was surrounded by smaller bungalows. When they get closer, however, he realized that what he was looking at was a single, massive confusion of a building, erupting over the top of the hill like a geometric melanoma. What appeared to be the oldest wing of the mansion was built in a straight Victorian style, while others were pseudo-hacienda; the most recent additions appeared to have been built along traditional Japanese lines. Gracefully curled pagoda roofs abutted at odd angles with Spanish arches, high-windowed garrets overlooking gilt temple dogs.

"I've heard of this place. It's the old Stone mansion, isn't it?" Jonny asked.

Conover nodded. The Cadillac stopped by a pond full of fat, spotted carp, and he stepped out. Jonny followed him; a grinding pain was building up in his shoulder beneath the anesthetics. "Yes, this is the Stone place. I'm surprised anyone still remembers it. Old Mister Stone made a fortune selling tainted baby formula in Africa and the Asian subcontinent, encouraging the mothers to stop breast-feeding and use his poison. After he died, Mrs. Stone got it into her head that the ghosts of all those little dead children were coming to get her. She kept building onto the place, sleeping in a different room every night for thirty years. The architects were given a free hand to build in whatever style was popular at the moment. This"—he gestured toward the mansion— "is the result. What do you think? Is this a vision of insanity, made whole and visible, or just the maunderings of a bored old biddy with too much money? Doesn't really matter. The place is very comfortable. The old lunatic only used the best materials."

"It's a great setup," said Jonny. "You must suck an awful lot of power up here. Aren't you afraid someone's going to trace it back to you?"

"We're set up for solar and there are darius windmills on the surrounding hills," said Conover. He gave Jonny a small smile. "The rest of what we need I've had Watt Snatchers route through the police power grid."

Jonny laughed, slapped the hood of the car. "I love it!" He felt weak and hot. He wanted to sit down.

From the madrones came a series of long hysterical cries, rising in pitch until they peaked, fell, and started again. Answering calls came from deeper in the trees.

"What the hell was that?" asked Jonny.

Conover gestured toward the hills. "Samangs," he explained. "Apes. We're right below Griffith Park. When the zoo was destroyed during the Protein Rebellion, some of the animals escaped and bred. It's not advisable to walk through these hills alone at night. The apes won't bother you, but there are tigers."

Jonny nodded, watching the madrone branches move in the light breeze. "Kind of chilly out here, isn't it?"

"Perhaps you'd like to see the inside of the house? I've picked up one or two baubles from some local museums that you might find interesting."

"Art is my life," said Jonny, following the smuggler lord inside.

The Japanese wing of the mansion was almost empty; Jonny was not sure if this was through style or neglect, but it smelled pleasantly of varnished wood, incense, and tatami mats. Many of the rooms they passed were closed off by rice-paper doors painted with pale watercolors of cranes and royal pagodas. Conover took him deep in the cluttered Victorian wing, where artificial daylight shone through stained-glass windows full of saints and inscriptions in Latin. Carpeted staircases appeared suddenly around corners, behind urns of blond irises and fat pussy willows, leading to corridors that seemed to turn in on themselves in impossible ways. Jonny's room was papered in a floral design, thousands of tiny purple nosegays, and furnished with delicate French antiques: a walnut armoire, small idealized portraits painted on glass, white hand-carved chairs with tapestry cushions, and a canopied bed, all lace and gold leaf. He smiled at Conover, but was inwardly revolted by the place. It was like living in the underwear drawer of a very expensive prostitute.

When Conover left him, Jonny sat on the edge of the bed and closed his eyes. He felt drained, both mentally and physically, but could not relax. The long walk to his room, Conover's fairy tale about his security and the wild animals in the hills, had been obvious warnings. Jonny was not to leave the grounds. That thought made him uneasy. He was afraid to touch the antique furniture and had not seen any signs of video or hologram viewers. Just these damned paintings everywhere, he thought. They lined virtually all the walls of the Victorian wing, set in carved wooden frames and lit by small halide spotlights recessed into the ceiling. He's an art freak, too, thought Jonny. Like Groucho. But the anarchist's art had affected him differently. It had shown the process of the artist's mind and made full use of his or her obsessions, revealing a wealth of personal symbols that were the landscapes of dreams. Conover's paintings reminded Jonny of grim family snapshots. Groucho's art (the art he and the other Croakers had not created themselves) had also been copies, cheap reproductions clipped from books.

Jonny looked above the desk at the portrait of a sorrowful-eyed man whose body was riddled with arrows. A small plaque below the painting read: El Greco. It meant nothing to him. He went out into the hall, touching each painting he came to, running his hands across the still eyes, the centuries-old canvas. They were all alike. One-percenters commissioned by noblemen to paint their faces, he thought. Old masters, he had heard them called. Most of Conover's paintings appeared to be portraits, although there were a few landscapes, also meaningless to him. Pictures of men on horseback wearing red jackets and chasing what reminded Jonny of big rats. Names: Goya. Rembrandt. The faces in all the portraits had the same leathery texture of old oil paint.

"I'll take Aoki Vega or Jimmy Gagarin any day," he said to a Renaissance Madonna with child.

On the wall above a heavy, darkwood Gothic table was a painting Jonny recognized: *Blue Boy,* by Thomas Gainsborough. He remembered seeing a postcard of the painting as a teenager, glued by sweat to the bare buttocks of the young woman he was with in the ruins of the Huntington Art Gallery. Jonny ran his fingers along the boy's plumed hat.

Finely ridged plastic.

Jonny touched the painting again. When he leaned close to Blue Boy's face he saw that the texture of the paint was an illusion. "A hologram," he said, very surprised.

So Conover does go for fakes, he thought. For some reason, that made him feel better. Jonny touched the plastic face one more time to reassure himself, then went back to his room. Inside, he undressed and ran water for a shower. Before he got in, he took two dilaudid analogs that Conover had given him for the pain in his shoulder. He stepped into the stall and stood for a long time under a spigot that was a golden wrought-metal fish, turning the water on hard so that it hit his back in a stream of warm, stinging needles.

Back in his room, he found that a maroon silk robe had been laid out for him, and a silver tray with ice, gin, and a bottle of tonic. The analog was just coming on. Standing by the desk, surrounded by antiques and the smell of clean sheets, he had a sudden vision of the world as an orderly place. His teeth melted gently into his skull. He poured himself a shot of gin and drank it straight.

His shoulder hurt as he lay down on the bed, but the pain came from somewhere deep underground, lost among dark roots and grubs. He fell asleep and dreamed of Ice and Sumi. He found them at the top of an ornate spiral staircase, but when he touched them, they were plastic holograms.

Jonny woke in a sweat, hours later. Someone had turned off the lights. He stumbled around the dark room until he found the gin. He brought the gin bottle with him, setting it on the floor next to the bed.

He lost track of the days.

He slept a great deal. Conover had a private medical staff, mostly Japanese and painfully polite. With many apologies, a young nurse called Yukiko stuck him with needles—antibiotics for the wound in his shoulder, protein supplements and mega-vitamins for his mild malnutrition. In a small, tidy lab in the Japanese wing, they grafted new nerve tissue into the damaged area of his shoulder. They hooked him to a muscle stimulator that used mild electric shocks to tense and release his muscles, building back the strength in his shoulders and arms. Yukiko spoke no English, but smiled a great deal. Jonny smiled back.

In the mornings, he tried to do t'ai chi, but the movements felt odd and unfamiliar, as if he had learned them in some other body. He took the lace-trimmed pillows from the bed and sat crosslegged on them in one corner of the room, staring into the interface of two flowered walls, trying to meditate. Despite the fact that his sitting had become haphazard over the years, he still held a certain belief in meditation's power. He had once had a master, an ancient Zen nun with creased olive skin like old newsrags, and cheap, second-hand piezoelectric eyes that could only register in black and white. "The colors are here," she would say, and point to her skull. "All this is illusion." She would point to the room. "But also important: so is this." She would point to her head again and laugh delightedly.

But the emptiness always eluded Jonny, the void that was filled when the self was lost. He remembered all the Zen words, all the theories. He sat on the old French pillows, pain shooting like hot wires down his knees, and chanted the Sutras, trying to imagine himself as a bird. In the past, this had sometimes helped. Leave yourself, become the bird. Leave the bird, become nothing. But his concentration was gone, replaced with a wavering self-doubt compounded of fear, drugs, and guilt. He thought often of Ice and Sumi.

Days came and went without any information about the Croakers. They seemed to have disappeared en masse. What Conover found out was that shortly after he had picked Jonny up, a second group of Croakers had attacked the Committee boys at the warehouse. There had been heavy losses on both sides. But he had no information about the Croaker leader or Ice.

Jonny discovered that if he turned a stylized cloisonné elephant on his desk counterclockwise, the wall would slide away and reveal a large liquid crystal video screen. He decided then that bed was his karma, the theme of this incarnation in the world of flesh, pain, and illusion. He did dilaudid analogs and watched Link broadcasts. Learned experts still clogged the wires with panel discussions on the Alpha Rats; Jonny flipped past these quickly, finding himself drawn day after day to the Pakistani newscasts on a restricted Link channel that Conover's satellite rig was somehow was able to unjam.

Jonny was delighted to find that the thin Muslim spoke in the same rapid and mock-smooth tones employed by Western newscasters. Although Jonny did not understand a word of Pakistani, the look of the commercials was familiar and the music had a universal sing-along jingle quality to it. The advertisements seemed to be mostly about new fusion power projects and injured war veterans.

Jonny's favorite part of each broadcast came at the end. That was when the ritual flag burnings always occurred. Sometime the flags they torched were American, sometimes Japanese. Jonny took to toasting the young uniformed hashishin (each with a gray metal key around his neck that was the key to heaven) until he remembered that Muslims did not drink. Then he would simply cheer and pound the bed, drunkenly singing along with the battle songs.

The news show often featured pictures of the moon, fuzzy satellite shots that showed ruined geodesic domes and the crystal mounds of the Alpha Rats' ships on the barren lunar surface. On one broadcast, Jonny saw a street that looked familiar. It was a jumpy rolling shot, as if taken from the window of a moving car or truck. Polychrome marquees above crawling neon. Hollywood Boulevard, Jonny thought. The newscaster's face grew serious as he spoke over the grim footage. Pictures of lepers in the streets—they seemed to be everywhere; shots of gangs (he recognized the Lizard Imperials right away), hookers, and nine-to-fivers from the Valley. Burning funeral ghats along the concrete banks of the Los Angeles River. A quick-cut to people being loaded into the back of a Committee meat wagon.

The show ended when the newscaster lowered his head and a caricature of Uncle Sam and a samurai appeared on the screen. Both figures were yelling "Banzai!," the samurai swinging a long sword, cutting a deep trench into a map of the Middle East. Jonny's hands were shaking when he turned off the screen.

Jonny sometimes ate dinner with Conover in a cavernous room at the far end of the hacienda wing. A cantilevered stucco ceiling with bare wooden beams so old that they were probably real wood crisscrossed two stories above the dining area, a lighted island of silver and crystal in a sea of plundered art. Sitting at the dining table, the walls of the room were lost to Jonny. Old masters, bathing scenes and hunts, orgies and crucifixions, some several meters long, were stacked three deep along the baseboards or perched on aluminum easels between sixteenth-century Roman warrior-angels and Henry Moore bronzes. Buddha and Ganesh shared space with porcelain clocks on the mantel above a bricked-in fireplace.

Jonny came to dinner dressed in one of Conover's black silk shirts and a pair of light cotton trousers. He was drunk, but he had given up on the dilaudid. Although the analog was technically nonaddicting, it gave him the sweats and cramps when he did not take it regularly. To counteract the symptoms, he had prescribed for himself daily doses of dexedrine. Despite all the drugs, he was aware that Conover's medical staff had done a considerable repair job on him. He felt healthier and stronger than he had since he'd quit the Committee.

Except for those times when Jonny joined him, Conover always seemed to eat alone.

They were served their meals by an efficient and mostly silent staff of ritually scarred Africans. The food was French and Japanese—snow peas or glazed carrots arranged with surgical precision around thin and, to Jonny, mostly tasteless cuts of beef. When he commented on this to Conover, the smuggler explained to him that the meat came from Canadian herds that still consumed grain and grazed in open fields, not the genetically altered beasts that hung from straps, limbless and eyeless, in the Tijuana protein factories.

"What you miss, son, is the taste of all those chemicals. Plankton feed solutions and growth hormones."

Jonny shrugged. "I'm just a cheap date," he said.

Conover laughed, sitting across the table in a chair of padded aluminum piping. Wires trailed from his chest, ears, and scalp (pale tufts of sparse white hair) to a vital-signs monitor on his left. One of his sleeves was rolled up and a tube ran from a rotating plasma pump mounted on the side of the chair and under a strip of surgical tape on his left arm. "Twice a week I have to endure this," he explained. "Blood change and cyclosporin treatments. My body is rejecting itself. Most of my organs are saturated with Greenies by now. Those that aren't, my body no longer recognizes and tries to destroy. The cyclosporin slows the rejection process." He took a sip of wine from a fluted crystal glass. "I clone my own organs. Have transplants once or twice a year. Heart, lungs, liver, pancreas, the works. Downstairs, I have everything I need to stay alive. That nerve tissue in your shoulder? We grow that here, in the spinal columns of lampreys."

He took a mouthful of beef and wild rice, chewed thoughtfully. "I've endured all types of nonsense to prolong my stay on this silly planet. I flew to Osaka once, let a quack remove my pituitary gland and install a thyroxine pump in my abdomen. I was told to gobble antioxidants, butylated hydroxytoluene and mercaptoethylamine. I took catatoxic compounds to boost the function of my immune system and now I take cyclosporin to inhibit it. I still have daily injections of dopamine because the production of certain neurotransmitters decreases with age." He shook his head. "My staff could cure me of Greenies addiction completely, of course. A little tinkering with my DNA and it's done. The problem is that afterwards they'd practically have to boil me down and build a whole new body for me. In the meantime, I'd be in some protein vat while the other lords and the Committee carved up my territory. It's strange, don't you think, that we expend so much energy trying to stick around a place we don't particularly like?"

Jonny picked at a piece of asparagus. "I think I could help your people track down the Croakers," he said. "I've got some experience, you know."

Conover continued chewing. "You're drunk," he said.

"That doesn't have anything to do with anything."

"And what are you going to tell the Colonel when he picks you up?" Conover asked.

"You think he can get to me again?"

"There's no question of it. You are a commodity of some value to him. Plus, your face is well-known. He or one of his informants will find you."

Jonny grunted. With his fork, he moved the tasteless meat around his plate until he could not stand to look at it anymore. "So I wait here forever, is that the plan? Well, forget that. I can take care of myself," he said. "Besides, what if I was picked up? What makes you think I'd tell Zamora anything?"

Conover set down his fork and glanced at the monitor. "Jonny, I understand your worry, believe me. You miss your friends and you've been drinking. What I should have said was that it would be very foolish for you to leave here. The Colonel wants you because he wants me, and he is not careful with his prisoners. When he pumps you full of Ecstasy and starts burning off your fingers, you'll tell him everything he wants to know."

Jonny picked up a crystal carafe and slopped some wine into a glass for himself. Conover pushed his glass forward, but Jonny ignored it and the smuggler lord had to pour for himself.

"In any case, you're better off staying away from the Croakers," Conover said.

"What does that mean?"

"Just what I said," Conover replied.

"The Croakers are all right. They're just trying to help people."

Conover rang a silver bell by his plate. Young African men in white jackets began clearing away the plates from the table.

"Why is it Americans always insist on making everything into a cowboys and Indians movie? Just because you label one group the Bad Guys, you immediately assume that the group they are in conflict with are the Good Guys. The world isn't that simple, son."

"You think the Croakers are the Bad Guys?" Jonny asked.

"I didn't say that. But they are destabilizing Southern California far more effectively than the Alpha Rats or the Arabs could ever hope to."

Jonny leaned his elbows on the table. His dinner churned with the liquor in his stomach. "The Croakers are the only effective force we have against the Committee."

Conover gestured to one of the waiters and dessert was served: a raspberry torte like a lacquered sculpture. "The Committee is a fact of life. What we do, you and I, all the dealers and smugglers, is poetry. Haiku. A form defined by its restrictions. The sooner you learn to work within those restrictions, the happier you'll be."

Jonny tossed his fork onto the plate and stood up. Wisps of vertigo floated around the inside of his skull. "Thanks for dinner. I'm going to get some sleep."

As Jonny started out of the dining room, Conover called to him. "You know I'm doing all I can, don't you?"

"I know," said Jonny, without turning around.

"And you believe me when I tell you I'm trying to locate your friends."

"Yes, I do."

"And you have to know I'm right about the Colonel."

"I know about all that," Jonny replied quietly. "I just don't know if I care anymore."

He drank from the bottle of gin he had taken from his room. He stood in a darkened storage room, the third one he had explored that night, a refuge from his latest failed attempt at meditation.

The room was silent, the air musty. Light danced on a circular dais at the far end. A camera obscura, he saw. There was a worn metal wheel mounted on the wall. When he spun it, the brilliant panorama of Los Angeles swept across the dais like a video on fast forward. He focused the image on Hollywood, moving the wheel until the luminescent tent of his home slid into view, glowing beyond palm trees and neon. For a while he found it comforting, but soon he felt pangs of self-consciousness, imagining himself a peeping Tom getting his kicks.

Is this how we look to the Alpha Rats? Jonny wondered.

Padded zero-G crates with five-year-old shipping codes from some lunar engineering plant were stacked against the far wall. Jonny took another pull from the gin, slid one of the crates to the floor, and opened the top. Inside were a dozen smaller boxes, each packed with capsules in blister packs, two capsules to each blister. The manufacturer's code indicated that the red capsules were an inhalant form of atropine. The purple capsules were unmarked, but Jonny had seen them before. His stomach tightened. It was a popular combination in some circles: atropine and cobrotoxin nitrite.

Holy shit, he thought. What's an engineering company doing with Mad Love?

He tore open one of the packs, slopping gin on the floor, and popped a purple capsule under his nose. The cobrotoxin came on like a slow-burning volcano, boiling along the surface of his brain—not enough to kill him or cause permanent damage, just enough to cop the killing euphoria from the cobra venom. His body was molten glass and treacle. No flesh, no bones, just a sizzling mass of plasma, fried eyes, and melting genitals. Thirty seconds later, he popped the modified atropine (its molecular web constructed in the mirror image of the cobrotoxin) and the inside of his skull iced over. The room exploded into negative as white glacial light blazed behind his eyes and shot down his spinal column. His nerves (he could feel each individual fiber vibrating in harmony like some kind of cellular choir) were cut crystal and gold. "A las maravillas," he said. This was it. Zen. Oneness. How could he have forgotten? Anger, greed, and folly were gone, replaced with a heightened awareness that was what he had always imagined enlightenment to be like.

Then the feeling was gone.

When he could move, he tore two more capsules from the pack and repeated the process. A few years before, Mad Love had been a big problem for Jonny. He had avoided the stuff for years, neither dealing nor using it. In some ways it had been easy; Mad Love was almost impossible to find in the street, at any price, since the Alpha Rat takeover of the moon. Yet here he was with hundreds of hits.

He felt expansive, filled with love for his fellow man, wanting nothing more than to share his good fortune with the world. Jonny laughed. It was the drugs talking to him, he knew. He did not want to share this with anybody. Stumbling to his feet (the atropine causing his muscles to fire erratically) he pulled down more crates, taking a quick inventory of his stash.

The first three containers were empty, but the fourth held another bonanza: twelve more boxes of Mad Love. He grabbed for more crates, caught the glint of something shining dully on the wall. Gilt wood. He pulled the boxes away, could see the carved frame. Then—*Blue Boy*. The original.

He ran his fingers over the old lizardskin paint, from the plumed hat to the gold-leaf frame. There was a catch at the edge. He pushed it and the painting swung away from the wall with a faint *click*. Behind it were shelves piled high with books and a bulging manila folder. Jonny picked up the foxed folder, took it back to the camera obscura, and dumped the contents on the dais. It was several seconds before Jonny understood exactly what he was looking at. He fingered a yellowed Social Security card, shiny with wear. Then, in the pale Los Angeles nightscape he turned the pages, rapt, reading a collage version of the life of Soren Conover.

A driver's license from Texas, two thousand and ten. Discharge papers from the United States Army, nineteen fifty-seven. Passports: British, Belgian, Egyptian, all under different names. Ancient news clippings concerning drug wars in Central America and the collapse of the government's genetic warfare programs. Photos on some of the older documents showed a handsome oval-faced man in his thirties, with intelligent eyes and a nose that had been broken more than once. Jonny double-checked any dated documents he came across, trying to find the oldest. From what he had seen so far, he was calculating Conover's age at around one hundred and fifty, possibly one hundred and sixty years.

There were photstats of OSS documents, brittle with age. Conover had apparently been involved with an operation to assassinate the Russian head of state in the early nineteen fifties. The American president had canceled the operation and pensioned Conover off. There was nothing from the nineteen sixties or seventies, but from the eighties there were several letters on CIA stationery bearing Conover's signature, along with a report marked "Confidential." The report carried no date, but detailed the workings of a Honduran-based CIA drug operation helping to finance right-wing revolutionary and counterrevolutionary forces in Central America. There was a black-and-white photo of men in jungle fatigues standing before mortar tubes and M-60 machine guns. One tall man held a cigarette in a short black holder. The hand-lettered date on the back of the photo read 1988. It occurred to Jonny that if these documents were genuine, then Conover had been in the drug business for close to a hundred years.

That's a long time to do one thing, Jonny thought. He continued through the papers as the silent city light played over them, and wondered at the process of the smuggler's life. How he had parlayed those CIA drug contacts into his own private business. Jonny found the gin bottle by the boxes of Mad Love, took a drink, and laughed. He and Conover had something in common, he now knew. Conover was a smuggler lord now, but once he had been like Jonny, an agent gone native.

L.A. glimmered on the dais, just out of reach.

The atropine was still buzzing inside Jonny's skull. He picked up handfuls of Mad Love packets and stuffed them into his pockets, then returned to the dais, gathered up the contents of the folder, and put them back behind the painting. He restacked the zero-G crates and, just before leaving the room, he spun the wheel that adjusted the camera obscura's lenses. The city blurred by on the dais, streaks of light like tracer rounds. The picture came to rest on the Japanese wing of the mansion. A snow leopard was strolling gracefully down the driveway.

Conover will understand, Jonny thought, popping another atropine cap.

He went out through the kitchen. The African staff had a music chip going full blast, some Brazilian capoeira band. A coltish young woman who had been dancing as she stacked Wedgewood in a cabinet stopped to stare at him. Jonny crossed quickly to the door, avoiding the Africans' eyes. Copper pots flashed bronze suns onto the wall above his head.

"Dad'll kill me if I don't get the trash out," he said to their unmoving faces.

He found Ricos alone in the garage, the workings of a robot rottweiler strewn across a wooden workbench. Rather than injure the man, Jonny wrapped an arm around Ricos's

neck and jammed a knuckle into his carotid artery, cutting off
the flow of blood to his brain. When he was out, Jonny went
through his pockets and found the silicon identification card.
He got into Conover's car, gunned the engine, and backed out.

He took the Cadillac at a leisurely pace down the drive,
eyes ahead, ignoring the men among the madrones. At the
foot of the drive, Jonny nervously punched the ten-digit code
he had memorized weeks before into the dashboard key pad.
He was surprised and relieved when he saw sections of the
hologram disappear. When the road was clear, he turned off
the roof lights and drove slowly down the hill.

The night was clear and hot.

He steered the Cadillac down the winding road, following
a series of rolling brown-outs through the suburbs, cracked
solar panels, astroturf on the lawns, a deserted shopping mall
that once had served as a holding area during the Muslim
Relocation programs at the beginning of the century. The razor
wire was still in place atop double layers of hurricane fencing,
a grim reminder of the war that had never quite gotten off the
ground.

Jonny popped another atropine cap and rode the high all
the way into Hollywood, confident that if called upon he
could count each strand of muscle tissue in his body. He left
the car behind a Baby Face plastic surgery boutique on Sunset
and made his way in and out of the stalled traffic to Carnaby's
Pit, taking a detour through the weekend mercado. The smell
of cook smoke and sweat greeted him, scratchy salsa disc
recordings, all the familiar sensations. The crowd was thick
with Committee boys. Jonny kept his head down while old
women tugged at his sleeves and children ran after him with
broken electronic gear, an artificial heart of chipped milky
white plastic, ancient floppy-disk drives. Jonny saw no Link
documentary makers and he took this to be a good omen, but
he kept mistaking women in the crowd for Ice and Sumi.
There were a lot of lepers in the mercado. He spotted them
easily—they were the ones wearing gloves or scarves or
longsleeved shirts of radio-sensitive material, drawing eyes
from their lesions to the random Link videos bleeding across
their clothing.

There were more lepers in the Pit's game parlor, frying in
their disguises. The air conditioning was down, leaving the air

sauna-hot and moist. Jonny felt as if he had stepped into an
oven. The scarves and gloves the lepers wore could almost be
taken for some new fashion, Jonny thought. Under other cir-
cumstances, they might have been. A blond woman plugged
into Fun in Zero-G wore a facial veil and a long chador-like
garment patterned with dozens of colorful corporate logos, but
the billowing material could not hide the mottling along her
hands.

All that atropine had left Jonny with a crushing thirst. He
pushed his way to the bar and ordered a Corona. Porn jumped
and jittered on the video screen, colors slightly out of register.
(What does that look like through skull-plugs? he wondered.)
Taking Tiger Mountain was not playing. The music was a
computer-generated recording in the style of numerous Japa-
nese bubble gum bands. The club was only half filled and the
crowd seemed edgy, voices louder than usual. Random came
back with his perpetual half-smile and set down Jonny's Cor-
ona. "Haven't seen you for a while," the bartender said.
"You're looking exceptionally handsome and vital these
days."

"Thanks," replied Jonny. "Took me a little out-of-town va-
cation. Dude ranch in the hills. Had an oil change, lube job,
the works."

The bartender nodded. "Vacation, huh? And you came
back? You must be a glutton for punishment." Random, too,
was wearing a scarf, folded cravat-fashion in the folds of his
sweat-stained white shirt, hiding something. He polished a
glass absently on the front of his spotted apron.

"Crowd's looking a little abbreviated tonight," said Jonny.

Random nodded. "Fucking *A*, man. You can thank the
Committee for that. They just passed an ordinance cutting the
number of people we can have in here in half. Supposed to get
a handle on the leprosy."

"While keeping things convenient for themselves," said
Jonny. "If it's illegal to get together, then the Committee can
raid any gang councils they get wind of."

"Exactamente," the bartender said. He set down the glass
he had been rubbing. Through some method Jonny could
never quite understand, the bartender could polish glasses all
night, and they never seemed to get any cleaner. "You hear
that bit of nastiness just came over the Link? Seems that some

person or person unknown set off a small nuke a few kilometers above Damascus."

"Jesus," said Jonny. "Was it us?"

"Nah. Very high burst. Didn't cause any property damage, but the emp fucked up communications, computers, et cetera for a few hours. Seems from the device's trajectory that it came from beyond Earth orbit."

"What, they think the Alpha Rats are dropping bombs on people?" Jonny asked. He took a long drink of the Corona.

Random shrugged, leaned his elbows on the bar. "Buddha said 'Life is suffering.'"

"Then this must be life," said Jonny. He held up the empty Corona bottle and Random bought him another. When the bartender set it down, Jonny said, "What do you hear about the Croakers?"

The bartender shook his head. Jonny could almost hear the gears shifting. Business mode. "Don't know if I've had the pleasure," said Random.

Jonny palmed a packet containing a half-dozen hits of Mad Love and passed it to the bartender. When Random realized what he was holding he glanced at Jonny, registering genuine surprise. Jonny was delighted; he had imagined the bartender incapable of any emotions beyond a certain rueful irony.

"If you had nicer legs, I'd marry you right now," Random said, tucking the packet away under the bar. "You're aware that I could open my own place if I had a mind to sell what you've just given me."

"If you had a mind to sell it."

"If I had a mind." Random leaned closer, running a soiled gray towel across the old dashboards that formed the bartop. His breath smelled of old tobacco. "Word is, Zamora's cut their balls off. They're gone, man. Closed up shop. Adios. All kinds of crazy talk about them. Like they're trying to get arms for those New Palestine guys or trying to steal a shuttle to go to the moon. Maybe they're the ones that nuked Damascus." Random laughed, all air. "Like I said, crazy talk."

"That's it?" asked Jonny.

"Hell no. That's the crazy talk. People with a few synapses left say they're holed up somewhere up the coast, past Topanga Beach. The Committee's coming down hard on all the gangs."

"So I've heard," Jonny said, draining half of his beer. He

glanced at the tense faces around the bar. "Anger, greed, and folly."

"Perhaps you've hit on it. Perhaps the Committee's nothing more than an instrument of karma."

"More like a stairway to the stars. If you're an ambitious prick."

"Que es?" said the bartender. "You think the Colonel wants to be addressed as 'Mister President'?"

Jonny shrugged. "He wouldn't be the first one."

"What's the old joke? 'Don't vote. It only encourages them.'" Random shrugged. "Maybe it's not that funny. Anyway," he continued, "if I were you, I'd consider taking my act on the road. Between the heat and the lepers, Last Ass ain't no place to be right now." The bartender moved down the bar to serve a group of well-dressed movie producers and their dates. They were drunk and tan and radiated the slightly forced humor of store-bought youth, hard, sleek bodies surgically sculpted into something as functional and anonymous as next year's jets.

"Jesus Christ," Jonny said. "It makes you crazy."

Later, when he was working on his third Corona, Random stopped in front of him. "You think about what I said?"

"About leaving?" Jonny asked. "No way. I'm a businessman. Got deals to make. Grande deals. Enorme deals."

"In that case," said the bartender, "I think somebody over there wants to talk to you."

Jonny turned in his seat and saw Nimble Virtue, the slunk merchant, waving to him from a corner table. "Thanks," he said to the bartender.

"It's your movie, man," said Random. "Be careful."

Jonny picked his way through the crowd to the corner table where Nimble Virtue sat by herself. She was dressed in a loose-fitting kimono patterned with water lilies and delicate vines done in gold and turquoise. Dropping into a seat across from the smuggler lord, Jonny had a perfect view of a couple of her men, two tables away, drinking iced vodka with some of the local Yakuza. Jonny smiled and waved to them. One of the Yakuza men laughed and made a circular motion with his finger to indicate madness.

"Dear Jonny-san," began Nimble Virtue. "First, allow me to apologize for the uncomfortable circumstances under which we last met. If I had had any inkling as to Colonel Zamora's true intentions, I can assure you that he would never have gained a single syllable of information from myself or any of my people."

Nimble Virtue was small, a skeletal, middle-aged woman with a flat nose and pale skin through which you could see the blue veins around her skull. The way Jonny had heard it, she had been born into prostitution on one of the circumlunar sandakans that had served the mining trade from the moon; it was not until the Alpha Rats' invasion had destroyed the lunar mining business that she had ever set foot on Earth. Once there, she had become the mistress of a powerful Yakuza oyabun and thereby escaped the sandakan.

Having spent much of her life in zero-G or reduced-G environments, on Earth Nimble Virtue was forced at all times to wear a titanium alloy exoskeleton. This helped her move about, and a ribbed, girdlelike mechanism worked her diaphragm, her chest cavity having grown too small for her lungs to breathe the thick air of Earth's surface. It was also rumored that she never went anywhere without a velvet-lined case bearing the fetuses of her two stillborn sons.

"You're a liar," Jonny said. "You'd sell your grandmother for sausage if you thought you could hide the wrinkles. The only thing I don't understand is why nobody's ever put a bullet through your brainpan."

Nimble Virtue covered her mouth with pale metal-wrapped fingers, and giggled. "Some have tried, Jonny-san, but, as you can see, none have succeeded. Many people find it more pleasurable to work with me rather than against me. Could you not?" Nimble Virtue lifted an empty wine glass and waved it at the table where her men sat. One of them got up and went to the bar. "Have a drink. They keep Tej here for me. Have you ever tried it? It's an Ethiopian honey wine. Wonderful."

"I don't drink with people who sell my ass out from under me," said Jonny. "But since you got me over here, you can at least tell me why you turned me to Zamora."

Nimble Virtue ran her index finger around the rim of her glass and licked off the remains of the wine. In the second of silence between the prerecorded songs, Jonny could hear the insect humming of her exoskeleton. "I gave you to him as a gesture of goodwill. I thought the Colonel and I had a deal, but things have not worked out for us." She gazed after her

man at the bar. "A bit of free advice, Jonny. Never develop a
sweet tooth. It is much too expensive a vice in a city like
this."

"What's this goodwill business you're talking about?"
asked Jonny.

"I thought you would be the expert on that."

"Don't be cute," said Jonny. "I could snap that skinny neck
of yours before any of your boys even draws his gun."

Nimble Virtue smiled at him. "And then we would both be
gone, and wouldn't that be a waste? No, much better that you
should hear me out," she said. "I have a business proposition
for you. It's very simple: I want you to forget the Colonel.
Come and work for me."

Jonny leaned back on his chair. "What could I give you
that you can't buy already?"

"I know that Zamora had you picked up because he wanted
information about Conover. I also know that the Colonel is
planning a massive raid against all the smuggler lords. It only
stands to reason that you two have made a deal. That's why he
let you go. Correct, Jonny-san?" She paused and took several
deep, ragged breaths. Talking, it appeared, put her out of
synch with her breathing apparatus. "You are a dealer and can
move freely among the lords. You are gathering information
about us for the Colonel: our strength and our movements. I,
too, wish to bid for your services. Work for me. All I need is
the date and time of the raids. For that information, I will
provide you with ample protection, as well as a permanent
place in my organization when we cut the Colonel down."

"I don't know anything more about the raids than you do,"
said Jonny. "And I'm not working for Zamora, and if I was, I
sure wouldn't give you any information."

One of Nimble Virtue's men arrived, carrying a heavy
green bottle from which he poured a clear gold liquid. The
man set down a second glass and poured Tej for Jonny before
heading back to the other table.

"Thank you, my dear," Nimble Virtue called after the man.
She took a sip of the syrupy liquid and looked at Jonny.
"Really, Jonny-san, these threats and the names you call me
mean nothing, but do not insult my intelligence. I know that
you have spent these last weeks at Conover's mansion in the
hills. Gathering evidence, yes? I know all about Conover's
hologram dome, and I know in my bones that you are working

for Colonel Zamora." She paused again to catch her breath. "In truth, I admire the subtle way you set up the Croakers for the Colonel. Groucho is not a stupid man. You are to be congratulated for taking him so thoroughly."

"Keep talking. You're digging your own grave," said Jonny.

Nimble Virtue crossed her hands on her lap and gave him an indulgent, matronly look. "Do you know the expression 'Little Tiger,' Jonny-san?"

"I've heard it."

"You are the Little Tiger," she said. "You make loud roars, but you have little strength and no cunning. I like you because you make me laugh. But circumstances force me to limit the amount of time I can expend on any one enterprise."

"Don't let me keep you," said Jonny.

She waited a moment. "Then you are committed to the Colonel?"

"I'll deal with Zamora in my own way," he said. "I don't work for him and I won't work for you." Jonny started to get up, but Nimble Virtue laid a hand lightly on his arm.

"I would think twice about leaving here if I were you," said the slunk merchant. "After betraying the Croakers, you have very few friends left in L.A. I could make it ever so much hotter for you—"

Jonny swept his arm across the table, knocking glasses, bottles, and wine to the floor. "You sell me like your goddam slunk and then you want to make a deal with me? Fuck you, old lady."

Nimble Virtue made a fluttering gesture with her hand. Jonny turned and found three of her men pointing Russian CO_2 pistols at him, assassin models, chambered for explosive shells. The men were young and handsome, wearing tight black jeans and sleeveless T-shirts with coiled dragons on the front. They were cool and expressionless, mechanical in their movements and stance. But they were not ninja. If they were, Jonny knew, he would be dead by now.

Nimble Virtue got to her feet and waved for her men to put their guns away. As they did so, she turned and gave Jonny a small bow. Her face was flushed and she was breathing heavily. "I will be going now. I wish you luck, and time to grow wise, Jonny-san. It would be best if you stayed out of my way," she said.

He watched them as they left. Taking Tiger Mountain appeared on the stage to indifferent applause. As Saint Peter kicked them into their first number, Jonny pushed his way out the heavy fire door at the rear of the Pit.

If he pressed his back against the wall of the alley, Jonny could get a pretty good look at Sunset Boulevard and the entrance to Carnaby's Pit. The repair job on the front of the bar had been a sloppy one. Smears of resin and cheap construction foam covered the bullet holes in the Pit's facade. The charm was definitely wearing off the place, he decided. Hot wind brought the smell of frijoles and burning carnitas down the alley from the mercado.

A scrape. A corpse's whisper: "Lord, if thou wilt, thou canst make me clean."

Jonny started to move. Metal, cold and sharp, bit into his neck. "Now, now," said Easy Money. "Long time no see, Jonny, old pal, old buddy." Easy spun Jonny around. Satyr horns, tattooed knuckles around the grip of a knife. "You know what I hear? I hear you want to do me."

Other feet shuffled up behind them; other hands gripped Jonny's arms. Easy released him and lowered the knife. "Bring the car around," he said. Footsteps moved off. Then to the others: "This guy wants to fuck me. But he's so simple you gotta love him, you know?"

Jonny leaned back, supported by the grasping hands, and snapped the steel toe of his boot up into Easy's groin.

Later, after they beat him and he was laid out on the floor of the car, their feet on his back and a canvas hood over his head, he comforted himself with the image of Easy Money rolling up into a fetal position on the pavement in the filthy alley.

8

THE MENACED ASSASSIN

"YOU'RE A VERY stupid boy, Jonny-san."

Water hit him and someone pulled the hood away. He found himself face down on the riveted steel floor of an abattoir. His shirt was gone; the freezing water cut into him like knives.

"How much of this have you taken?"

He stood and Nimble Virtue tossed a packet of Mad Love at his feet. It came to rest by the toe of his boot, where the water was icing up over a flaking patch of dried blood. Welding marks, like narrow scars of slag. The slaughterhouse had been grafted together from a stack of old Sea Train cargo containers. A cryogenic pump hummed at the far end of the place, like a beating heart, pushing liquid oxygen through a network of pipes that crisscrossed the walls and floor. Hanging from the ceiling, dull steel hooks held fly-specked slabs of slunk, gray and shapeless sides of old meat. Jonny looked at Nimble Virtue.

"We found your pockets packed with this. From the size of your pupils, I would guess you've snorted up a small fortune's worth." She wore a bulky floor-length coat of some opalescent sea-green fur. Shrugging, she turned away from him, a tense, mechanical gesture. Her exoskeleton whirred. "We could have extracted the information we need painlessly, with drugs. But that seems impossible now. Who knows what might happen when the mnemonics mix with the toxins you've ingested. We'll have to do it another way. But I want you to remember," Nimble Virtue said, "you've brought this on yourself." (He heard her voice overlaid with Zamora's then: "You beg for it, Gordon—")

Easy Money and a thick-necked cowboy Jonny knew as

Billy Bump stepped into his field of vision. Easy was wearing a sleeveless, gray down jacket, Billy a surplus Army parka. Each held a Medusa. Easy swung the whip end of his in a lazy arc before him. A bright, almost luminous fury welled up in his eyes. "So when is it, asshole?" he asked.

"When is what?" Jonny asked.

"When's the raid?" snapped the cowboy. He spoke in a thick south Texas drawl, the result of a quartz chip implanted in the speech center of his brain. He spit a rust-colored stream of tobacco juice onto the floor. Billy Bump had picked up his name as a teenager, when he had a habit of pushing people in front of moving cars for their pocket change.

"I can't hear you," Easy said in a mock singsong fashion.

"Why bother?" Jonny asked. "You're not going to believe anything I say."

"Jonny, please tell me when Zamora is going to move against us," said Nimble Virtue.

"I don't know," Jonny told her.

Easy Money whipped his arm out. The charged copper tips of his Medusa snapped into Jonny's chest, blinding him with sparks. The water radiated the shock across his arms and down into his groin. Jonny doubled up and came to, finding himself clinging to a side of gray meat for support. He could barely breathe.

"When are the raids?" asked Nimble Virtue.

"I don't know," he said.

"Asshole," said Easy.

Jonny pushed himself from the meat and took off between the stinking rows, but Billy was waiting for him. The cowboy jammed a big boot into Jonny's stomach and brought the Medusa down across his back. Jonny collapsed onto the metal floor.

Above him, Nimble Virtue's face appeared. Through his confusion and pain she seemed as gray and lifeless as her slunk. Hard bones beneath dead meat. Maybe that's her secret, Jonny thought dreamily. Not more Johns; she's found another way to sell herself.

Easy Money kicked him in the ribs and shook the coils of his Medusa over Jonny, sending sparks into his eyes. Jonny heard Billy and Easy laugh. "Well it's cryin' time again," Billy sang.

"Do you know where you are, Jonny-san?" asked Nimble Virtue.

Jonny nodded. "Meat locker," he said, trying to get his breath.

"Correct. And there is a warehouse full of my men just outside. There is no way out of here without my say-so."

"No way out," echoed Easy Money.

"I could have these young men beat you all week. Do you understand that?"

He sat up. Strange lights boiled around the edges of his vision. "Yes," he said.

"Good," said the slunk merchant. "Then why not be reasonable? When are the raids?"

"Tuesday," he said. Then: "Oh fuck, I told you: I don't know."

Easy and Billy were on him, snapping the coils of their Medusas down on Jonny's back and stomach. Pain and the mad dance of sparks overwhelmed him, merged with the flow of sensory data along his nerves until he was unable to tell where the white storm of agony ended and his body began. When they stopped, his muscles continued to convulse.

"When are the raids?" asked Nimble Virtue.

"I don't know," said Jonny. "Zamora didn't talk to me about raids."

"What did he talk about?"

"I don't remember." Jonny crawled to his hands and knees. Despite the cold, sweat was flowing from his arms and chest. "My life," he said.

"What?" Nimble Virtue demanded. She waited until he was in a kneeling position, then she slapped him hard across the face. Jonny felt the metal around her fingers tear his skin.

"Conover," said Jonny. "Zamora wants me to turn Conover."

At a signal from Nimble Virtue, Billy hit Jonny from behind. While he was stunned, Easy secured hard loops of white plastic around Jonny's wrists. Then Easy and Billy lifted him from the floor, Easy pushing Jonny's arms over his head so that when they released him, he was hanging by his wrists from one of the heavy steel hooks. The pain was instant and terrible. He screamed.

Nimble Virtue picked up the Medusa that Easy had left on the floor and approached Jonny. "Answer me quickly and simply," she said. She gathered the coils of the Medusa together and pressed the charged tips into Jonny's side. He convulsed on the hook and went limp. "What is your name?" she asked.

"Jonny Qabbala."

"Your real name."

It took him a moment. "Gordon João Acker."

"Where were you born?"

"The Hollywood Greyound Station," he said. Easy and Billy laughed again. It echoed. Jonny looked up; framed by the corroded bulkhead around a ventilation shaft, he saw his hands, blood on his arms.

"What is your profession?" Nimble Virtue asked.

"Dealer."

"When did Colonel Zamora tell you to expect the raids?"

"He didn't."

"Liar!" yelled Nimble Virtue. She pressed the ends of the Medusa into Jonny's stomach and held them there. "You stupid boy, I can keep you up alive for weeks! Cut off a piece every day and sell you in the mercado!"

When Jonny came to, he realized that he had blacked out again. Nimble Virtue was muttering in Japanese and making unpleasant sucking sounds as the exoskeleton breathed her. Jonny's arms and shoulders had gone numb. He thought he could hear music in the next room. When Nimble Virtue looked at him, he said, "I can't tell you what I don't know. Zamora just wanted to talk about the Alpha Rats."

Jonny saw something flicker over Nimble Virtue's face. "Take him down," she said. Easy and Billy moved under him, lifted Jonny off the hook and laid him out on the floor. Nimble Virtue moved closer and put a hand on his leg. The fur of her coat tickled his stomach. "Say it again. Say it or I'll have them put you back up."

Jonny looked at her eyes. Fear or relief, he wondered. His head swam. He wondered when the dream would be over and he would wake up next to Ice and Sumi. "There's a deal," he said and his head fell back.

"Wrap him up," Nimble Virtue told one of the men. "But leave his hands bound."

Jonny lay on the cold steel, hoping it had worked. Fear kept him still, but he was satisfied that they had bought the fainting act. A trickle of relief washed through him. He could hear the purring of Nimble Virtue's exoskeleton as she moved around the abattoir. "Get the Arab back here," she said. "Tell him we can deal."

Jonny listened to the footsteps: Billy's heavy and flat-footed, his cowboy boots coming down like open-handed slaps; Nimble Virtue's rapid and light, with insect hums and clicks. Easy Money moved in quick bursts, his clubfoot dragging behind him. Jonny knew he would have to wait at least until Easy or Billy had left the room before he could make a break. He willed himself to remain still, to use what time he had to rest and collect himself. The sweat on his right arm was freezing to the slaughterhouse floor. Just as he was beginning to worry about frostbite, he felt Billy (he caught a whiff of chew) wrap a rough woolen blanket around his shoulders.

"Don't want you croaking out on us, now," he heard the cowboy say.

There was a loud buzz from the far end of the room. Jonny kept his eyes closed, his breathing shallow. Movement, machinelike and delicate. "What is it?" came Nimble Virtue's voice.

Static. At first Jonny could not understand the voice. "—spotter picked up police vans headed this way. Looks like a raid," the intercom sputtered.

Nimble Virtue cursed in Japanese. "Not now. I'm not ready," she said.

Jonny heard Easy Money: "It's the cops, not the Committee. No sweat."

"Perhaps," she said. The coldness came back to her voice, the hard suggestion of efficiency. "Stay with him. You come with me." A confusion of footsteps, all three of them moving around the room at once. The abattoir door opened and closed. Then there was nothing. Jonny could not stand it. He opened his eyes.

At the far end of the room, Easy Money was leaning against the cryogenic pump, grinning at him.

"Ollie ollie oxen free," Easy said. He chuckled and steam from his breath curled around his grafted satyr horns. "Watching you's like watching porn. I mean, you're so fucking trite, but I can't help it. I still get off. Twisted, huh?"

Jonny got up from the freezing floor and pulled the blanket tight across his shoulders. "You gonna tell the teacher I was bad when she left the room?"

Easy shook his head. "Hell no," he said. "You think I care

about the bitch? I'm just watching the parade go by. Besides," he said, strolling toward Jonny, "I know what you really want. You want the stuff I took off Raquin. It's Conover's dope, isn't it? What is it? No, don't tell me; you'd only lie, and I'd get pissed. Anyway, after we're clear of this, maybe you and me, we can work out a deal. Meet me at the Forest of Incandescent Bliss in Little Tokyo." Easy nodded toward the door Nimble Virtue had just used. "That's one of Yokohama Mama's clubs."

"The Forest of Incandescent Bliss. Right," said Jonny.

"I assume you're in contact with Conover, and can get me a fair price."

"No problem."

Easy moved a little closer. He spoke to Jonny softly. "Tell me the truth, you were gonna blow me away that night at the Pit, weren't you?"

"Who, me? I was just stopping by to watch the movie stars."

"Liar," said Easy Money. He smiled. "We're gonna have to work that out, too."

"Whatever you say."

"But later," Easy said. Through the slaughterhouse wall came the muffled sound of automatic weapons fire. The lights in the abattoir went out. A few seconds later, emergency floodlamps flared to life over the doors, throwing the room into brilliant arctic relief. "They'll be back in a minute. You better get back on the floor." Jonny reluctantly lay back down and Easy bent over him. "One more thing," he said. "I'm not helping you, understand, but if I were you, I'd make a real effort to get out of here. You don't want to deal with the bitch's Arab friends."

Jonny nodded. "Thanks." The meat locker shuddered. Nimble Virtue and Billy hurried through the door.

"Bring him!" shouted Nimble Virtue. "It is the police, but I don't want him found."

Jonny smelled tobacco again. He went limp as Billy grabbed him around the chest and began hauling him toward the door. When they hit warm air, Jonny dug his heels in and drove an elbow into Billy's midsection. The cowboy groaned and fell back against a wall of yellow fiberglass packing crates. Jonny spun, put a boot to Billy's chin (just for fun, that) and took off running, Nimble Virtue shrieking behind at him.

He made one corner and hid between a cluster of rubberized storage cylinders and the angled steel wall supports. Men armed with Futukoros ran past him. Jonny's hands, when he looked at them, were blue and swollen. Running again, he saw police wearing breathing apparatus moving among the long rows of crates. Down another row, and he was gasping and stumbling, knee-deep in carbon dioxide foam. He tried to climb out over a wall of crates, but lack of oxygen muddled him. Black things with glassy eyes and tubes for mouths grabbed him. He swung his bound hands weakly, but missed. His feet could not find the floor.

And the foam swallowed him.

It seemed to him that he was always waking up in strange places. As if his whole life had been a series of dull, terrifying discoveries—trying to find some point of reference, finding it and having it swept away at the next moment. The feeling frightened and infuriated him even as he nursed it along, believing that if he ever lost his terror and rage he might lose himself, flicker and disappear like an image on a video screen.

Jonny woke up to a hot pain that extended from his shoulders, across his back, and down into his hands. When he moved his fingers, pins and needles stabbed him. The familiar smell of prison (human waste and disinfectants) turned his stomach.

"Christ," he said, opening his eyes. "Don't they know any other color but green?"

The door of his cell scraped open and a balding, waxy-faced young man peered at him from the hall. Evidently he had been waiting there for some time and Jonny's voice had startled him. Jonny was relieved to see that the man was wearing the blue uniform of the police department, and not Committee black.

"Hello?" said the cop.

Jonny swung his feet onto the floor and sat up on the pallet. The cop tried to cover it, but Jonny saw his head snap back in surprise. "I was just commenting on the accommodations," said Jonny. "They suck." Pain, like a tight cord, cut through his middle.

The cop frowned and closed the door. Jonny listened to his

footsteps as they faded down the corridor. Alone again, he pulled up the stiff gray paper prison shirt and probed his ribs with the tips of his fingers. Bruises and tender flesh there, but nothing seemed to be broken.

Surveying the cell, Jonny felt relief and a quiet kind of joy. Dealing with the police, he knew from experience, would be no problem. They were wired for failure, ridiculed even by the city government that supported them; in the street, they were considered a notch below meter maids as authority figures. Most of the department was staffed by boys who could not cut it in the Committee, had blown their chance through lack of cunning or nerve or the inability to zero in on and take advantage of the fine edge of madness that was absolutely essential in Committee work.

In their own odd way, the police were more vicious than the Committee, a brutal down-scale version of their sister agency. Their lack of power and the consequent pettiness of their concerns had, over the years, become a kind of strength for them, a license to use whatever savagery they thought required to complete the job at hand. And the jobs took many forms; mostly, they concerned shaking down small-time smugglers, dealers, and prostitutes for protection from the gangs. These were often the same people who were paying off one or more gang for protection from the police.

Jonny reflected that the cop who had looked in his cell was typical of the department: older than most Committee boys and lacking the spark of youthful certainty that death, when it came, would be looking for someone else. Jonny decided he would feel out the cop when he returned. See exactly what kind of story he wanted, cop a plea and get assigned to a road gang or one of the mayor's neighborhood renewal projects. Jonny knew that once he was outside, he'd be gone. With any luck, he figured he could be back on the street in a week.

It was about a half-hour, by his reckoning, before he heard footsteps again. Two sets, walking with a purpose. The door of his cell ground open and the cop he had seen earlier entered, followed by an older man wearing a worn blue pinstriped suit patched at the cuffs with thread-jell—a cheap polymeric fiber that hardened when it came into contact with air. The older man's tie was a shade too light to go with his suit and was at least two seasons too thin. Jonny made him for a bureaucrat; a public defender, or maybe a social worker. He

would be the one to work on. Talk about his deprived child-
hood, the violence in the streets . . .

"Officer Acker," said the older man. His eyes were red and
anxious. His shoes were injection-molded polyvinyl, vending
machine numbers. "I'm Detective Sergeant Russo, and this is
Officer Heckert."

Jonny smiled and shook the hand Russo extended to him,
but his mind was kicking into overdrive. New tack, thinking:
he called me "officer."

"I wanted to let you know, personally, that we're on top of
the situation," said Detective Russo, smiling as he sat down
next to Jonny on the plastic sleeping pallet. "You see, when
you were brought in with that bunch from the warehouse,
Officer Heckert here ran retinal scans on everybody to check
for old and foreign warrants—not something we usually do
until after arraignment, but considering the volume of goods
in the warehouse. . . . Then, when he saw Colonel Zamora's
note in your file, he crossed-checked your retinal print and
found your Committee record."

That's it, Jonny thought. This lunatic thinks I'm still in the
Committee. I can walk right out of here. "Good work, Of-
ficer," Jonny said. He nodded to Heckert. The cop nodded
back, obviously happy with his new-found status. "How is it
you happened to raid the warehouse when you did?"

"Anonymous tip," said Heckert. "A woman's voice syn-
thesized to sound male. We ran the call through the analyzer
and got a good print, but I guess she doesn't have a record."
The cop smiled. (Playing hard boy, Jonny thought. Type of
guy fails Committee application, becomes police department
and swears up and down he wanted to be a cop all along, not a
stuck-up Committee boy.) "Probably just some chippie tryin'
to get even with a boyfriend."

"Anyway," said Detective Russo, giving Heckert a disap-
proving glance, "we called Colonel Zamora and he'll be by to
pick you up soon."

"You what?" Jonny yelled. He was on his feet, feeling as if
the bottom had just fallen out of his stomach. "Don't you
know the Committee's been compromised?" He knew he had
to give them something. He made it up as he went along.
"Moles from the New Palestine Federation penetrated the
Committee months ago! I'm undercover, investigating Arab
terrorist cells operating in Southern California. They're insidi-

ous. Dumping mycotoxins in the water table. Releasing plague-infested rats in the suburbs. This is strictly top-level stuff, you understand. Eyes only. Washington and Tokyo are involved, Sergeant Russo. None of this can leave this room."

Russo's gaze passed from Heckert to Jonny and back again. His forehead was furrowed (unsure of his responsibility, his culpability, Jonny thought; unsure, also, whether or not he's being mocked). "But surely you can't suspect Colonel Zamora—" Russo asked.

"How do you know it was Zamora you were speaking to?" Jonny yelled. He was angling closer to the door. He could see they were buying the line of nonsense; it was there in the cops' eyes. Their colorless bureaucratic blood was bubbling to the surface. He knew they would let him go because they believed he was just like them: another link in the chain of command that bound them and defined them. But their gears shifted slowly, and Jonny felt he had to push them along. "Listen, pal, you may have blown my cover but good," he said. "And if the Arabs get wind that I'm in here, with the data I've got, we can all kiss our asses goodbye, 'cause they'll level this whole complex rather than have me get away."

"Well then, we better get you someplace safe," said a gravelly voice from the door. Jonny turned around. He had not even heard Zamora coming, and now it was too late to do anything about it. He turned back to the cops. "Wait, I was lying. I'm not really a Fed," he said. "I'm a Croaker! An anarquista! Arrest me and I'll tell you everything! Names and dates!"

Detective Russo rose from the pallet and turned to Zamora. A muscle jumped angrily along his quickly reddening jaw. "Colonel Zamora, I hope you can explain what's going on here," he said. "Is this or is this not one of your men?"

"Why, Detective Sergeant Russo," said Zamora, "of course he is." The Colonel smiled at him and Jonny felt ill. "Didn't you see my notation in his record? Agent Acker has been under deep-cover for some time now. Working among terrorists for so long, he's had a breakdown. Convinced himself he's one of them. It happens sometimes in these deep-cover cases. But we'll get him all the help he needs."

Russo grunted. "This man has wasted all our time, Colonel. And put this department in an embarrassing position. I hope you get him some help soon." He shook his head, jammed his hands into the pockets of his shabby suit, and started out of the cell. "Colonel Zamora," he said in a tired voice, "the next time you're having trouble with your men, I'd appreciate your notifying the department. I realize that the police aren't held in quite the same regard as the Committee, but really—"

"You're absolutely right, detective," said Zamora. "Communication. That's what it's all about."

Russo and Heckert left the cell (the younger man fixing Jonny with a look of absolute loathing) and went one way down the corridor, while Zamora and a couple of heavily armed Committee boys led Jonny in the opposite direction. In a waiting area painted in two tones of blistered green paint, Zamora grabbed Jonny (tearing the cheap prison shirt) and punched him in the stomach. "That's for being a smartass," said the Colonel.

Zamora shoved Jonny, still doubled up, into an elevator. Someone pushed a button and they started moving. Jonny saw his reflection in one transparent wall, ghostly with receding rooftops and cumulus clouds. The overcast sky burned muddily through the grime and mirror-glazed Lexan that encased the rising car. Straightening, Jonny looked at the Committee boys who flanked him. They appeared to be about fourteen years old, radiating waves of amphetamine tension. Both were skull-plugged into multiplexers set to coordinate their Futukoros with the Sony targeting matrices that webbed their chests and backs in tight diamond mesh. Each boy had a powerpack around his waist and a datapatch, also jacked into the array, covering one eye.

"The best we have," said Zamora, indicating the boys. "See all the trouble I go through for you?" He smiled sympathetically. "Look at me, Gordon. I'm an avalanche. And I'm coming down hard on you this time. You should not have blown our deal."

"What deal?" asked Jonny. He rubbed his sore ribs. "We never had a deal. You put a gun to my head and gave me an order. Bullshit, that's what that is."

Zamora shrugged. "Call it anything you like. The fact of the matter is you fucked me over and now you've got to pay the price." He looked away and Jonny followed his gaze as it settled out over the docks. White articulated-boom cranes were offloading bright silver boxcars from container ships, sliding on their induction cushions like the skeletons of immense horses.

An old and familiar anger enclosed Jonny, like a fist tightening in his chest. He choked; it reminded him of speed, the reckless and undirected anger of the comedown.

He looked at the floor, trying to clear his mind. Strands of plastic-coated copper wire coiled at angles from around the dull service panel beneath the elevator button pad. Jonny gained some small sense of control by telling himself that he had denied Zamora the thing he wanted most—Conover. But he's got me, thought Jonny. And he knew that Zamora would eventually get Conover anyway. That thought brought the anger back, stronger than ever.

"I see right through you, Colonel," said Jonny.

Zamora raised an eyebrow, amused. "Oh really?"

"Damn straight," Jonny said. "It came to me while I was up there in the hills. I haven't worked out all the details, but I know you're in bed with the Arabs. I saw broadcasts from L.A., on a restricted Arab Link channel. Obviously, if there are Arabs operating in the city, you know about it. And if you know about it, it means you're being paid off."

"What if I told you you weren't even warm?"

"You'd be lying. Cause it's that Arab connection that makes you so nervous about Conover. He's got CIA connections that go back decades. You're afraid he's on to you, that he'll cut a deal with the Feds and that you'll end up in a sterile room somewhere with wires in your head, spilling every thought you ever had."

"What makes you think I'm not prepared to go up there and drag Conover down by his skinny neck?"

"Because you don't want a war. Conover's not stupid. Obviously, you know where he is. That hologram dome is just a carny trick to impress the locals and the other lords, but he's got that haunted house set up really nice against any kind of assault. You'd have to flatten the whole hill to get him down. But if you did that, people would start asking questions and you'd be back in the shit again. That's why you told me that fairy tale about the Alpha Rats. You thought I'd be all impressed and terrified of your heavy connections, that I'd get Conover off that hill and come sucking around to you, looking for table scraps."

Colonel Zamora shook his head, let go with his throaty

lizard laugh. "God, kid, you've really gone around the bend. Maybe we should get you to a hospital after all," he said. "Naturally there's Arabs operating in Last Ass. Hell, Washington and Tokyo've got some of the most influential Mullahs in Qom and Baghdad on the payroll. It's the way of the world. Economics, remember? But these L.A. sand-scratchers are just a propaganda cell. Bureaucratic pussies that couldn't keep me in lunch money."

The elevator was still climbing. Jonny knew then that they were headed for the hoverport on the roof. He shook his head. "I know that you were lying that night back at the warehouse. You don't have Sumi. If you did, you'd have brought her up already. Used her to threaten me or something."

Zamora smiled. The elevator was gradually slowing its ascent. "You sure about that, Gordon?" The Colonel reached out and gently fingered the rip in Jonny's prison tunic. "You ready to bet your life on it?"

"You telling me I got anything to lose?" Jonny asked.

Zamora laughed again. "No, probably not."

The elevator shuddered as magentic bolts locked it into place below the hoverport. They were still two floors from the roof. Like most port-equipped buildings in L.A., this one had a special restricted-access elevator they would have to use to reach the port. "Get ready," Zamora told the Committee boys. Neither boy directly acknowledged the order, but each moved, adjusting datapatches, wiggling their shoulders to smooth the targeting webs. The boys were living on a different level, Jonny knew, in the extended sense-field of the targeting matrix, experiencing a digital approximation of expanded consciousness. For a moment, Jonny found himself envying them. He shook his head at the absurdity of his own mind. Nothing to lose there, he thought.

The elevator doors whispered open and Jonny was propelled into the hall; Zamora came behind him, the Committee boys on either side. The Colonel moved quickly to the other elevator, slid his identification card into a slot under the key pad, and pushed a button. A few meters down the corridor, a prison maintenance worker was using a caulk gun to apply a clear silicone sealant around the edges of an observation window. The corridor itself was silent and anonymous with beige walls and brown institutional carpeting; Jonny was relieved to find that the vile prison smell did not extend up to this level.

Time was definitely slowing, Jonny decided. He felt as if he were moving through some heavy liquid medium, acutely aware of his surroundings, pulsing with the exaggerated senses of the dying and the doomed. Objects had taken on an almost holy significance. Potted palms by the windows. Dull chrome lighting fixtures. The blue overalls of the maintenance worker, his mottled skin, pink shading to black. Something in his hand: silver bolt in a crossbow pistol.

The name came out involuntarily. "Man Ray," Jonny said. But by then it was over. The Committee boy on his right was dead, a slender length of superconductive alloy bursting through his chest, glittering there like a bloody spider, the ribbed filaments bent back, tangling and shorting the targeting web—frying the boy in his own sense-data.

The other boy was firing down the corridor, spraying the walls with hot red tracers. Jonny spun and roundhoused him in the kidneys. An arm clamped around Jonny's throat, jerking him backwards. "No!" Zamora shouted. The Committee boy had turned on them; stoned and red-faced with rage, he had his gun pressed to Jonny's jaw. There was a subdued hiss and the boy fell back—his throat split with a spidery bolt.

The elevator doors opened and Zamora pulled Jonny through. In death, the second Committee boy's eyes were like those of a bewildered child. Jonny felt for him, but then his head was snapped back savagely to meet the barrel of Zamora's Futukoro. "It's not that easy!" the Colonel yelled. He flicked the barrel of his gun at Man Ray and blasted between the closing doors, the sound thundering through Jonny's head. Man Ray leaped the bodies of the dead Committee boys and rolled clear of the shot. The elevator doors closed with a soft thud and the car began to rise.

"Nothing," Zamora whispered in Jonny's ear. "Not a move, not a breath, not a sound." The arm around Jonny's throat tightened, threatening to lift him off his feet. "You think your compañeros are cute? They're assholes. Got nothing going for them but card tricks."

"Maybe," said Jonny, "but your boys are still dead."

The car shivered gently to a halt and the doors opened under the towering lighting gantries of the hoverport. The Colonel's Futukoro pressed to his temple, Jonny crossed the tarmac, the Colonel hugging his back. Smog-light bloodied the sky, the setting sun burning feebly through hydrocarbon-laden mists. "Heads up, children!" Zamora bellowed. "There's Croakers in the building!" Boys moved in the dusty desert light.

A dozen broad circles were laid out evenly across the roof, like illuminated manhole covers. The hovercar landing pads were essentially waffled discs of carbon steel inset with guidelights, set on a bed of leaking shock absorbers. At the moment, there was only one car on the roof, resting on a pad at the far end of the port; Zamora was pushing Jonny toward it as a dozen running Committee boys and cops fanned out behind them, preparing to lay down covering fire across the rooftop. Off to Jonny's left, a young cop with a lightning bolt tattooed on each side of his bald scalp was sending the aircraft elevator to the basement, sealing the roof from the rest of the building. Horns sounded and crimson warning beacons revolved. The platform dropped about two meters and stopped. The roof lights flickered and died.

"Power's cut!" someone yelled.

Zamora shoved Jonny forward, into the arms of a couple of slope-browed Meat Boys. The taller of the two, an acne-scarred chollo, tall even by Committee standards, said, "Where's Rick and Pepe?"

"Shut up," said the Colonel. "They're gone. It's the asshole's fault. Take him to the car."

At the moment that the Meat Boys' brutal fingers death-gripped Jonny's shoulders, something fluttered in the air. The Mitsui Pacific Bank complex, dark a moment before, glowed a pale, snowy gray, and a black-and-white hologram of a woman's face coalesced in the air, gridded with windows and shining robot washers. The image refocused, tightened until only the eye remained. And the profile of a man with a straight razor in his hand. The gray eye covered ten stories at the top of the bank as the razor slid through the cornea, cutting it neatly in half. On every side of the roof, buildings flared behind tides of phosphenes. Pale dustings of porn flesh. The wet red of an autopsy instructional. Collaged ads, too fast to follow: shoes, cars, new eyes, cloned pets.

From somewhere, a loudspeaker blared metallically: "We are the revolt of the spirit humiliated by your works. We are the spark in the wind—the spark seeking the powder magazine!"

"Get him out of here," said Zamora as the first concussion shook the roof.

The Croakers were above the hoverport when Jonny saw them, high enough to still be silent under the whirling blades of their ultralights. He figured they had launched themselves from the nearby buildings under cover of the holograms. They were circling now, dropping garlands of roses, playing cards, flocks of mechanical doves, which spun on convection currents to the roof below, where they exploded, ripping steel and tarmac from under the boys' feet, billowing choking pink clouds of CS gas.

"What'd I tell you?" Zamora said. "They're hotdogs. It's going to be a turkey shoot."

But the power cut in, and the carbon arcs atop the light gantrys glowed to life, blotting out the winged figures. "Shit!" Zamora yelled, hurrying across the roof. "Get him to detention," he yelled to the Meat Boys. "Lose him and it's your asses."

The shorter Meat Boy, a WASPish blond with bad teeth, nodded and pushed Jonny in the direction of the hovercar. "Name's Stearn," he said. "This is Julio." He jerked his thumb at the taller boy. "We'll break your back if you get cute." At about sixteen, Stearn was nearly a meter taller than Jonny, his voice unnaturally deep, his speech slurred by his distended acromegalic jaw.

At the base of the hovercar platform Jonny panicked, knowing what would be waiting for him when they reached Committee headquarters. He twisted in Stearn's grip, the cheap paper shirt splitting at the shoulders, and vaulted up and over the hovercar. He caught a glimpse of the pilot inside, an amber death's head in the backwash from the navigation console. Down on the other side, Jonny leaped off the platform and ran for the edge of the roof, waving his arms and yelling at the Croakers: "Here! I'm here!"

A fist the size of Jonny's head caught him between the shoulder blades and knocked him flat. A moment later, he was dragged to his feet. The Meat Boys doubletimed him back to the hovercar. On the far end of the roof, Croakers were bringing their ultralights down, coasting to a halt amidst a wash of tear gas and Futukoro fire.

"All right!" yelled Jonny. "They're gonna use your balls for paperweights, Ubu!"

Stearn released him and Julio shoved Jonny backfirst through the canopy of the hovercar. He fell, staring up at the huge boot that hovered above his face and then passed over him as Julio settled into the seat on his right. The Meat Boy hauled him up as Stearn got in and sat, boxing Jonny in on the left.

Outside, the amplified voice continued: "I am here by the will of the people and I won't leave until I get my raincoat back."

Stearn snapped down the canopy and tapped the pilot on the shoulder, yelling "Go!" The pilot hit the cut-in switch for the engines. Subsonics rumbled in Jonny's gut as the hovercar's four Pratt and Whitney engines burned to life. Ultralights settled to the roof a few meters from the platform, and Croakers came scrambling for the car.

"Go! Vamonos!" yelled Stearn.

Jonny jammed his leg between the forward seats and swung his boot at the pilot's head. "Keep still," muttered Stearn, shoving an elbow into Jonny's throat.

In a tear-gas fog, the hovercar rose about two feet off the platform. And banged down again. Something silver flashed by the window. The pilot pushed the throttle forward, feeding more power to the engines. The hovercar slowly began to rise, and swung out over the street. Jonny saw Zamora below them, waving frantically. One of the Meat Boys cursed and Jonny looked up.

The sickle end of a *kusairigama* was wrapped around the light rack atop the car. Flash of a face in the window. Noise from the roof. Jonny whooped at the sight. Three Croakers were chained to the roof as the hovercar flew unsteadily twenty stories above the city.

"I can't keep it steady," the pilot said. "There's something wrong."

Julio leaned forward. "Look up, stupid," he said.

The pilot turtled his head forward as an axe cracked the windshield just above him. He pulled back on the control stick, rocking the hovercar violently from side to side. The sound of metal and fragmenting plastic came from above. The Croakers were spread out on the roof, methodically hacking away at the canopy.

Stearn had his gun out, pointing it up at the crotch of a Croaker kneeling on the canopy above him. The pilot was still struggling with the stick. The car pitched to the left, a complaining animal, and the boy lost his aim.

"Hold it still! I can't get a shot off!" he yelled.

"No!" screamed the pilot. "You might hit the stabilizers! It's hard enough to control now."

"Then shake them off," said Stearn.

"Right; hang on."

The pilot cranked the stick hard to the left and the hovercar flipped. Jonny's feet left the floor. He reached out for the ceiling, dangling a few centimeters above the seat by his safety belt. The Croakers were still outside, secured to the car by their chains.

"I can't hold it," said the pilot. "Load's too much."

"Hold it!" Stearn ordered. He took aim at the Croaker by his window.

Jonny braced his back against the roof and rabbit-punched the Meat Boy with both fists, driving his face into the glass. The Futukoro went off, blasting out the window. Shattered glass blew in on them like a thousand flying knives. The sound of hot wind and the scream of overworked turbines.

The pilot righted them. The Croakers clambered back onto the roof and went to work, hacking away at the body of the hovercar. Stearn turned and stared at Jonny, jagged wedges of glass embedded around the boy's eyes and mouth glittering there like savage jewels. Stearn lunged and locked his thick fingers around Jonny's throat, squeezing. Jonny went for the boy's eyes, but missed, felt muscles in his neck tear, felt his breath stop, the world begin to slide away.

"Stop it!" Julio's voice cut through the wind. "We've got to get him to detention," he said. "He's not yours!"

But Stearn kept on squeezing. Jonny heard a muffled explosion and felt the fingers on his neck go slack. He struggled back. Stearn had jerked upright, his shoulders twitching convulsively. Then he fell forward, revealing a wet hole in his back.

"Move!" yelled the Croaker with the gun. She was leaning in the broken window, upside down, trying to get a shot at the other Meat Boy.

Jonny threw himself down on Stearn's body, heat of gunfire across his back. When he dared to look up, Jonny saw the Croaker out the window, lifeless puppet, chain slipping from around her wrist, dead already as she tumbled from the car.

Julio grunted some obscenity in Spanish. Jonny found him stuffing a handkerchief into the hole in his shoulder. The Meat Boy smiled.

"I won't kill you," he said, and pressed the barrel of his Futukoro into Jonny's groin. "But I'll make you wish you were dead."

"We're near the detention center!" shouted the pilot. "I'm going to set us down there."

"Do it fast," Julio said. He pressed his back to the shattered window and slid partway out.

Jonny felt his skin prickle at the thought of returning to Committee headquarters. The hovercar was skimming over the roofs of blacked-out skyscrapers. They neared Union Bank Plaza, with its dry fountains and dead, brittle trees. Jonny saw the freeway. If he could get the pilot to put the hovercar down there, he thought, he and the Croakers could hijack a car and disappear. Jonny glanced at Julio and saw the boy occupied with a Croaker who refused to hold still and get shot.

Using Stearn's body for cover, Jonny stamped his boot down and drew out his long-bladed knife. Leaning between the forward seats, he touched the tip of the blade to the pilot's throat, pressing just hard enough to draw blood. The pilot's head snapped back.

"Set it down by that fountain," Jonny whispered.

"Yes, sir," he said, and started a slow bank toward the Plaza.

Jonny heard a voice: "What the hell are you doing?"

He swung around. Julio was pulling his head in through the window, and Jonny caught him on the chin with his boot heel. Two leather-clad arms shot in behind the Meat Boy, latching onto handfuls of his hair, dragging him back out the window. Julio seemed to panic then; he waved his Futukoro all around the cabin, pointing it one moment at the Croaker who had him, then swinging the gun back at Jonny. As the Croaker disappeared out the window, he pulled the trigger. The pilot's head exploded, and the hovercar angled forward, nosediving for the pavement.

Jonny reached under the body of the dead pilot and grabbed the stick. Above him, he could hear Julio still struggling with the Croakers. A shot went off through the roof. Jonny pulled back hard on the stick, trying to forestall the crash. The hovercar banked steeply, scraping down bellyfirst through the trees in Union Bank Plaza.

Across the street, amidst a jumble of rotting patio furniture, sat the mirrored bulk of the Bonaventure Hotel. Jonny looked up just in time to watch his own reflection crash into the building across the street.

9

THE TREASON OF IMAGES

A LIGHT CRUSTING of salt on his lips. The smell of damp cement and fish.

Los Angeles closed over him like the wing of a bird, distorted like the image of a diamond caught in the concave surface of a parabolic mirror. Distended, the city shattered; it could not hold. All the gleaming office towers and prisons, all the cars and guns, the junkies and the dealers, the dead and the dying came raining down on him from the back of a wounded sky. And everybody seemed to know his name but him.

It occurred to Jonny that for someone who basically just wanted to be left alone, he was spending an awful lot of time waking up in bandages.

That he was alive at all was less a surprise to him than a burden. He kept wondering if there was some reason for it, some purpose other than for other people's amusement. The back of his head felt as if it had been pried open with a can opener and filled with dry ice. He laughed at something—not entirely sure what—and found the edge of the bed with his hand and sat up.

The smell of fish was stronger. There was a chittering, like the voices of dolphins, rooms away. No light, though. He felt bandages on his face, multiple layers of gauze and surgical tape. Scars on his cheeks. He had had surgery. Below the line of the dressing, he touched his lips. They were swollen, his front teeth loose. His nose was probably broken, too. Still, it could have been worse, he thought. His eyes ached.

His eyes.

Somewhere in the back of his mind, a voice was screaming. His own: like the roar of turbines, like metal twisting on metal.

Eyes.

The world tilted then, burdened by the weight of a single word. "Blind," he said. It barely registered. He found he could hold it back, if he tried, could examine the word from a distance, scan the contours and convolutions of it, while never quite allowing it to take on conscious meaning. But the weight of it was such that he could not keep it away indefinitely; it fell, bringing memory crashing down on him like the windshield of the hovercar. He was blind.

I am blind.

"Jonny?" It was a man's voice. Amplified. "Stay there. Don't get up."

Below his bare feet, the floor was cold. He felt damp concrete, limp strands of kelp, and, a few steps later, the rusted grillwork of a floor drain. He could hear the ocean, very close by. Something skittered across his right foot—a tiny crab. He felt others move away each time he brought his foot down. A wall. He needed a wall, something substantial to hold onto. He started back to where he thought the bed was, then stopped. Unsure. He turned in a circle, shouting, his head thrown back, his hands reflexive claws tearing at the gauze. When it was all gone he was still standing there, panting. No light at all.

"Jonny, don't move."

He started at the sound, took a step—and was falling. A hand closed on his shoulder and right arm, pulling him back. He lay on the floor, his hands to his face, the dampness seeping through his pants legs.

"I told you to stay put. You almost walked into ten meters of empty air just then." The voice was familiar.

"Hey, Groucho," Jonny said. "Guess what. I'm blind."

"I already knew. You didn't have to go to all this trouble to prove it to me." The anarchist hauled him to his feet and walked him back to the bed, a distance Jonny judged to be no more than fifteen meters.

"Christ, I'm a fuckin' veg," Jonny said.

"Don't be stupid," said the anarchist. Jonny felt the distribution of weight on the bed change as Groucho sat down. "You have your hands; you have your mind. We sealed off what was left of your optic nerves. There wasn't much more we could do."

"Great," Jonny said. "What about implants?"

"I don't know. We could probably rig something to give you some kind of vision. Eventually. Splice some nerve cells from somewhere else in your body into your optic nerve tissue and see if we can generate something to rebuild with. I'm not sure. The trouble is, we're limited in what we can even attempt out here in the hinterlands. We lost a lot of our equipment when the Committee came down on us." Jonny felt him move. Some kind of gesture. "Sorry, man."

Jonny nodded. "Yeah. So where are we?"

"A fish farm. It's been out of business for years. That's what you almost fell into, one of the drained feeding tanks. Before it was a farm, the place used to be a marine mammal center. There are pens outside where the dolphins still come looking for a free lunch. I'm afraid we've been encouraging them," he said. "They're beautiful animals."

"Gee whiz, tell me all about it," said Jonny. He took a deep breath and swallowed. "Listen, I gotta know. Do I—I mean, what do I—?"

"Your face is fine," said Groucho. "You may even consider it an improvement. Although you have enough plastic and metal in your skull now to qualify as a small appliance."

Jonny shook his head. He tried to conjure up the image of Groucho sitting next to him on the bed. The bed itself was easy. Running his fingers around the edge, he felt bare metal and soft rubberized bumpers, locked wheels beneath. A specimen cart, he thought, covered with a foam sleeping mat. But Groucho's face eluded him. Jonny could never recall people's faces unless he was looking right at them. He tried to picture the room. Bare concrete, enameled tanks with chrome ladders leading to the bottom, drains in the floor—

Forget it.

It was a shopping list, not a picture. He could imagine himself (also faceless), Groucho and the bed, but beyond that was a void, terra incognita. Nothing existed that was farther away than the end of his arm. "Get used to it, asshole," he mumbled.

"What?"

"So what happens now?"

"We go back to plan one," said Groucho. "The Croakers

have friends in Mexico. We should be able to get you down to Ensenada in a couple of days, then over to the mainland. It's going to be a while before we can do anything about your eyes."

"Don't shit me, okay?" said Jonny. "If my optic nerves are as gone as you say, then we're just blowing wind talking about nerve splices. Realistically, we're really talking about a skull-plug run through a digitizer and some kind of microvideo rig. You, or any of your people, got the chops to fix that up?"

"No. You've got to go to New Hope or some government clinic for that kind of work."

"Well, there you are," said Jonny flatly. The bed moved as Groucho got up. Jonny studied the overlapping echoes of the anarchist's footsteps as he moved around the room, counting the number of beats between each heel click, imagining that this might give him some sense of the room's layout or size. It did not. There were other sounds: the white noise of surf, dolphins, the clicking of crabs across the floor, all equally distant and unreal, as if, in the absence of any visual stimulus, his brain were busily manufacturing sensations for itself. "Maya, man. Sometimes I think this is all just smoke and mirrors."

"I thought that was acknowledged," said Groucho. The anarchist's voice came from across the room, a little off to his left.

"It used to make me crazy," Jonny said. "The roshis told me that this was all an illusion. Well, man, if this is all illusion, it must be somebody else's, 'cause I wouldn't make up this shit." There was a scraping on the concrete, a rustling of paper. Jonny thought Groucho might be moving boxes.

"That's just avoiding the issue," Groucho said. "It also sounds like an elaborate excuse for suicide. Do you want to die?"

"I don't know." Jonny shrugged. "Sometimes. Yeah."

"It's hard. We've become so numbed by the presence of death that we toy with it, use it like a drug, building it up in our minds as the great escape. The fallacy there, of course, is that death is an illusion, too."

"You're a three-ring circus, man," said Jonny. "But it's all just words. The Catholics got half the city under their thumbs with cheap lighting effects and stained glass, the Muslims tell the hashishin that dying for Allah is a ticket to heaven, and

Buddha says life is suffering, which means I shouldn't bring anybody down by pointing out that being blind—that this whole situation—is completely fucked."

"Don't you see, that's what illusion means? You're blind, you say? I say, there's no one seeing and nothing to be seen. How can you miss what never existed?"

"That is such bullshit."

"Ice told me you had a roshi once, that you used to sit. What happened?" Groucho's voice was close again. He pressed something into Jonny's hands. "Your boots. Sorry, somebody polished them. They're black again."

Jonny leaned over the edge of the bed and started to pull on his right boot. He said, "Yeah, I used to sit. I was young and it was fashionable. Teeny-bopper Zen. Like lizardskin jackets or green eyes."

"You don't seem the type for that game."

"Sure I am."

"No, you like to believe you are, because it's easy and it fits in with an image you have of yourself. But I don't think you're nearly the cynic or fool you like to play at."

As Jonny pulled on his other boot, he said, "That was you guys tipped the cops to Nimble Virtue's warehouse, right?"

Groucho sighed. "Taking you from the cops was going to be a breeze. We never dreamed the idiots would call in the Committee. Ice made the call, actually. She's safe, you know."

Jonny smiled. "Thanks."

"Sumi, too."

"Jesus," he said. "Is she here?"

"Yes. She practically rigged all the lighting out here single-handed. She's running the juice through the transit authority's power grid."

"That sounds like her," said Jonny. "Where is she? Take me to her." He stood, but Groucho pushed him back on the bed.

"You stay here. She and Ice are on a scavenging party to some of the old oil platforms nearby. When they get back, I'll let them know you've come around."

"Thanks, man," Jonny said. He touched the neat rows of tiny plastic staples they had used to close the incisions in his face. Tight meridians of pain. He felt very tired.

"The confidences of madmen. I would spend my life in

provoking them. Take this." Jonny found a small cylinder of soft plastic pressed into his hand. "Auto-injector," Groucho said. "Endorphins. If the pain gets too bad, just remove the top to expose the syringe, and hit a vein."

When the anarchist left the room, Jonny popped the top of the injector with his thumb and pressed the needle into the crook of his left arm. A spring-loaded mechanism pumped home the drug. Immediately, the pain was gone, replaced with a gentle, disembodied warmth, as if his blood had been replaced with heated syrup. He lay down on the bed, feeling his muscles uncoil, and let the drug and the deeper darkness of sleep wash over him. He listened to the ocean and the dolphins, licked the salt from his lips, and hoped he would not dream.

Sleep did not stay long. The drug did its work well, holding the pain an arm's length away, but it left too much of his brain in working order. He was just aware enough to notice the ghosts as they floated high above his bed. Hot red and electric blue, moving fast, like falling rain or static on a video monitor. He swung at them open-handed, but missed. They were not there. They were inside. Inside his head.

A trick of the surgery, he told himself. Random signals twitched from fried nerves, entering the visual center of his brain. Fireworks, he thought. Great timing. Thank you very-fucking-much.

When he fell asleep again he dreamed of machinery, an underground refinery, like a buried city. Cooling towers and steam and choking clouds of synth-fuel fumes. He had run away from the state school again. Jonny, ten years old, fat and out of breath, ran on trembling legs and hid among the dull hills of cooling slag. A man came after him. He wore a cheap plastic poncho and carried a gun. Silent as death; half his face hidden behind a pair of mirror shades. When the man found him, all Jonny could do was raise his blistered hands to cover his ears. At the last moment, he saw his burned face reflected in the man's glasses. The refinery roared and spat smoke. He cried, hoping he would not be able to hear the shot.

"Wake up, Sleeping Beauty. Hey, Jonny, come on, move your ass. Somebody made little railroad tracks all over your sweet face."

Startled, he awoke. He could still see the ghosts, but there were fewer of them now. His skull was full of cotton. "Ice?" he said.

"Who else, doll?"

He sat up in bed, reached out and touched wet leather, cool and smelling of the ocean. "Hiya, babe," she said, and kissed him with salted lips. "I got a present for you." She guided his hand to the right, until it touched something. Graceful planes of skin and bone defining cheeks; below that, a strong jaw and mouth. Something happened in his chest, a jolt, like pain, that instead was pure pleasure. Later, he thought that if he had had eyes, he probably would have made a fool of himself by blubbering. "Sumi," he said.

"Can't put anything over on you," she replied.

He held her, held on to her to keep from falling. If he let go, he knew the floor would open up and swallow him. But he felt Ice's arm join Sumi's across his back. They stayed that way for some time, huddled there together, Jonny's head on Sumi's shoulder. His drugged brain could hardly handle the input. It kept misfiring, triggering emotions and memories at random. Fear. Love. A melted circuit board. Desire. Mirror shades. A gun.

"Where the fuck have you been?" he asked, finally. They relaxed and moved apart on the bed, but remained touching.

"You know Vyctor Vector?"

"Sure," he said. "She's only el patron of the Naginata Sisters."

"Well, I was setting up power out at her place; she's got this squat in an old police station in Echo Park. The Sisters are using it as their new clubhouse. Built-in security system, a gym, working phones, you know? Anyway, when I finished up there I went back home, but when I got there the place was crawling with Committee boys. I thought one of them might have spotted me, so I hightailed it through some movie crew downstairs, and back to Vyctor's. The Sisters were cool. They put me up for a while, then got in touch with some smugglers they muscle for, who put me on to the Croakers. And here I am."

"Here you are," said Jonny. "Christ, we probably missed you by maybe a couple of hours." He shook his head. "I thought you were dead."

"And *we* thought you were dead," said Ice. "'Course, be-

fore that, Sumi thought I was dead, and I thought, oh shit—"
She laughed. "Let's face it, everybody wrote off everybody
these last few weeks. But we made it. We foxed 'em."

"We got lucky," Jonny said.

"Maybe it's the same thing," said Sumi.

"Maybe it doesn't fucking matter," Ice said.

"I'm so out of touch," said Jonny. "What's it like on the
street? The Committee's push still on?"

"Yeah. We thought, with so many people sick, they'd for-
get about it and back off," said Ice. "No such luck. They're
just pumping the boys full of amantadine and sending 'em out
on search-and-destroys, using the virus as an excuse to come
down on anyone's ever looked cross-eyed at the Committee."

"That's why the Naginatas were moving," said Sumi.
"Vyctor said the Committee closed the Iron Orchid, where
they used to hang out."

"Public Assembly Laws, they call them." Ice all but spat
the words. "No gatherings of more than a certain number of
people within a kilometer of Los Angeles. The Colonel must
be going nuts," she said. "He's getting positively medieval."

"Does anybody have any ideas on how the virus is spread-
ing?" Jonny asked.

"On a molecular level, the thing's just a lousy cold bug. A
rhinovirus. Vanilla as you can get," Ice replied.

"What I saw on that micrograph at the clinic sure didn't
look like a cold virus," said Jonny.

"Right," said Ice. "It's like one of those Chinese puzzle
boxes. You know, open up one box and there's a little box
inside; you open up the next box, there's a smaller one inside
that, and on and on. On one level, this thing looks like a
phage, on another level, it's just a cold bug. But the levels
keep going. The molecular structure of this thing's dense. We
know something else, too. At least, we're reasonably sure."

"Sure of what?" asked Jonny.

"It's man-made."

"How do you know?" Jonny wished he could see Ice's face
as she talked. He could usually learn as much from her ex-
pressions as from what she said.

"Partly it's just a hunch." (She would be frowning now.)
"But natural bonds just don't feel like this mess. It's like
somebody tried to squeeze ten pounds of ugly into an eight-
pound box."

"Tell him about the war," said Sumi.

"What war?" asked Jonny.

"I'm coming to it," Ice said. "It looks like what we got here is an ultra-complex retrovirus, something that back in the 'nineties they called a layered virus. A primary bug attacks a system—in our case, the bug is a viral analog of leprosy. It causes whatever damage it can, but eventually the system's defenses kill it. Here's the tricky part, though—"

"There's another virus," said Jonny.

"You got it, doll," said Ice. "At some point, we don't know what triggers it, but a secondary virus is activated. It uses the damage caused by the first virus to attack the already weakened system. In our case, the secondary virus uses the peripheral nerve damage caused by the leprosy to travel backwards, on a substrate of nerve cell axons, up into the brain. Almost the exact reverse of neuroblast migration. We think it might be modeled on that."

"What's the pathology of the second virus?" Jonny asked.

Silence. "Syphilis," Sumi said.

"Jesus."

"Parenchymatous neurosyphilis, to be exact," said Ice. "A really hyped-up version. Years' worth of nerve damage gets compressed into a few days. Death occurs a week to two after the symptoms manifest." She took a breath. "It's a motherfucker, too. Physical, mental, and personality breakdown, epileptic attacks, lightning pains, tremors; the full whack. Patient's pupils get small and irregular."

"Argyll-Robertson pupils," Jonny said.

"Right. Looks like they got bugs in their eyes." Ice's voice trailed off; then it came back loud, full of frustration. "And the syphilis is modified too, of course. So none of our standard therapies are worth shit. Personally, I wouldn't go through it—"

"Who would?" asked Jonny.

"I mean I wouldn't want to die that way," said Ice. "I think if I found out I had the bug, I'd do myself before I'd go through all that."

"Yeah," whispered Sumi. He could feel the woman move, leaning toward Ice to comfort her.

Jonny thought that it was probably night outside. Even in the relative quiet of evening, the sounds and smells of the ocean lent a subtle sense of life to the old fish farm that Jonny appreciated. Raw sensory data, enough to keep from feeling completely disconnected with the world, poured through the seaward vents, sounds and scents changing radically with the passing of the day. There were no chittering dolphin sounds now, just the quiet lapping of water and the scratching of crabs in the empty pools. Farther away were human sounds. Occasional hammering, voices, the momentary roar of a car engine. It would not be unpleasant, thought Jonny, to spend the rest of his life here.

"Tell me about the war," he said.

"Down by the port, we liberated this warehouse of some guns and fuel, and ended up with this case. Had some floppy disks full of declassified military documents. The war was that Arab and Jap thing back in the 'nineties," said Ice. "Seems NATO's bio-warfare arm was working on something a lot like the layered virus we're looking at now. Operation Sisyphus. Trouble was, back then they couldn't always trigger either virus, and when they did, they couldn't always protect their troops. A lot of people died. There's apparently still a zone in northern France that's off-limits to civvies. After all that, the project got a bad name; the research was considered too expensive and too dangerous, so when the war talk cooled down, the project died. And the techs went back to making the world safe for conventional warfare."

"You think our virus could be the same one they were working on back then?" asked Jonny.

"A much more refined version, yeah. I'd be real surprised if, in the last fifty or sixty years, some of that original data didn't get walked out of there from time to time," Ice replied. "I mean, we weren't even looking for it."

Jonny nodded and his chin momentarily brushed Sumi's hand, which rested on his shoulder. "It fits," he said. "There's a New Palestine cell operating in the city. They've been beaming leper videos to the folks back home. Zamora told me they were just a propaganda unit, but he was lying."

"Hell, could be Aoki Vega or the goddam Alpha Rats, for all the difference it makes," said Ice.

"She's right," said Sumi. "If this is some germ warfare thing, we're probably not going to find any easy treatments for it."

"Fuck it—if the Arabs want this city, they can have it,"

said Jonny. "Groucho already talked to me about Mexico. He says we can be down there in a couple of days."

"I'm not going," said Ice. "Sumi'll take you, and I'll come later."

"You still playing the artistic anarquista?" Jonny asked.

"Fuck you," snapped Ice. "I've got commitments here. I'm a Croaker and that means I'm part of this revolution, no matter what you think of it."

Jonny turned to her voice. "Excuse me, but wasn't that you a little while ago telling me how much you wanted us to be together again? Well, here we are." He waited for her to say something, and when she did not, he said, "What's the matter? You bored already?"

He felt her get up and leave the bed; an emptiness developed in her wake, a sense of loss that was more profound than the simple lack of her physical presence. He put out his arm, but she was not there and he could not find her. Ice's practiced steps were light and almost silent from months of guerilla raids and street warfare. Her sudden absence reminded him of his helplessness. "Ice?" he said.

"I'm doing this." Her voice was firm and low, the tone she always used when she wanted to project assurance but was afraid her voice might crack. "You can help me or not, make this easy or hard, but I'm in for the duration."

"Why are you being such a shithead, Jonny?" asked Sumi. She shook his sleeve gently. "What's the matter?"

"I'm afraid," he said. "I'm afraid for her and you. And I'm afraid for me. I don't want to end up alone."

"You won't be alone," said Sumi. "I'm going with you. Ice will come."

"He's afraid I'm going to take a walk again," came Ice's voice.

"Shouldn't I be?" he asked.

"No."

He breathed deeply. His fingers picked idly at a paint blister on the bed's molded metal handle. "I hate politics. It's the lowest act a human being can sink to."

"Yeah," said Ice, drawing the word out to the length of a breath.

"Why don't you come here?" Jonny said.

She came back to the bed and he kissed her for a long time. Then he leaned back and kissed Sumi, and when he moved away he found himself pressed in the warmth of two bodies as the women's mouths met over his shoulder.

The undressing was a haphazard affair. Jonny yanked at the boots he had just put on and tried to help each woman out of her clothes. Without his eyes, though, he just succeeded in tangling them in their shirts. Sumi pushed him down on the bed and held him there, reminding him that a couple of days was not a very long time, and that maybe he should not help them.

Eventually, they bent together, in one three-way kiss. Hands moved in phantom caresses and scratches over Jonny's body. The women pressed him to the bed, embracing each other on top of him, exciting each other while moving in slow undulations over his body. Occasionally their rhythm would change and he would feel a tongue or hand sweeping over his belly or up his thigh. They were teasing him, he realized. Making his blindness a part of their lovemaking. He loved it.

The women changed places, moving back and forth across his body. He lost track of them, could no longer tell one from the other. One bent to his penis and he leaned back, shuddering pleasurably against the other's breasts. The smell of their bodies overwhelmed him.

While the one remained on his cock, he tilted his head back into the sweet-sour folds between the other's legs. He and the one he was tonguing (he thought it might be Sumi) came together—in that instant he felt his life drain out into both of them, as theirs drained into him.

The one on his cock stayed there until he was hard again and mounted him from the top. The other woman moved between them, biting, scratching, caressing the two of them as they moved together. Then the women switched places and a new warmth enveloped him. He felt the one riding him—Sumi, he was sure—lean across his chest and brush her lips across the other's labia. Ice trembled to a climax as he kissed her and the life moved between the three. The smells of concrete and rust, sweat and sex flared and merged with his own orgasm, lighting, for a moment, the vast and eyeless darkness in a small act of binding.

And then the light was gone and he was blind again, but this time he did not feel so alone.

* * *

"Big trouble." It was Groucho's voice.

Jonny sat up in bed and fumbled for a light switch, then remembered where he was. He felt Ice and Sumi stirring on either side of him. "What's wrong?" he asked.

"Zamora," said Groucho. "He's got the city sealed off. There are goddam jetfoils patrolling not a hundred yards out from here. Roadblocks on the freeways and secondary roads. Aerial recon on the desert. Nobody's going anywhere."

"How'd you hear about this?" Ice asked. Both women were up now. Fabric rustled softly as they pulled on their clothes. Jonny waited for someone to hand him his.

"A rescue team just brought in a driver from up north," said the anarchist. His voice was tired, hoarse. "She was riding point for a camel train moving down the coast from San Francisco, bringing in antibiotics and amantadine. Seems that everything was clean and clear until they hit Ventura. Some of Pere Ubu's boys were waiting and all hell broke loose."

"She going to make it?" asked Jonny. Someone dropped his clothes in his lap and he started to dress.

"I doubt it," said Groucho. "She's shot up pretty badly. Gato just gave her the last of the endorphins. I've been on the radio all night. Ubu's got the town sealed up tight."

"Think he's ready to move on the lords?" Ice asked.

"No question about it," Groucho said. "This driver said they made a run on New Hope, hoping they could pick off a warehouse. The place is deserted."

"Then we're fucked," said Jonny. "They've moved the heavy money out of the way of war."

"We're still safe out here, aren't we?" asked Sumi.

"Not any more," said Jonny, pulling on his boots. "It's standard Committee procedure to let a few people get away from any raid, just to see where they run. They probably had that driver tagged all the way out here."

"Which is why we're going back to the city," Groucho said. "I have people packing up anything we can use. The rest gets dumped. We've got a few kilos of C-4 wired to pressure points all along the superstructure of the building. When Ubu's boys get here, it will be waiting for them."

"What happens to Jonny?" Sumi asked.

"Funny, that was my next question," Jonny said.

Groucho sighed. "What can I tell you? We're pretty good for weapons, but we have to coordinate with the other gangs before we can hit the Committee. We can find something for you to do once we get set up."

"Like rolling bandages and hiding under beds when the shooting starts? No, thanks. I got other plans."

"What?" asked Groucho.

"Well, I don't mind telling you, Mister Conover was pretty choked up when I took off from his place. He'll be glad to see me."

"You sure you can trust him?"

"Absolutamente," Jonny said. "He's always been right by me, and besides, if there's any way to move stuff out of town, he'll know about it." He stood up from the bed and pulled on his shirt. The sounds of movement, clattering tools and footsteps, things being dragged across concrete, echoed through the complex; there was tension in the voices Jonny heard, a frenetic buzz that he recognized as the prelude to combat. At that moment he no longer had any desire to remain at the farm, thinking: the Colonel's taken that away, too.

"I'll need a driver," he said.

"That's me," said Sumi.

Jonny reached toward her voice and felt a hand close over his. "You should go with them," he said. "They can use your help. If Conover can't move me, it could mean sitting on our asses for a long time."

"We had a deal," said Sumi firmly. "I don't see where this changes anything but the location. I go with you now and Ice joins us later."

"When the girl's right, she's right," said Ice.

"You sure?" asked Jonny.

"Completely," Sumi replied. "What about a car?"

"No problem." Groucho's voice was farther away, near the noise from the door. "Be ready to go in thirty minutes," he said.

As the anarchist left, Jonny said, "He says that like we got to pack or something."

"He just wants to give us time to say good-bye," said Ice.

Jonny laughed. "I don't think a half-hour is going to be enough," he said.

* * *

Sumi took his hand, pulling Jonny through long and curving corridors that buzzed with the staccato beat of voices (too many languages at once, he could not understand any of it) and hurrying feet. The smell of nervous sweat hung in the air, an undercurrent, like a faint static charge.

Outside, a cool salt breeze lapped at his face. The sun warmed him. Sumi took him down two switchbacks and then out over hard sand that crunched like broken glass under their feet. It was a sound from his childhood. Fused silicon. He knew where they were now, could picture the scene in his head. The smell of burning fossil fuels came from his right, along with the growling of primitive combustion engines. The sun was dead ahead. Yes, he could picture it. The vehicles that had been hidden under the pylons of the fish farm were being rolled out onto the blackened beach, leaving feathery webs of cracks in the dead glass of the Pacific Palisades shore. Jonny had visited the beach before.

The summer of his twelfth birthday, he and a boy named Paolo went over the wall from the Junipero Serra state school. In Santa Monica they stole a small launch. Paolo piloted it up to the Palisades and they weighed anchor at the sight of a wrecked Venezuelan freighter. Liquid-natural-gas explosion, Paolo had said. Wiped out the whole town. Jonny nodded, trying to look cool, but he could barely keep his lunch down.

There was not much of the freighter left above the surface. In the leaking wet suits and respirators they found on the launch, they went swimming through the wreckage of the ship's engine room. It had been blown, nearly intact, onto an outcropping of rock a few dozen meters below the water level. The big furnaces were crusted with bright streamers of coral and undersea plants, like some weird ice castle. On their way back to the surface, Jonny spotted something. An odd shape below the big mussel-studded steam pipes. He swam closer. A skeleton, blackened with the sea and time. The back of the skull and ribs had melted when the ship had burned, flowing in the same pattern as the bulkhead walls, fusing with them. Hermit crabs and barnacles had claimed the skull.

Standing on the beach now, Jonny wondered if the sailor was still out there, washed by the Pacific tides. He was the first dead man Jonny had ever seen.

* * *

Sumi took his hand and placed it on the warm metal roof of a car. Jonny felt his way along the smooth finish until he came to a seam where the roof met the door. He pulled the door open—it swung up, not out—as an arm slid around his midsection. "You take care, killer," Ice whispered. She pecked him below the ear.

Jonny nodded. "You, too," he said. The sun was making the scars on his face itch. He heard the women up by the headlights, speaking in low tones. A rustle of fabric as they embraced. Then footsteps as someone crunched away quickly across the sand. A hand touched his arm. "You have to step up to get in," said Sumi, trying hard not to let her voice crack.

Jonny put a leg up over the side of the low-slung car, and settled onto rotten leather upholstery. When he touched the dashboard, he felt weathered wood. His fingers smelled lightly of varnish and mildew. As Sumi got in, he ran his hands over the stick shift and instrument panel and felt an embossed logo. It reminded him of another car he had been in. Something Italian. Lamborghini? he wondered.

"There's a shoulder harness to your right," said Sumi quietly.

Buckling in, Jonny said, "She's going to be all right."

"Right."

Someone came running up to the car. "Here, take this." It was Ice, breathless. She put something in Jonny's hands. Half a meter long, and heavy, it smelled of cordite and machine oil, had two chopped-off cylinders mounted on a short wooden stock. A sawed-off shotgun. "Figure you can't use a pistol right now, but if someone gets close enough, this'll modify their opinion."

Jonny weighed the gun in his hands. "I love you, too," he said.

"Need any amantadine?"

"No, Conover'll be holding."

"Right." Ice touched his shoulder. "Gotta go." And she was running away again, off to where he could hear the other cars warming up their engines.

Sumi gunned the Lamborghini and slipped the car into gear. "She's not coming back," Sumi said.

"Just drive," said Jonny.

* * *

It began to rain as they entered the city. They were driving along Wilshire Boulevard, right through the withered heart of the financial district. Jonny imagined he could feel the heat of the lights as they passed Lockheed's brilliant torus and the flat black sphere of Sony International, Sumi trying to blend the old Lamborghini into the hesitant flow of rush-hour traffic. Groups of Croakers had preceded them, heading north and south from the beach, hoping to pull away any surveillance teams that had followed the camel train driver.

Rain needled across the asphalt as they cruised through Beverly Hills. Jonny thought it sounded like frying eggs. For the last hour, a spring had been steadily working its way through the ruined seat and into Jonny's back. He listened to thunder roll in the distance, like a collapsing mountain, growing faint until it faded completely somewhere to the south. When they were in Hollywood, Jonny told Sumi to head up into the hills.

"Exactly where are we going?" she asked.

"Up high," said Jonny. "We want to rattle Conover's cage so his security'll come and check us out."

"Great. How do you know they won't just blow us away and ask questions later?"

"They won't."

"How do you know?"

"I know."

"How?"

"Actually, I don't. But I've still got this," he said. From the top of his boot he slid the black card with the gold bar code. "Cops didn't search me when they decided I was Committee meat. The card transmits an identification code. They won't kill us if they scan us for I.D."

"If they scan us."

"Right. If."

He told her to park the car in the driveway of one of the derelict houses in the Hollywoodland development. They waited there in the rain. Jonny popped the door on his side to let in a little of the breeze that swept down through the hills. The air smelled of sage and manzanita. The staples on his face alternately itched and stung. He thought about the endorphins Groucho had given him back at the fish farm, wished he had some now. He consoled himself with the thought that Conover would have all the drugs he needed to feel better. Better than better, Jonny thought, remembering the stash of Mad Love. Quite a mixed blessing, that. It would be a bad time to bliss out again, with Ice in trouble and Zamora's push so near. They might have to move on a moment's notice. And he knew that Sumi hated to see him wasted. It brought back bad memories for them both. The Committee. Ice running away. Sumi doesn't need that crap, he thought, not now. "How are you feeling?" he asked.

"Tired," said Sumi. "My head hurts. Stomach, too. I wish we'd had a chance to eat something today."

He wanted to tell her about the Mad Love, ask her to help him keep clean. "Conover's got these great cooks," he said. "They really lay it on. You'll feel better once you've eaten." He started to mention the drugs. His lips moved, but the words would not come.

Folly, he thought. Greed and folly.

An hour passed. No contact with Conover or his people. Jonny heard Sumi yawn. Her head settled on his shoulder, soft hair against his cheek. He wondered if it was night yet. He was unaccustomed to the sounds of the hills. Each gust of wind, each snap of a twig made him jump. A part of him wished his hearing had gone with his sight. Living by half-measures was getting to him. Sumi jerked her head up.

"What is it?" he asked.

"Shh," she whispered. "Something's moving."

"Conover's men?"

"No. An animal."

"What kind—"

Sumi screamed and something slammed into the front of the Lamborghini like a truck. Then it was on the roof, clawing and pounding on the canopy, trying to force its way in through Jonny's half-open door. He grabbed the handle and held on. "What the hell is it?" he yelled.

"A tiger!" screamed Sumi. She pounded on the glass. "Get off, fucker! Demasu! Demasu!"

The cat growled like rolling thunder. Jonny's door lifted a few centimeters and something slid in. He felt wind on his face, heard claws tearing up the dashboard. "Shoot it!" he yelled. Something cut the air before his face. In his mind's eye he saw mad knives, bent silver blades that smelled of musk and sweat coming for his scarred face. "Shoot it, god-damit!" He pulled harder on the door, but could not budge it.

"Where's the gun?" yelled Sumi.

Jonny twisted in his seat, trying to keep his shoulder from the ripping claws. He had slid the gun down between his seat and the car wall. He felt along the rotten leather, coming up with spiderwebs and dust. Then his hand fell on a wedge of polished wood. Something sharp tore at his shoulder, scraped bone. He cursed once and fell back against his seat, pulling the gun up and letting off both barrels through the window.

At first there was nothing. When the roaring in his ears died down, he was aware of a gentle but persistent hissing beneath the sound of the rain. There was a peculiar chemical smell in the air. Almost metallic.

"Christ," said Sumi. "It's a robot." Jonny heard her release the latch and lift her door open. A creaking of springs as she stood in her seat. "Looks like you got it in the neck. Took its head clean off. Jesus, you ought to see this. Steam, fiber optics, and circuit boards all over the place. Some kind of supercooled liquid. It's bubbling the paint right off the car."

"Get back in," said Jonny. "They'll be coming soon."

"I think they're here," said Sumi. Jonny heard her slide back into her seat.

Footsteps ground on stone off to the left. They came right for the car; it sounded like three of them, making no attempt to mask their approach. They would be armed, Jonny knew. And nervous when they saw the ruined cat. Conover's rail guns could turn the Lamborghini to slag in a few seconds.

A man barked harsh Spanish near the front of the vehicle. "Fuera! Fuera! Vamanos!"

Jonny held up his hands. "Ricos! That you, man?"

Someone came around the car and raised the shattered door over Jonny's head. A low laugh. "Hey, maricón. I was all planned to kick your ass, but I see somebody do it for me, no? Lucky for you."

"Yeah, I must be about the luckiest guy in Last Ass," said Jonny.

"Mister Conover es muy enojado, you take off like that," said Ricos. "He be happy to see you." The man moved closer. "Quien es?"

"That's Sumi," said Jonny. "She's a Watt Snatcher. Friend of mine."

"Not bad, maricón," said Ricos.

"You keep staring, ass-eyes, you're gonna find out how bad I am," Sumi said. Jonny smiled.

Ricos tapped Jonny's shoulder. "Come on," he said. Then: "Hey maricón, you bleeding."

Jonny put his legs over the side of the car and slid to the ground. Sumi came around the front and took his arm. "It's the story of my life," he said.

"We fix you up good," said Ricos, pushing Jonny toward the trees. "Watch your step."

"Very funny," Jonny said.

"A nasty piece of work, son," said Mister Conover, turning Jonny's face in his hands. "You're never going to learn to take care of yourself, are you? The plastic surgery looks first-rate, though. Tell me, what condition are the optic nerves in?"

"Shot," said Jonny. Sumi sat next to him on the plush sofa in the Victorian wing of Conover's mansion. The room was warm and the air smelled of aged wood and patchouli. The smuggler lord had given them Earl Grey tea spiked with Napoleon brandy. Jonny was working on his third cup, rolling with the buzz, letting it build up slowly. He was warm and, despite everything, was feeling pretty good. Conover was having one of his twice-weekly blood changes. Jonny could hear the medical techs moving quietly around the room, mumbling to each other, adjusting tubes and compressors. "The optic nerves are sealed, but they're pretty useless."

"Interesting," said the smuggler lord. "I'm sorry my tiger mauled you tonight."

"That's okay," said Jonny. He moved his shoulder, feeling the tight weave of gauze where the techs had dressed his wound. "Sorry I had to blow its head off."

"Completely understandable, given the circumstances," said Conover. "I'm sorry, too, in a larger sense, that any of this had to happen. All this was avoidable, if you had just stayed put. But you're still young and sometimes your energy outstrips your sense. Considering what you've been through, I think I could forgo the I-told-you-so's."

"I'd appreciate that," said Jonny.

The blood change took another hour. After that, Conover announced that he was going to bed. On his way out, the smuggler lord paused by the sofa and said, "Nice to have you back, son," and, "Thank you for not hurting Ricos that night in the garage."

Jonny smiled toward Conover's voice. "All I wanted was the car. Did you get it back?"

"Of course," said Conover. "I took the fact you didn't do Ricos any real damage as a sign of your goodwill. That you were not Zamora's man, after all. But please—"

"I know—"

"Don't run off like that again." Conover's tone was friendly enough, but there was something underlying it that chilled Jonny. He nodded at the lord.

"No problem," he said.

"Good," said Conover. "Fela, here, will take you to your room when you're ready. I'm putting you in the same one you had last time, Jonny. Since you're already somewhat familiar with the layout, I thought you might be more comfortable there."

"Yeah, thanks."

"'Night all."

"Good night," said Sumi.

After Conover left, they finished their tea in silence. At three, dozens of clocks, porcelain and grandfather, cuckoo, music box and free-standing, chimed, rang and called the hour, slightly out of sync, so that the sound had the effect of a musical waterfall. When the sound died down, Jonny asked Fela, a member of Conover's African house staff, to take them to their room.

To his surprise, Jonny found that without his eyes to trick him the mansion was much less confusing than the last time he had been there. He was learning the place by touch, sound and smell, not sight, so the false doors and back-lit windows, the peculiar angles of the floor and wall joints, could not throw him off. He memorized as much of their trip through the house as he could, mentally comparing what he was touching to what he had remembered seeing in the mansion. He knew when they reached the corridor where their room lay. Inside, he was greeted with the familiar feel of filigreed wood on the French antiques. He felt a kind of elation, a childish sort of pride, completely out of proportion to what he had accomplished. He smiled and staples stung him.

Fela left them (silently, as always) and Jonny took Sumi

out into the hall, walking her past the paintings, describing each he could remember. "That's a Goya, picture of a nude woman lying on a couch. This is a Rembrandt, right? Dark portrait of an old man with no teeth. On that table's a sculpture. I forget who did it. Bronze of ballerina."

Sumi made appreciative noises as they walked along. He could not tell if she was admiring the art or his memory or neither. He did not really care, either way. He had a surprise for her.

When Jonny felt the edge of a heavy gothic table, he stopped and pointed to the wall above it. "What do you see?" he asked.

"A painting of some kid dressed all in blue. He's holding a big feathered hat," Sumi said. "Am I supposed to like this guy or something? He's not my type."

"It's *Blue Boy* by Thomas Gainsborough. And it's a fake," Jonny said. "The only one in the hall." He nodded back the way they had come. "Touch it. The texture's just a holographic trick." He waited a moment. "Well?"

"Well what? What's supposed to happen?" asked Sumi.

"It's plastic. Didn't you notice?"

She grunted. "I don't think it's plastic."

"Of course it is," insisted Jonny. "I found the real one in a storage room—" His fingers brushed wormed wood, but where he was expecting thin, ridged optical plastic, he felt fleshy mounds of oil paint. "Is this the right painting?" he asked.

"It's a young boy dressed in blue," said Sumi.

Jonny shoved his hands in his pockets. He turned around in the hall, confused, suddenly unsure in which direction their room lay. He touched the painting again. Sumi took his arm and walked him back to the room.

He sat up the rest of the night brooding, wondering who had changed the painting. Sumi tossed in her sleep. The brandy had upset her stomach and she sweated with a low-grade fever. By dawn—he could tell the sun was up by the warmth that came streaming through the lace curtains—her fever had broken. He lay down beside her on the damp sheets and fell asleep. He dreamed, but there were no images, just darkness. Endless, unbroken night.

* * *

"It's the 'nineties all over again," Conover told Jonny and Sumi. Silent waiters set bowls of what smelled like miso soup before them on the low, lacquered table. They were in the Japanese wing. Conover had gone all out for the dinner, the third the three had shared. Silk kimonos had arrived at Jonny and Sumi's room earlier that evening, along with split-toe socks and wooden sandals. The scent of sandalwood incense filled the house, and koto music, fragile, ancient quarter-tone melodies, coming from the halls and every room, flowed from speakers hidden in the walls. The three of them sat cross-legged on tatami mats, firm, pumpkin-sized pillows resting against their backs.

"It was an exciting time. There was blood in the air then, too," the smuggler lord continued. Jonny thought he sounded a little drunk. He had been celebrating by himself the completion of some big business deal. It amazed Jonny how, in the midst of what seemed to him to be absolute bug-fuck madness, Conover could calmly carry on with business as usual. Earlier that evening he had mentioned this to Conover and the smuggler lord had explained that it had mostly to do with his age. "Nothing much surprises me anymore. Or frightens me, for that matter," he had said. "It's all reruns now. Has been for years."

Now, Conover said, "Nineteen ninety-six was the year of reckoning. How good is your history, Jonny?"

"'Bout as good as my math," he said between sips of hot soybean soup.

"How about you, my dear?" Conover said to Sumi.

"Ninety-six? That was the year of the Saudi revolution. When the oil ran out, right?"

Conover laughed and slapped the tabletop. "An educated young woman, how delightful. Yes, indeed, in ninety-six the oil ran out. For us. The West. Of course, it was still there—in the ground—but there was so little left that the New Palestine Federation wanted to freeze all exports. That's what brought down the House of Saud. They opposed the embargo and down they came, like a house of cards."

"That's it?" asked Jonny. Someone took away his empty soup bowl and set a plate before him. He sniffed. Pickled cabbage. "That's what that whole stupid non-war was about? They wouldn't sell us their oil?"

"No, no, no," Conover said. "That was part of it, to be sure. But it goes much deeper than that, back years and years. If you read histories of that period, they'll tell you the shooting started when somebody blew up the Malaga fusion reactor in southern Spain. The CIA claimed the Arabs took it out with a surface-to-surface missile from Tangier. For their part, the Arabs claimed that radical members of the Green Party or some other environmental group did it without knowing the damned thing was on line."

"Did they really blow up the reactor?" Sumi asked.

"Yes indeed. Wiped out a hundred square kilometers of prime Spanish real estate, too. But as to starting the war—it's like saying the assassination of the Archduke Ferdinand started World War One. In a way it's true, the ultimate outcome is accurate, but the event becomes meaningless when you remove it from its context."

"Who's Archbishop Ferdinand?" asked Jonny.

"It was Islam itself we had to kill," said Conover. Jonny heard the smuggler lord sipping tea. He picked at his pickled cabbage, waiting for Conover to continue. Even drunk, the man was interesting.

"This goes back to the nineteen seventies and the early oil embargos. When the Arabs first let the world know they were aware of their own power. You have to understand that world communication was still at a very primitive stage. There was no World Link, no skull-plugs. Your average Westerner knew nothing of the middle east. Muslims scared the hell out of America. All most people knew of Islam came from the old broadcast news services. Videos of hostage-taking, flag burnings, young men driving trucks full of explosives into the sides of buildings. Utterly alien images. American power was based on fear, but how were we to frighten these people? We couldn't. There we were, the most powerful country on Earth and we were powerless to stop a handful of radicals. 'Fanatics' we called them. 'Muslim extremists.'"

"Terrorists," said Jonny.

"Oh yes. A very flexible word," Conover replied. "Generally used to describe anybody the authorities don't like. But the Arabs—after all the years we had been shitting on these people, they were starting to shit back, and that was unacceptable. It was bad for morale and, more importantly, it was bad for business. We had to squash them. It was going to be Central America all over again. Boom!" Conover yelled. "Flat as a pancake."

Jonny set down his chopsticks and, not finding a napkin, licked his fingertips. He had picked up the habit of keeping one or two fingers on his plate at all times. It was the only way he could find his food. "You really think that old mess is heating up again?" he asked.

"I was speaking metaphorically," Conover explained. "I simply meant to draw an analogy between that old war and our current situation in L.A."

"Who's the Arabs and who's the U.S.?" asked Jonny.

"I suppose we'll figure that out when we see who wins."

"The war in ninety-six died down in a few days, right?" asked Sumi. "Nobody really wanted to start World War Three."

"The war plans died, yes, but it was more like a few years," said Conover. "Don't forget that's where our economy went, right down the black holes of all those oil fields we didn't own. The moment they signed the Reykjavik treaty, we were dead. All those booming war-time industries collapsed overnight. Then, when the Depression was at its worst, the Alpha Rats landed on the moon, cut off the mines and our lunar research labs, and finished us off. We're probably the first country on record to ever go into receivership. The Japanese picked us up for a song." The smuggler lord was silent, as if remembering. "Some people think it comes down to accumulated bad karma. My dear—" Conover said suddenly, "are you all right?"

Jonny reached out and found Sumi's hand. It was hot and moist with sweat. "I'm fine," she said irritably, pulling from his grip. "The food up here's too rich for me. I can't keep it down."

"She's been running a fever on and off for a couple of days," said Jonny. He touched her face. She was burning up.

"Don't do that," she said.

Jonny heard Conover get up and move around to their side of the table. "Please," the smuggler lord said quietly. He was quiet for a moment. Jonny knew the lord was checking Sumi's eyes. Hepatitis was still common in the city, and the D strain was a killer. "Why didn't you tell me about the fever sooner?" Conover asked.

Jonny shrugged. "We were out at that fish farm. It was wet. I thought maybe she got a cold. It just didn't seem important," he said, and saying it, he knew he was lying. He and Sumi had both been afraid of the same thing when she became ill, and at moments of stress it was easy to fall back on old habits. A year before they had avoided talking openly about Ice's leaving and the daily knowledge of it had eaten them up. Now they could not discuss Sumi's illness, could not take the simplest measures to treat it because to treat it would be to acknowledge its presence, and that was impossible. Sumi could not be ill, not with what they both knew was loose in the city.

"I'm going to have my techs check you out, Sumi." Conover's heavy footsteps moved across the straw mat. A light door slid back.

"Please don't—Mister Conover? Please—Jonny, make him stop. I don't—want to know—"

Jonny pulled her to him and she put her arms around his neck. She shook with fever and wept quietly. Jonny found himself supporting more and more of her weight. "Hurry!" he yelled.

It was like waking up blind all over again. His mind was working, racing, in fact, like an overheated engine, but nothing was getting through. The information, the possibility that Sumi might be fatally ill, was utterly unacceptable. Bad dreams, bad data.

"It's all right, babe," he whispered. "Everything's gonna be all right."

Medical techs were coming down the hall, preceded by the smell of antiseptic. Something followed them. Jonny heard it brushing against the rice-paper walls, something that floated forward steadily on an induction cushion. The techs pushed it up to sliding doors and left it there, humming quietly. He felt Sumi being gently lifted from him. Opening his arms, she slipped away into a space occupied by smooth, reassuring voices, the smell of scrubbed skin and betadine.

"Jonny?" He heard her as they set her on whatever they had brought with them. "Don't let them take me, please. Jonny? They're wearing masks. I can't see their faces." He sat there at the table as they took her away. "Jonny? I'm scared. Jonny?" Footsteps. The buzzing of induction coils.

He cradled his head in his hands. "Jesus-fucking-Christ."

He took deep breaths, pressed his fists to his temples. And hit himself. And again. And again.

"Stop it." Conover held Jonny's fists. "You're not helping her with that. We have to wait for the lab results."

"You know what it's going to say," Jonny said.

"No, I don't," said Conover. "And neither do you, unless you've developed some special sense you haven't told me about."

"It's the virus," Jonny said. "She's got the fucking leprosy."

"This is a good med team. Russians," said the smuggler lord. "I'm moving them for a private clinic in Kyoto. Now they can earn their keep."

"She's been all over the city," Jonny said. "It was her job. Watt Snatcher goes anywhere people need power. She's been all over. Probably been exposed to it a hundred times."

Conover sat down next to him. "We'll know soon enough."

Jonny stretched out his legs on the tatami mat, running his fingers over the scars on his face. He thought of the micrograph of the virus he had seen at the Croakers' black clinic: the pseudophage's distorted head, its thin insect legs holding it in place while it pumped out its genetic material. Then the cloning of the plague. The cell exploding. Poison in the bloodstream.

"Mister Conover," Jonny began quietly, "if I asked you a couple of personal questions, would you be straight with me?"

"If I can." The smuggler lord's voice was deep, guarded, rumbling from the depths of his belly.

"I can't help thinking that you know more about this leprosy analog than you've been letting on. Let me ask you— that stuff Easy Money took off you, was that connected with the virus? Maybe a specimen?"

At first, Jonny did not think the lord would answer, but as he was putting together another question he heard, "Yes."

"I've moved a few disease cultures and infected organs myself," said Jonny, "to gangs into research. But this virus is something else. It's like something a government lab or a multinational would come up with."

"I just move merchandise," said Conover. "I have no idea who the original owner is. The deal was conducted through a third party."

"Any chance that original owner is Arab?" asked Jonny.

"I have no idea," Conover replied.

"Do you know if Easy Money has any Arab connections?"

"Not to my knowledge."

"But it is possible."

"Easy Money would work for Colonel Zamora, the Arabs, or Mother Goose if she had cash," said Conover.

"Right. And if Easy was moonlighting for the Arabs, what better place to work than with you, using your connections and your protection If he knew about that virus shipment and was waiting for it, he could have been tipped by a go-between that you had it, snatched it, and taken off."

Conover dragged something across the table. There was the sound of liquid being poured. Jonny felt a small cup pressed into his hand. He sniffed the liquid. Saké. He gulped the whole thing down. "Easy says he has a second vial from the shipment and he's willing to sell it. Is it unreasonable to assume that if there are two vials involved, one might be the virus and the other, something to kill it?"

"No. That's not unreasonable at all," said Conover. "Do you know where Easy is?"

"Maybe," said Jonny. "What I can't figure, though, is that if Easy is working for the Arabs, why is he willing to sell us the second vial?"

"Easy is greedy," said Conover. "Why should he turn a single profit when he can double his money by splitting the vials and selling them individually?"

"Yeah. That's just the way he'd do it."

"So what are we going to do about this?" asked the smuggler lord. "It's obvious you know where Easy is hiding, but you won't tell me."

"I didn't say I wouldn't tell you. I just want to make a deal first."

Conover laughed. "Why didn't I see this coming?" Jonny heard him pour out more saké. A cup was pushed into his hand. "Your terms?" Conover asked.

"If Sumi has the new leprosy," Jonny said, "when I get this stuff from Easy, she's the first one to get a shot."

"I have no problem with that."

"There's more," said Jonny.

"My," said Conover appreciatively, "you're growing up, son. You're finally beginning to think like a businessman."

"The second part is that I'm in on the pick-up. I want to be right there when the deal goes down. I want to hold the vial in my hand and know it's safe."

"You of all people should know how stupid an idea that is," Conover said. "The last time you left here you were healthy. Now you have a face that's half plastic and no eyes at all."

"It's a yes-or-no proposition," said Jonny. "No go, no show."

Jonny could sense the smuggler lord thinking. He sipped his saké and waited, confident that he knew what the lord's answer would be. He felt an odd, distant amusement at having bested Conover in a business deal. Below them, behind reinforced concrete doors, layers of steel, and emp shielding, was Conover's underground clinic. Jonny knew that the techs were down there studying Sumi's blood, running tubes into her arms, down her throat, taking tissue samples and watching her on video monitors from distant rooms, manipulating diagnostic devices with nursing drones, checking her for signs of infection, but keeping well away from her. There was a ball of acid burning in the pit of his stomach.

"I'll accept your deal," Conover said finally. "But before we can proceed, I have a deal of my own that you must accept."

"What is it?"

"It's simple, really, and not terribly unpleasant. I just want your word that you and Sumi, when she is well, will remain here as my guests, with complete run of the house and grounds, for as long as I deem necessary."

"That's it?" asked Jonny.

"That's it."

There were footsteps coming down the corridor. Jonny picked at a loose piece of tatami as Conover went to the sliding door. Low voices. "Thank you," Conover said, and sat down again next to Jonny. "It's the test results."

"I don't want to hear it. If it was good news you'd have said so from the door," Jonny said. "Shit. People like me, we spend our whole lives tripping over our feet. But Sumi, she doesn't deserve this." He tried to conjure her face, but he could not find it. The inside of his head felt hollow, as if someone had scooped his brains out and chromed the inside of his skull. "You've got a deal," Jonny said.

"Excellent," said Conover. He poured them each another

cup of sake. "A drink to seal the deal, and off to bed for you. You're going to need strength tomorrow."

"Yeah, dealing with Easy's a real drain."

"You won't be cutting any deals tomorrow, I'm afraid. Tomorrow, you're going under the knife."

"What do you mean?"

"I mean," said the smuggler lord, draining his cup and smacking his lips in satisfaction, "that at this time tomorrow, you'll be in surgery. If you're going back down into that madhouse, it seems to me the best way to make sure you find your way back here is to fix you up with a new pair of eyes."

__ 10 _____

SECOND SIGHT: AN
ADVENTURE IN OPTICS _____

HE COULD NOT SLEEP. He spent the night listening to the
World Link viewer in his room, restlessly changing the chan-
nel every few seconds, program to program (damned Alpha
Rat documentaries, he thought), language to language, and
pacing. The old house creaked, settling deeper into the earth
on its century-old foundation. Jonny tried not to think of Sumi
and Ice, tried to keep his mind numb. He felt his way into the
hall once, found *Blue Boy* and ran his fingers over the uneven
layers of paint. He knew that he was probably on somebody's
security camera, but he did not care. Jonny wondered what
would happen if he put his fist through the damned painting.

Later, in his room, when the little enamelled clock on his
desk chimed seven times, they came for him.

They injected him with something and, against his will, he
felt himself relaxing. He was pushed through the halls on a
padded chair that hovered a few centimeters off the parquet
floor on an induction cushion, wondering if it was the same
chair they had used to take Sumi away. Conover walked be-
hind him, smelling of clove cigarettes.

"You have good timing, son," said the smuggler lord. "In
another week, these techs would be gone. Off to Japan. My
own staff is good, but these people are special. And expen-
sive, too. I'm turning a nice profit on this deal. They're Rus-
sians, did I tell you? I had them brought in from a sharaska
near Leningrad. You wouldn't have believed the state they
were in when they got here. Pathetic. The Russians had stuck
neural scramblers in all their heads. One hundred meters
beyond the prison walls, their brains went into vaporlock. It's

not easy, you know, taking a neural scrambler out of a brain and having anything but Spam left over. The Japs developed the technique. My staff performed the actual surgery. We lost two, but the rest came through with flying colors." Jonny was pushed into an elevator. He heard the doors hiss closed, experienced the slight vertigo of descent. Then the doors opened and they pushed him to a room where the smell of antiseptic hit him like a slap in the face. "Doctor Ludovico is the prize, the reason the Japanese financed the operation. The others are his staff. Ludovico is a specialist in xenograftology. He'll be doing your surgery."

The techs elevated the chair a half-meter and let down the back, sliding Jonny onto a narrow table in a single, practiced motion. Someone began covering him with small sheets of sterile cloth, moving up his body to his throat, leaving his head bare. Fingers touched his forehed, pulled the lids back from his empty eye sockets. Jonny gasped.

"Relax," said Conover. "It's Ludovico. He just wants to have a look at what he has to work with." Ludovico, Conover explained, spoke no English. He smelled of expensive cigars and cheap cologne. Jonny did not like the man, did not like having a stranger's fingers prying into his head, did not like the idea of a bunch of possibly brain damaged ex-cons cutting him open, and he was about to say so when a needle hit him in the arm and an anesthetic mask slipped down over his nose.

"I'll be seeing you," said Conover. "And with any luck, you'll be seeing me."

"It hurts," Jonny said. Two days later, his hair was just beginning to come back in. The Russians had removed the staples from his face, sealing the scars with a protein glue. A lightshow played in Jonny's head. No images, just silent fireworks. He had not had any contact with Sumi since the surgery. She was in quarantine, and from the noises Conover was making, Jonny thought she might be on life-support. Unconsciously, he found himself relying on the old wisdom to keep going. It was a matter of accepting each moment as a unique entity, allowing observer and the observed to merge and thus keep the panic and horror from overwhelming him. The Buddhists were right in that at least, Jonny thought. He found that he was able to meditate for short periods of time and that seemed to help.

Now, something was tickling his eyes; ants crawled up his optic nerves, marched through his skull to his brain, where they laid tiny eggs that burst into supernovas, scattering colors he could not name.

He was downstairs again, in a different room, sitting up this time. Ludovico was there, mumbling to his assistants and operating a Cray minicomputer, trying to calibrate the frequency response of Jonny's new eyes. Exteroceptors, someone had called them. The front of Jonny's head felt huge, bulging with the new hardware. The techs had assured him that the feeling would wear off in a few days, but Jonny had his doubts. He was convinced that he would look like a bug for the rest of his life.

"It's a bridge he's built," said Conover. "That's the key to this procedure. Ludovico's bypassed your optic nerves completely and implanted silicon sensors in your sight centers. The chips receive data from a broadcast unit at the back of the exteroceptors. Your retinas are really modified Langenscheidt CCDs. Any pain or unusual light patterns you are experiencing are the effects of the electrical field around the graft stimulating what's left of your optic nerves."

Jonny laughed. "People've been telling me I ought to get a skull-plug for years."

"Now you've done them all one better. An entire digitized sense."

"I don't know," said Jonny, squirming in the exam chair, trying to find a comfortable spot. "I've always been a little afraid of grafts and implants, you know? Like maybe I'd forget where the machinery ended and I started."

Conover breathed heavily, making a sound that could have been a sigh. "It's all a gamble," he said. "Every moment you're alive. Would you rather be blind?"

"No way," Jonny said. He shook his head. "Some choice."

Ludovico said something and a woman with a heavy Japanese accent translated. "The doctor is going to bring up the exteroceptors now. He wants you to describe everything you see."

Jonny settled back in the chair, consciously controlling his breathing. Burning violet rimmed his field of vision.

"Keep your eyes open," someone said.

Hot fear. Something was moving up his throat.

Give me anything, he thought. Just a little light. A little

light. Over and over until the words lost all meaning and it became a chant, a mantra—

Then it flowed into him, obliterating all else, a flood of sensations, solid mass of bent spectrum, vague things moving within. He turned his head, letting the colors blur across his vision. *His vision.* He was seeing children's blocks, a rainbow chess board—no—a grid, like fine wire mesh. Each individual segment was throbbing neon. Then shapes. A man was seated before him. His right hand appeared to be burning.

"There's a lot of colors coming through a grid," Jonny said. "Looks like some kind of pixel display. There's someone there. His hand—it's like it's on fire." The woman translated into Russian.

The man-shape typed something into the Cray and the colors dropped suddenly in intensity. They were replaced with more distinct shapes. The burning hand was no longer burning, but remained faintly aglow, splashes of pastels shading the fingers and wrist like an old map, different colors indicating geographic regions. The hand belonged to a fat man, Jonny could see, and the burning, he realized, had come from a pencil-sized flashlight the fat man had been shining into his eyes.

The pixels had the effect of distancing Jonny from what he saw. He felt that he was watching the room from a video monitor, shooting through thousands of individual squares of beveled glass.

Something flared off to his right. Jonny turned and saw Conover. The smuggler lord was lighting a cigarette, the flame on his lighter burning red and ludicrously large.

"These eyes have thermographic grids," said Jonny. "Some kind of computer-enhanced infrared scan."

"A bonus," said Conover, a variegated skull, dead patches of skin registering as holes in his face. "There are some other sub-programs in there, too. You'll find them and learn to control the sensitivity of the pixels."

"I can make out shapes pretty well, right now," Jonny said. "Are the colors going to be like this all the time?"

"No, you're just registering infrared because the lights are out."

"Well, fire them up. This heat vision is weird."

"Is that all right, Doctor?" Conover asked. A woman spoke to Ludovico, whom Jonny recognized as the fat man. The

Russian nodded, extra chins spilling over his collar. "Da," he said, and someone turned on the lights. Normal spectrum canceled out the infrared. Jonny looked at the room, the people, the blinking lights on the diagnostic devices. The colors were just a shade or two hotter than normal.

"Fucking beautiful," Jonny said. He was laughing. It was all he could do.

Conover put a hand on his shoulder. "It's all right now, isn't it?"

"It's incredible, man," Jonny said. "When can I go see Easy?"

"Soon. Tonight, maybe, depending on how you feel. Before you go, though, there's something we have to talk about."

"Yeah, I know. You want one of your people to go with me."

"That's right. Ricos. But that's not what I want to talk about." Conover dropped his cigarette to the floor and ground it out. There was something wrong with the techs' faces. They were not looking at him like someone they had just cured. More like someone they had just saved from meningitis only to find cancer. Jonny recognized a woman in the corner as Yukiko, a member of Conover's private medical staff. She had been kind to him when he was here before, he remembered, but now she would not look at him. "What's going on?" asked Jonny.

"You know," Conover said gently, "living out here in the fringes, we sometimes find ourselves forced to fall back on raw ingenuity and imagination." He picked a set of forceps off a metal tray table, turning them over in his hands. "We learn to improvise."

"What did you improvise?"

"You have your sight again."

"What's wrong with me?" He scanned the room again. "Have I got the virus?"

"Nothing like that," said Conover. "I just want you to understand the context of your operation."

By then Jonny was up, pushing the Russians out of his way, looking for something. Near the scrub sink, a chrome cabinet on the counter. Leaning on the Formica, white flecked with gold, he pressed his face close to the metal. And cursed, his fist denting the side of the cabinet before he could think. "What have you done to me?" he yelled.

"We gave you back something you had lost."

Jonny looked back at the dented metal, searching for his face, but it was not there. Sockets black and threaded with the purple and red of broken blood vessels. Something alien stared back at him. Yellow-eyed, with pupils that ran vertically from lid to lid. At certain angles, there were flashes of light, green and metallic. Tapetums, he thought.

"That tiger I blew away," Jonny whispered, feeling the strange machinery in his head. "You gave them to me."

"We had no choice," Conover said.

Jonny turned to him. "Great trade, man. One short hop. Cripple to freak."

"You're no more a freak than I," Conover said. His face tightened, smoke trailing from the scar of his nose. "Do you think I always looked like this? You learn to live with it."

Jonny kept staring. "Look at me. I ought to be in a fucking carnival."

Conover moved up beside him. "You wanted eyes, you have them."

Jonny walked numbly back to the examination chair, fell into the seat, covering his face with his hands. "Oh, man—"

"It was the best we could do," the smuggler lord told him. He smiled. "And you have to admit—in this city, they're really not such a strange sight. In a few weeks, they'll be old friends."

"Oh, Christ!" Jonny looked at his hands. "Don't get the idea I'm sorry about the operation," he said. The grid was still visible, subtly, clipping the tips of his fingers straight across. He looked at Conover. "I'm glad I can see again, really. It's just kind of a shock."

Conover nodded. "I understand." He looked at his watch. "Listen, I'm going to have to leave for a business meeting. You should go to your room and try to get some rest. I'll send Ricos by later. You can tell him then if you want to go tonight or wait."

"Right," said Jonny. As Conover started to leave the room, he called out. "Mister Conover—"

The smuggler lord stopped in the doorway. "Yes?"

Jonny shrugged. "Thanks," he said.

"My pleasure."

"Think you could do me one more favor?"

"What is it?" Conover asked.

"Could you have somebody take the mirrors out of my room?"

Conover smiled. "Done," he said, and left.

Jonny leaned on the counter, letting his nearly bald head fall back against the laminated cupboard doors, and stared at the Russians staring at him. Yukiko brought him tea in a white styrofoam cup. With a little effort, she looked at him and smiled. "Thank you," he said.

The trip back to his room was a nightmare. He kept his head down, but the peculiar layout of the house forced him to look up frequently and his reflection seemed always to be there, waiting for him in the glazing on a Ming vase, in the glass front of an antique china cabinet, the polished chrome of a seismic meter.

Golden-eyed monster.

He had refused the induction chair; a couple of the Russian techs followed him from the clinic, keeping a respectful distance. When he got to his room, he closed the door in their faces.

Inside, he remained by the door and looked the room over, checking for any reflective surfaces. When he found none, he went straight to the bed and lay down.

The transparent lameness of Conover's story had been so obvious to Jonny that he knew it had to be deliberate. That meant that giving him the freakish eyes was, to one degree or other, a calculated move. The smuggler lord had obviously planned to show his displeasure with Jonny in some way, and Jonny's blindness presented him with a convenient method. The eyes were a punishment and a warning. Punishment for stealing the car and running away, and a warning that he had better not do it again. Like a Yakuza ritual, Jonny thought. Make a mistake, lose a finger joint. Look for the guys with no fingers, they're the real fuck-ups.

What does that make me? he wondered.

It surprised him, but he felt no real anger toward Conover for what he had done. He could have done a lot worse, Jonny knew. And the smuggler lord had been right all along. The moment Jonny had left the hill, he had set himself on a course that led right back into Zamora's hands. Living with funny eyes, he thought, would be a hell of a lot easier than living with whatever the Colonel had planned for him.

"Hey, maricón."

Jonny sat upright in bed. He had no memory of falling asleep and feeling himself shaken awake, the loss of control it implied, frightened him. Jonny looked at Ricos and saw that he was not the only one who was startled.

"Joder, man," Ricos whispered. He was wearing a red motorcycle jacket and striped leather pants. "What you let them do that to you for?" Ricos was staring at Jonny as he might have stared at an open sore or a road kill, not trying to hide his disgust. For that, Jonny was grateful.

"I didn't have a lot of choice," said Jonny, swinging his legs off the bed and getting up.

"Carajo. I kill anyone do that to me."

"Your boss included?"

"Anyone."

Jonny smiled at the man. "You're really full of shit. You know that?" He went to the dresser, found a pair of black slacks his size, and started to put them on. "We're going to need ID," he said. "Something corporate. Multinational."

"No problem," said Ricos.

On the top of the dresser somebody had left a dozen pairs of sunglasses, laid out neatly in three horizontal rows. Their sleek designs, so out of place against the pale wood of the French antiques, reminded Jonny of one of the Croakers' strange sculptures. Without thinking, he picked up the mirrored aviators and put them in the breast pocket of the gray tweed jacket he had taken from the closet.

"All right," Jonny said. "We'll pick up the ID, get you some better clothes, and be on our way."

"What's wrong wi' my clothes?" asked Ricos, offended.

"Nothing man, if we were going to Carnaby's Pit." He headed out the door, Ricos a few steps behind him.

"So where you takin' me, maricón?"

Jonny spun and jammed a finger into the man's stomach. "Little Tokyo," he said. "Where they shoot people like you and me on sight."

* * *

The car was an old alcohol-powered Brazilian coupe, modeled on a turn-of-the-century Mercedes design. Ricos drove; he wore a powder-blue Italian suit and tugged constantly at the collar of his pearl-gray shirt. Jonny and he were carrying the ID chips of dead men.

They abandoned the car near Union Station, an art deco hulk sprouting cracked brick and I-beams like exposed ribs. A ruin of stripped cranes and power generators surrounded it, heaps of ferro-ceramic track turning black under the moon, under the Alpha Rats' gaze, waiting for the bullet-train that never arrived.

A maintenance shaft beneath the battered transformers of an out-of-commission Pacific Gas and Electric sub-station ended in a short crawl space that gave out at the false bottom in a section of vent, part of the massive air recirculation system that served the Little Tokyo arcology. Jonny removed the loose bottom panel from the vent and he and Ricos crawled inside, careful not to get their new clothes dirty. The dimensions of the vent were such that they were able to duck-walk their way to an access hatch, a hundred meters or so upwind from where they entered. It was like strolling into a tornado the whole way.

Manipulating the lock from the inside, Jonny opened the hatch and they jumped down to the floor of the recirculation plant. The place was fully automated, Jonny remembered, the human crew making no more than a cursory round of the place once or twice a night. Jonny could hear Ricos behind him, breathing above the din of the air circulators. The man was tense and jittery, starting at every grunt and hiss of the equipment. Jonny led him into a corridor that rose in a slow spiral toward the surface. Cinder-block walls painted the teal and orange of the Hundred Dynasty Corporation bulged with rot.

They found the ladder Jonny was looking for behind a wall of fifty-five gallon drums stacked on modular racks, pushed away a grating at the top, and emerged behind a French discoteque, La Poupée.

In the pastel half-light that bled over the rooftops, the skeletal superstructures supporting neon graphics and holo-projectors, Jonny took a last quick look at the dead man's ID. Jonny was Christian van Noorden, a Dutch-born systems analyst for Pemex-U.S.; Ricos had a chip identifying him as

Eduardo Florentino, a security coordinator for Krupp Bio-
Elektronisches. Jonny slipped on his mirrored aviators and
headed for the boulevard, Ricos on his heels, and merged
unnoticed into the crowd of strolling tourists, the cream of the
multinationals' crop.

Walking just ahead of Jonny and Ricos was a group of
young Swedish aerospace techs. They were fair and slender,
strikingly attractive, each with the same narrow jaw and deli-
cate, long-fingered hands. Jonny wondered if they might be
clones. They were all shirtless and the hard muscles of their
torsos were exposed, flexing as they moved beneath transpar-
ent polycarbonate bodysheaths. Their muscles had been dyed
different colors to accentuate the movements of various
groups. They were like living anatomy charts, Jonny thought.
Across the street, high in the air, appeared the parting lips of a
hologram vagina—a pink, idealized orchid, a toothless mouth
that seemed to engulf the image, becoming a roller coaster
flesh-tunnel, the glistening walls blurring by.

At the corner, Jonny had to stop. He pretended to watch the
animated menu display outside a Burmese restaurant. The
menu explained the meals in different languages depending on
where you stood, but Jonny hardly noticed it. His hands were
shaking.

It was an impossible psychic leap. He was a kid again,
seeing Little Tokyo for the first time, nailed in his tracks by
the light, the air, the impossible wealth and beauty of the
place, the blatant and cherished waste of energy. Little Tokyo
was a transcultural phenomenon, its name having long since
been rendered meaningless, indicating a city geosector and
giving hints to the place's history, but little else. It was Japa-
nese and European chic filtered through American sleaze,
through generations of exported television, video and Link
images, visions of Hollywood and Las Vegas, the cheap gang-
ster dreams of the Good Life, haven and playground for the
privileged employees of the multinationals. Little Tokyo was
loud and it cost the corporations dearly, but they loved it and,
in the end, came to need it. What had once been their play-
thing now defined them.

There were clubs offering all varieties of sexual en-
counters. Death-fetish clubs, where controlled doses of eu-
phoria-inducing poisons had replaced drugs as the high of
choice. It was in one of these clubs, when he was seventeen,

that Jonny had first tried Mad Love. Right now, he thought, he would kill for a hit. There were the computer-simulation clubs, offering those with skull-plugs close encounters with violence, madness, and death. A block ahead was the Onno-gata, where members of various cartels gambled time in the regeneration tanks for data on next year's computers, synth-fuels, and pharmaceuticals.

Other clubs offered similar opportunities, and anyone could play. Hit a losing streak, and you could leave parts of your body scattered all over the boulevard. Organ removal and installation were all part of the standard hotel services. Those who lost badly enough were put on life-support systems, sometimes gambling away even those before the company jet could arrive to take them home. No one had died in Little Tokyo for over a century. Not permanently.

Ricos was staring at Jonny. "You want to eat now?" he asked.

Jonny looked at the man, then back at the menu, which was describing a chicken and rice dish in over-eager French. "No," he said, "just thinking."

He took off across the clean, broad street, walking, want-ing to get the feel of the place before he got down to business. He had not been in Little Tokyo in years. Warm breezes car-ried the faint smell of orange blossoms, a wholly contrived sensation. Jonny had seen drums full of the scent back in the recirculation plant.

Conover had been right about the eyes, Jonny noticed. Half-consciously, he had begun to manipulate them, changing their focus at first by mistake, then by repeating the mistake until he could control it. He turned to Ricos, who seemed unaffected by the place, colors slurring slightly off-register in his peripheral vision. "You see it?" asked Jonny.

"Que es, maricón."

"No one's sick here. No one's old," he said. They were walking by a man-made lake. One- and two-person robot hover-vehicles were cutting up the glassy surface of the water, shuttling between the shore and a five-story pagoda on a small island near the lake's center. Wings of jewellike foam spread from beneath the little disc-shaped crafts, setting off the tai-lored evening gowns and tuxes of the riders. "Not a leper, not a liver spot, not a paper cut in sight."

"Si," Ricos replied, nodding toward a young couple displaying their customized genitalia to some friends. Chrome winked from between their thighs. "Estos carajos, they come in kits. Comprende? Cut 'em, they don' bleed."

The entrance to the Japanese club was flanked by two man-sized temple dogs carved from some dark, supple wood. Ricos walked past the place, but Jonny stopped, drawn by something—perhaps the odd angle at which one dog's head had been carved. He realized at the moment he stopped that the dogs were not statues but were, in fact, alive. The dogs, pure-bred Tosas, sat on their haunches, watching the crowd with the impassiveness of sunning lizards, the pink of a tongue appearing now and then to lick massive jaws, their necks and backs bulging with muscle—the end-product of controlled breeding and genetic manipulation. As Jonny looked at the animals, a frozen image of the bodysheathed Swedes imposed itself on his vision, the street by La Poupée clear in the background. Then it was gone. Jonny blinked, tensing the muscles around his eyes. The image of the Swedes flashed back. He held it this time, made it move slowly, forward and backward. It made perfect sense that the eyes would have a recording chip, he thought. Couple of days ago, they were part of a security system. Download pictures of intruders for the law. He blinked off the image and said "In here" to Ricos.

The uniformed Japanese doorman bowed and held the door for them as they went in, touching a hand to his right temple as Jonny and Ricos walked past. Scanning for weapons, Jonny knew. He cursed silently, wondering if they had been made already.

Inside the club it was very dark, the architecture traditional: tatami mats, low tables glowing with buttery yellow light of painted lanterns, white-faced geishas serving pots of hot saké to the mostly male, mostly Japanese and American middle-management crowd. There was a lot of noise coming from a room beyond the bar. Jonny slipped his hand to the small of his back as if to hitch up his pants, and touched the grip of a small SIG Sauer handgun. The body of the weapon was of a liquid-crystal polymer, impossible, he had been told, to pick up on metal detectors. The shells were a Gobernacion

standard issue, commonly known as Rock Shot. Each bullet
had a synthetic quartz tip. When it struck an object and com-
pressed, the minute charge from the quartz was conducted
through a medium of liquid polypyrrole where it ignited sus-
pended particles of C-4 plastique. Ricos was carrying a similar
weapon in his jacket.

Jonny ordered saké and motioned for the geisha to bring it
to them in the next room. She bowed. He smiled uncomfort-
ably at her, unsure if he was supposed to bow back or not. He
bowed, and the geisha giggled at his gaijin stiffness. "Keep
your eyes open for Easy Money," he told Ricos.

They split up in the next room, climbing opposite sides of a
flat-topped pyramid constructed of multiple tiers of polished
mahogany beams. The smell of sweat and blood was heavy in
the smoky-booze air, but Jonny was still shocked by what he
saw when he reached the top tier, pushed his way to the front,
and peered down into the wooden pen.

The winning dog was just receiving its award—outline of
a golden lotus on a small banner of purple satin—from a pale,
doughy-faced man in shirtsleeves. One of the dog's front paws
was twisted and badly mangled. Jonny watched the losing
dog's body being dragged out of the enclosure, its humiliated
owner and assistant careful not to get blood on their white
shirts.

A moment later, the whole thing was starting again. The
doughy-faced man made an announcement in rapid-fire Japa-
nese and blessed each corner of the arena with salt. Then two
more dogs, enormous Tosas again, bigger than the previous
pair, easily a hundred and fifty kilos each, were led in from
opposite sides of the pen at the end of heavy carbide-steel
chains. The money chips were out; Jonny caught the flash of
silicon embossed with gold phoenixes as the crowd sur-
rounded the house bookmakers, touching their chips to the
little multiplexer he carried, hoping to get their bets in before
the dogs were released and the odds started dropping. Jonny
looked around for an exit and found one, down by the far end
of the enclosure. He was just starting for it when he heard the
dogs hit, the dull thud of meat on meat, low-throated animal
grunts, primal death-talk. He looked around for Ricos, nodded
when he saw the man on the other side of the pen, eyes wide,

watching the animals tear each other apart. Jonny smiled. Ditching Ricos had been easier than he had ever expected.

Heading down the tiers toward the exit, Jonny heard one of the dogs yelp frantically, the sound of it painful through the club's P.A. system. Jonny was almost to the floor when he turned and darted back into the crowd. Some time during the few seconds it had taken him to find Ricos and walk down the steps, a Meat Boy had stationed himself at the exit. Jonny shouldered his way through the screaming mob, moving back the way he had come, eyes on the gamblers' faces, trying to keep the dog fight out of his sight. Animal screams and human cheers. He spotted another Meat Boy by the entrance to the bar. The giant was talking to someone. The doorman. Jonny looked around, hoping that maybe there was an exit he had missed. But he found none, and when he turned back the way he had come in, he saw the doorman—pointing right at him. Jonny ducked back into the crowd, scrambling along the top tier, the Meat Boy moving through the crowd like a pock-marked ice breaker.

Up, one leg over the rim of the dog pit. For an instant, the crowd fell silent. Then he had the gun out and the noise came back, shrill and frantic this time. He fired twice, but the stampede was already underway, and when the shells hit, blasting away one end of the dog pen, the frightened Tosas took off, all teeth and claws, headed for the only way out. The Meat Boy chasing him, big as he was, was helpless, dragged back by the press of bodies. The last Jonny saw of Ricos, he, too, was being swept along by the human tide. His gun was out, his eyes wide and furious. Jonny did not stick around to see what happened.

He headed for the rear of the club, which was nearly deserted, and made it out the rear exit. Down the alley for the rest of the block. When he came out onto the street again, he fell in with a crowd that was staring back at the club. Dark-suited men were still pouring out the front. The Tosas were headed down the sidewalk, scattering pedestrians and snarling the evening traffic.

Jonny took the long way around the block, just to make sure he did not run into anybody from the dog club. Eventually he ended up back at the man-made lake. Hovercrafts churned up the water. The pagoda glittered on the small island, its finial a solid chunk of carved rose quartz, twenty meters high. Around the pagoda's base was a grove of crystal trees, a tangled thicket of prisms. The Forest of Incandescent Bliss.

No more screwing around. It was time to find Easy Money.

__ 11 _____

OBJECT TO BE DESTROYED _____

"GOOD EVENING," said the little hovercraft as Jonny stepped aboard. "For your safety and comfort, please hold onto the handrail provided. The trip across will take two minutes."

"Fuck you," he told the machine.

"Very good, sir," it said. The non-skid rubberized matting on the passenger platform vibrated softly through the soles of his feet as the craft's engine rose faintly in pitch, lifting him and the vehicle out and over the water. A light mist of warm water blew up from the sides of the craft, settling on his skin. The feel of Sumi's fevered body and Groucho's theories on art and revolution came back to him as he skimmed toward the bright pagoda in the distance. Flashes of carp and fat prawns below the surface of the lake. His thoughts of Sumi disturbed him. The images revolved around plastic tubes and pumps, dumb machines that could never know or understand her, that might, in their ignorance fail—not perceiving her value, the absolute need he had for her to be alive. Revolution, when he considered it, was a phanton pain, nothing more. Like his eyes. He felt them itch, but he knew that they were plastic and unreal, and therefore they could not itch. Yet his desire to rub them was constant. Revolution was like that. A delusion, a pipe dream that when the lid closed over the eye, it could be rubbed and the itch would go away, that the flesh would be restored.

Before he had run into the Croakers, Jonny had known a number of revolutionaries. Bomb throwers and pamphleteers, graffiti artists and assassins. Some of them had meant it, others were revolutionaries of fashion, of convenience. In the end, they had all failed. Jonny had already spotted a dozen of the old faces in the corporate crowds of Little Tokyo. Maybe they were the smart ones, he thought. The ones who went over. Maybe they were the ones who were dead before they started. He could not decide.

The crystal trees at the base of the pagoda grew in detail and complexity (molten-glass light webbed through with burning diamonds) as the hovercraft approached. A battery of white-gloved attendants shaped the trees, carving the branches and leaves from a base of modified aluminum sulfate crystals. Easy Money was somewhere in the structure beyond, Jonny knew. He would get the second vial from Easy, kill him if he got the chance (because he had not forgotten Raquin's murder). That was all the revolution he could expect. As for the other, Groucho's anarchist dreams, there wasn't a chance in hell for those. The best that could be hoped, Jonny decided, was for Sumi to get better and for Ice to come back; to not get hurt for delusions, for dreams of old eyes.

Once inside the Forest of Incandescent Bliss, he went straight to the bar. It was a low affair, horseshoe-shaped, attempted art deco, with gilded mirrors behind the bottles and ridged tiles that glowed with a soft internal illumination. The two bartenders, an Asian male and a blond Caucasian female, were each under a meter tall, but perfectly proportioned. Everything behind the bar, bottles and corks, sponges and mixing utensils, was scaled down to their size. Everything except the glasses in which they served the drinks; these were meant for someone Jonny's size and looked absurdly large in the bartenders' childlike hands.

Jonny ordered gin and tonic, watched as the little man retrieved a hundred-year-old bottle of Bombay gin that had been sealed, at sometime in its past, in dull blue wax. Jonny sipped his drink and handed the man his ID chip. It failed to register the first time the bartender tried to call up the account, and when it failed a second time, Jonny started to get nervous. On the third try, though, the transaction went through, the computer deducting the amount of the drink and a large tip from the dead man's company account. Swirling the cool antiseptic-tasting gin in his mouth, Jonny swallowed one of Conover's endorphin tabs. His new eyes were hurting, a constant pain cutting right through his head to the back of his skull.

Something was moving in the gilded mirror behind the bottles. Jonny turned to the darkened lounge, which took up

most of the pagoda's ground floor. Aged oyabuns playing end-
less games of Go, moving with the ancient and deliberate
grace of mantises; younger men talking earnestly, toasting
each other, skull-plugged into tabletop translators. Mostly Jap-
anese faces, but many American and Mexican, too. Jonny
knew a few, had seen others in the newsrags. Many of the
Japanese were missing finger joints. Yakuza. Must be their
hangout, he thought. Neutral ground. Mafia, the Panteras de
Aureo, Triad families—they were all there, criminals in a
league beyond anything Jonny had ever known or experi-
enced. They were like him, but, he understood, their immense
wealth had insulated them, enabled them to live far enough
removed from ordinary life that they were almost mythologi-
cal figures, shaping the course of nations with their wealth.

Kaleidoscoping in the air above the gangsters' heads was a
crystalline holographic light display, like a sculpted cloud. It
seemed to follow the shifting mood of the room, colors
brightening when the voices rose, muting when the talk was
low. The man next to Jonny addressed the bartender in Portu-
guese. He wore an Irezumi jacket—tanned skin of a heavily
tattooed man, cut bomber-style, with fur around the collar,
one of the most expensive garments in the world. He was not
the only person wearing such a jacket.

In the end, Jonny thought, they were not very much like
him at all. So where the fuck was Easy Money?

He turned, seeing her at the same moment she saw him.
Quick eyes, face the color of night.

"Hey, gaijin-boy, you lookin' for a date?" she said.

"What the fuck are you doing here?" he asked. Ice smiled,
looped an arm in his, and drew him away from the bar. She
wore a tight brown pin-striped dress, cut like a man's suit at
the neck, tapering to a pleated skirt that fell just above her
knees. Her legs were bare. On her feet she wore rolled-down
white socks and strap-on Mary Janes. "Jesus Christ, you turn-
ing tricks for the revolution?"

"Relax," Ice said, holding the smile. She took him to a
corner of the bar below a spiral staircase whose railings were
mahogany dragons, curled around each other in battle. Soft
quarter-tone melodies came from a wall-mounted Klipsch
speaker above their heads. "Now," she said, apparently satis-
fied that no one could hear them. "Keep smiling, babe. I'm
not turning tricks for nobody. See?" She showed him the

cork-bottomed tray she carried. "I just serve drinks. These Yakuza boys like to be around gaijin girls. 'Specially us dark exotic types."

"But—" he began.

"But that doesn't mean they can have us."

"Fuck," he said. He could not pinpoint who or what he was angry with—the club, Ice, or himself. "So what are you doing here?"

"I was going to ask you the same thing," she said. "Where's Sumi?"

He touched her shoulder, smiled for the first time. "She's fine," he lied. "I left her up at Conover's. I'm supposed to meet Easy Money here."

"Por qué?"

"Deal I made with Conover," he said. "I've got to get some of his merchandise back for him."

Ice looked at him and her smile wavered. "You okay?" she asked.

"Fine."

"Something's wrong. Is it Sumi?"

"She's fine." He bit off the sentence abruptly enough that he knew Ice could tell he was lying. "You shouldn't be here," he told her.

She shrugged. "I'm undercover," she told him. "There's other Croakers and some Naginatas, too. We've staked this place for months. Zamora comes here sometimes."

"Zamora?"

"Yeah. This is where we first got wind of the raids. Figure the next time he comes in"—she pressed two fingers into his ribs—"boom! Buenos noches, Colonel." She pulled a wad of bills from her pocket. "Besides, the tips are great."

He shook his head in wonder. "I'm glad to see you."

"Ditto, babe."

"I know this is sick," he said, "but you're making me incredibly horny."

"It's the club," she said. "Subliminals in that holo-display. They pump some kind of sex pheromone-analog through the air conditioning system." Her hands were up before he could stop her. Later, when he was alone, he would replay the picture of her face, studying the emotions there as she saw his new eyes: fear, bewilderment, concern.

"Oh, baby," she said. Jonny felt her hand on his cheek. He

turned his head, caught a distorted image of himself in the
upturned lenses of the aviators. Yellow eyes. Vertical pupils
glinted chrome green. He had forgotten about them, uncon-
sciously adjusting the exteroceptors' photosensitivity to com-
pensate for the mirror shades. He took the glasses from her
and started to put them on, but she reached out and stopped
him. "Oh, baby," she repeated. Then abruptly: "What's wrong
with Sumi?"

Seeing right through me, Jonny thought. He took a breath.
Not wanting to lie, he chose to remain silent. She would not
let go of his hands. "I have to see Easy Money," he said
finally.

"Tell me about Sumi."

"Please," he said. "She's going to be all right." Ice's face
changed with that. Rigid. He knew she understood. "Easy has
the cure," he offered.

"There's a cure?"

"That's what Easy took when he killed Raquin. Conover
didn't know what it was. He was moving it for some third
party."

She shook her head, releasing his hands at the same time.
"Hard to concentrate, sometimes," she said. "Makes you
wonder what we're doing here."

A particular head in the crowd caught his eye. "You going
to be all right?" he asked her.

She nodded, her jaw working silently, trying to contain the
rage and frustration. Jonny had felt it often enough to recog-
nize it. "Yeah." Then: "Liked your eyes; I did. Your eyes and
Sumi's hands. She has these callouses. Gives her character. I
liked that."

"Yeah, me too," Jonny said. He looked past her. The head
was moving. The one with the horns. "He's over there."

"Get moving," she said and kissed him, deeply, biting his
lower lip as she released him. "Against club rules, you know,
but what the fuck—it's probably my last night here anyway,
right?" She smiled at him.

"I'll get you on the way back."

"You better."

He left her then, feeling lousy at abandoning her full of
half-digested, half-understood information, but he concen-
trated on the head moving through the crowd before him. It
was odd seeing Easy in a suit. The tuxedo jacket fit him badly

across his narrow shoulders. Jonny caught up with the man and tapped him on the shoulder. "We've got business," Jonny said.

Easy turned at the sound of his voice, curling his lips in the distant approximation of a smile. "Love the new hardware, Jonny. I never thought you had it in you. We could get you a job upstairs anytime."

Jonny looked at his hands and realized that he was still holding the mirror shades. He slipped them on and followed Easy up the spiral staircase.

Upstairs were the prostitutes. The Water Trade, a tradition in Japan for hundreds of years, had provided for their presence. They were part of the decor, like the dwarf trees and the straw mats; an accepted style, part of the Floating World. And, as the "pleasure girls" had reflected their own time in the previous centuries of the trade, so the prostitutes in the Forest of Incandescent Bliss reflected theirs. They lounged about the halls on benches covered in thick brocades depicting scenes of ancient royalty and gardens where flowers formed intricate patterns like double and triple helices. They waited in doorways and on the railings of the stairways. Some of them were clothed in kimonos, most were partially nude, showing off their tattoos and grafts. A few wore nothing at all and those were the ones that disturbed Jonny the most. "Don't bother trying to guess their sex," Easy advised him. "Half of 'em can't even remember which way they started out."

At first, Jonny saw nothing special about the prostitutes, but that, he realized, was because he had not been prepared to understand them. Mouths like vaginas, vaginas and anuses like mouths. Hands that sprouted silicone elastomer penises instead of fingers. Each of the prostitutes seemed to have at least one extra set of genitalia, most (apparently) had moved or replaced their originals. Easy giggled and stroked the odd breast, the occasional scrotal sac as Jonny followed him. At one point, Easy snorted something from a plastic inhaler. Jonny caught a glimpse of the label: it was a cheap, mass-produced interferon nasal spray, Oki Kenko—Big Health—a common cold preventative.

Sniffing loudly, Easy said, "Now, what was that deal we were talking about?" They were on the upper floor of the pagoda.

"The second vial you took off Raquin," Jonny said. "Conover's authorized me to pay cash for it."

"Oh yeah. That." Jonny wondered if Easy was stoned. The horned man made a vague gesture with his hands, laughed drowsily. There were two other men in foreign-cut suits at the far end of the corridor. "Funniest damn thing, man," said Easy. "Remember back at the meat locker when you and me, we first talked about the deal? Well, the bitch had the place wired. Ain't that a scream? Heard every word of it. She's smarter than I thought."

By now, Jonny had stopped in his tracks and Easy was holding a Futukoro on him. "I'll take you apart, man." Easy reached behind Jonny, took his gun, then pushed him down the corridor. "Nimble Virtue's got the stuff now. I had to give it to her, you know? Get back on her good side. It's not like I can go back to Conover." The two men ahead—actually boys, Jonny saw; in different clothes they could have passed for Committee recruits with no problem at all—Jonny recognized the cut of their suits now. Like the Pakistani broadcaster on the restricted Link channel, long, almost knee-jackets and baggy, wide-waisted pants. Neo-Zoot, a current Arab style. "Anyway, you've got to deal with her now," Easy said. The Arabs never took their eyes off Jonny. The younger one, a handsome boy of about fifteen with black eyes and hair, gave him a wide feral smile and opened the door before him. "Muchas gracias, boys," said Easy, pushing Jonny through.

Inside, Nimble Virtue looked up, a tiny glazed tea cup poised before her lips. "My goodness," she said, her respirator sucking the words back down her throat. "We have a visitor." She sat behind an oversized desk constructed of opaque sheets of black glass supported by a frame of etched gold cylinders. An older man with salt-and-pepper hair was sitting across from her, also sipping tea and eyeing Jonny skeptically, as if contemplating the purchase of a used car.

"This is the man?" the gray-haired man asked Nimble Virtue. He was quite handsome, with hard, angular features, long, graceful hands, and the easy manner of someone used to being listened to. His suit was of better material than those of the boys in the hall—he had the same restless dark eyes as the one with the feral smile—but the style and cut were definitely Arab.

"Yes," Nimble Virtue said, pouring more tea, her exoskeleton whirring softly under her kimono as she raised and lowered her arm. Easy set Jonny's gun on the dark glass before her and leaned on an elaborate air purification system: ionizers, charcoal filter rigs, dehumidifiers. The room was very cold. Jonny thought of Nimble Virtue in the abattoir, the orbiting sandakan, unconciously recapitulating her childhood in her office, constructing within it a low-key approximation of the frozen vacuum of space.

"So whose little doggie are you?" Jonny asked the Arab.

"Jonny!" hissed Nimble Virtue.

The Arab smiled, turned to Nimble Virtue, and laughed. "You were right. His mouth works much faster than his mind. Still, this is no problem. It is his presence we require, not his intellect."

"You don't say. Who is this guy?" Jonny asked Nimble Virtue.

"Jonny, please," she said. "Sheik al-Qawi is a guest in my house. More than that, he and I have entered into certain business arrangements on behalf of the New Palestine Federation, of which he is a field representative." The words were clear, but her inflection was sing-song. An act for the new money, Jonny thought. Helpless geisha girl.

"I thought it smelled funny when I came here. That bad-meat political smell." He looked at Nimble Virtue. "You've finally found your place. You, Zamora, this clown—I hope you'll be very happy together."

Nimble Virtue's hand came to rest on a squat lacquered box that stood open on its end near the far corner of her desk. "Not political at all. Just the opposite," she said. A single jar sat in each side of the box. Embalmed things floating there, surrounded by dark purple velvet. Fetuses. "Sheik al-Qawi made me a very generous offer for the acquisition of—what? —an artifact. A bauble. I am merely acting as his agent in this matter."

"Right. And tell me those boys in the hall aren't hashishin," Jonny said. "These people consider going to the toilet a political act."

"It's funny that you should raise the question of political philosophies, Mister Qabbala," said al-Qawi, "since yours seems rather vague."

"That's because they don't exist," Jonny said. He checked his watch. The passing of time had begun to weigh on him.

Sumi was back on the hill. He thought of the second virus moving through her blood, waiting there like a time bomb. "You know, you guys slay me. Corporate types. Politicos. If I put a bullet through your fat face right now, they'd have you in a vat in ten minutes. And they'd keep you there till they could clone or construct or repair a body for you. That's the difference between your people and mine. We don't get a second chance. We're just dead."

The sheik brightened. "Then you are political!" he said. "Those are not the sentiments of an amoral man. Your manner and the company you keep bespeak a strong sense of purpose, even if you refuse to name it."

"Look pal, I'm just here to pick up some dope—"

"But surely you must agree that the imperialist forces now at work in Tokyo and Washington must be shown that plotting against the peoples of other sovereign nations cannot be tolerated."

"You want to deal or not?" Jonny asked Nimble Virtue. She turned her eyes up at him, still doing her little girl act. "Not now," she said.

"Then I'm out of here." Jonny headed for the door. Easy had his gun at the back of Jonny's head before he had taken two steps. "Hey, just a joke. I'd love to stay."

Al-Qawi stood and slammed his fist down on Nimble Virtue's desk. Her hand moved reflexively to the case containing her sons, steadying it. "I cannot believe such behavior," the sheik yelled. "That you can make jokes in the face of the hideous conspiracy in which your government is embroiled. That you, yourself, are a part of."

"Jonny-san," Nimble Virtue purred, "what Sheik al-Qawi is referring to are diabolocal plans hatched by certain war-loving officials in Tokyo and Washington to launch a sneak attack against the united Arab nations and bring about a terrible third world war."

Jonny looked at the two of them. He almost smiled, certain he was being gas-lighted. Nimble Virtue was not above setting up such a game just to confuse him and drive up the price of Conover's dope. However, there was something in al-Qawi's manner, a weariness around the eyes that was either very good acting or genuine anxiety. "Do you actually have the drugs?" Jonny asked.

"Yes, right there," said Nimble Virtue, pointing to a spot

on the floor before a screen inlaid with mother-of-pearl cranes.

"Let me see it."

"No!" shouted al-Qawi. "No more drug talk. As a man of God, I cannot permit it." His long hands cut the air in tense, rapid bursts. "Thanks to the good work of Madame Nimble Virtue, my trip to this sickening city has been a short and fruitful one. As you may have inferred, sir, you are the artifact I came here to find." He pushed a finger in Jonny's face. "Mister Qabbala, it is my duty and honor to arrest you in the name of the New Palestine Federation and the people of all oppressed nations everywhere."

"Great. Swell." To Nimble Virtue, Jonny said: "Did you sell this idiot my dope?"

"Do not play the fool with me, sir!" shouted al-Qawi. "Surely even you cannot endorse so mad an adventure as your government's alliance with the extraterrestrials!"

Jonny looked at the sheik, blinked once and inadvertently scrambled the resolution of the exteroceptors' pixel display. When the sheik's face came back, it had been reduced to a moving matrix of black-and-sand-colored squares. Easy Money sniffed loudly from his interferon inhaler. "I'll tell you exactly what I told the last lunatic that tried to tie me to the Alpha Rats: I don't know what the fuck you're talking about!"

"I do not believe you. I have studied your records, however. You live in the drugged ignorance of a man with a heavy burden," al-Qawi said. "It may interest you to know that the New Palestine Federation has intercepted a series of communiques between broadcast stations in Southern California and the moon. We now know that, using you as a go-between, your Eastern masters plan to link forces with the Alpha Rats, as you call them, and launch a sneak attack on Arab territories simultaneously from the Earth and the moon."

"Look, I've heard this moonman song before," said Jonny wearily. "The last time it was about dope. Now it's war. Why don't you people get your stories straight?" He shook his head, finally correcting the pixel display. Easy Money was behind him, sniffing and laughing to himself. "What's your story? You suddenly develop a political conscience?"

Easy shrugged, the hand with the gun resting by his side. "Don't ask me. You're the one hangs out with anarchists."

"I am, Mister Qabbala, prepared to offer you a deal," al-Qawi said.

"A deal?"

"Yes. Negotiate with the extraterrestrials on behalf of the New Palestine Federation. Convince them to turn their weapons on your puppet masters in the East. For this, the Federation will grant you a full pardon for crimes against the Arab people and"—he smiled at Jonny—"return to you a reasonable profit for your services."

"You're crazier than Zamora," Jonny said. "He only accused me of being a go-fer for a smuggler lord. You think I'm hanging fast and true with the Alpha Rats myself."

"Aren't you?"

"No!"

The sheik shook his head. "This world is an unkind place, Mister Qabbala. I am attempting to extend to you the hand of friendship."

"Why? So you people can finish that stupid war? Don't get me wrong—I don't think this place would be any worse under Arab rule, but any dirty little wars you guys start, it's the people in the street—we're the ones that get hurt." Jonny pointed out the window. "Not *your* people, fucker, *mine*."

Al-Qawi nodded gravely, hands clasped behind his back. "In that case, Mister Qabbala, you are my prisoner. You have obviously deserted your own government to work for terrorists and anarchists. However, you will not shirk your responsibility to the New Palestine Federation."

Jonny, knowing Easy was watching him, kicked his boot into Nimble Virtue's desk, knocking off the false heel. The Futukoro went off precisely where Jonny was not. He was rolling across his shoulders away from Nimble Virtue's desk, scooping up his own gun on the way. He kept it low, sending a round into the floor near Easy.

A sheet of flame hit the ceiling as the shell exploded in the hyper-oxygenated air. Easy landed in a heap across the room, over by the air purification set-up. Jonny sprinted to the door and threw the security bolts. Then he turned his gun on Nimble Virtue. "Give me that dope, goddammit!"

"What have you done?" she screamed. Shaking, Nimble Virtue rose from behind her desk and went to where al-Qawi lay, his legs twisted under him, his neck bent at a peculiar angle. Her respirator was clicking rapidly beneath her kimono;

Jonny could hear the air being forced in and out of her with-ered lungs. "He was taking me with him!" she shouted. Then, quietly: "He was taking me with him. It was part of the deal."

Jonny moved over to the floor safe. "Give me the dope," he said. Someone was pounding frantically on the office door.

Nimble Virtue ignored him, touching the stretched-out body of the Arab, attending him with quick, birdlike move-ments. "I was going away," she said, covering her face with her hands. No act this time, Jonny knew.

"Listen to me," he told her. "A friend of mine is sick. She needs this stuff badly."

Nimble Virtue turned and looked at him. "Good!" she said. "I hope she dies. Rots and dies like me—like I have to stay here. In this city." She stood and walked to the far side of the desk, rubbing at her red-rimmed eyes. "Zamora will kill me."

"Please, give me the dope."

"No."

The pounding on the door got louder. Jonny grabbed one of the bottles from the desk and held it over his head. The little fetus, disturbed in its fluid, bumped gently against the side. "Give it to me."

"Go to hell."

His arm snapped out and Nimble Virtue screamed. There was no crash. Jonny held out his hand, showing her the palmed bottle.

"All right," she said, and moved shakily toward him, dropping stiffly to her knees, her exoskeleton whining with the unaccustomed motion.

Jonny held his gun on her as she removed a segment of polished wood from the floor and entered a code on a ten-key pad. The soft hiss of pneumatic bolts withdrawing. As Nimble Virtue reached into the safe, Jonny stopped her. He pushed his hand past hers and found the old pistol lying near the top. A tarnished Derringer two-shot, yellowed ivory grip with over-and-under barrels, each holding a single .38 hollow-point shell. He pocketed the gun and reached in again, coming up this time with a brushed aluminum Halliburton travel case. Inside was a small black vacuum bottle. Taking it, he backed away from the safe, keeping his back to the wall. Nimble Virtue was standing over al-Qawi again, staring down at the sheik, her eyes flat and dull like blank video monitors. Over by the air purifier, Easy Money moaned.

A shot, then two more from the hall splintered the wood and metal of the office door. Jonny took a wide-legged stance and fired at it twice. What was left of the door exploded, peppering the room with burning wood and metal. He heard Nimble Virtue breathe in sharply. Over by the safe, the velvet-lined case lay on the floor, the two little bottles shattered amidst the glassy black wreckage of the collapsed desk, old alcohol reek filling the room. Nimble Virtue's mouth was open; a moment later she screamed—a single note, high and keening. Running down the stairs, Jonny could still hear her.

Pour gasoline on an ant hill; light it. Watch the insects pour from the mound, crazed and sizzling. That was the main floor of the Forest of Incandescent Bliss. At the sound of the first shot, paranoid gangster reflexes had kicked in. Half the club was making for the doors, sure the cops or the Committee— somebody in uniform—was raiding the place. Frightened old men threw handfuls of cash and pills at anybody who came near them.

The other half of the club had stubbornly stayed put, convinced that they had been led into a trap. Yakuza and Panteras lay bloody and dying across Go boards and tea pots where they had blown holes in each other at point-blank range. Prostitutes, orifices flexing in silent, convulsive screams, scrambled down the stairs. Jonny fell into step with them, hitting the main floor behind a curtain of manufactured flesh.

Ice was by the bar, signaling to someone. Rapid variants of Amerslan, fingers on lips, brushing the back of a hand. She spotted him when he waved and ran over. They huddled by the spiral stairs.

"You got the stuff?"

He held up the vacuum bottle. "Right here."

"Great. Zamora never showed. We gotta rendezvous with the others." She looked over his shoulder—"No!"—and pushed him to the ground as the gun went off.

There was a smoking hole on the center of Ice's chest, but no blood—the Futukoro shell having cauterized the wound even as it made it.

"Give me the dope, Jonny."

He swore the voice had come from inside his head. He looked at Ice, insane for that moment, and knew he had killed

her. A black metallic wind blew through his bones and he
heard the voice again.

"Hand it over like now, man."

Outside him that time. Easy Money. He was above them on
the stairs, one satyr horn broken off at the scalp, his left elbow
stiff, dribbling blood down his arm.

"I need that dope, man." Down a step. "The bitch's gone
nuts. Gotta have Conover's juice to stake myself. Com-
prende?" This time Jonny did not aim for the feet, but Easy's
head. He missed anyway. The explosion brought down a good
portion of the staircase, and Easy jumped clear on the far side.

Jonny kicked at the wreckage of carved wood, dragons in
splinters, pig-iron reinforcement rods sticking like bones from
the pile. He knelt beside Ice, who was staring down at the
hole in her chest, gingerly touching the blackened skin around
the edges.

"I always wondered what this felt like," she said, drunken
wonder slurred in her voice. He cradled her head in his lap,
gangsters, gunsels, and hangers-on still massing for the door,
clawing at each other. She looked at him and a shiver passed
through her body. "You're a big boy now, Jonny, whether you
like it or not. Sumi can't cover your ass like I can." Blood,
through tiny cracks like miniature lava flows, was beginning
to seep from her wound. "You gonna help us, Jonny? You're a
Croaker. Always have been. You walk away, though, you're
one of them. And they'll do us like this forever." She looked
at her wound, touched a bloody hand to his cheek. "Sweet
Jonny. You and Sumi—my babies—"

He let her still head slide off his lap and stood, trembling
and crying. His new eyes did not permit tears, but kept flash-
ing him stored images of the last few hours. The dead fetuses.
Dogs, massive and terrified, tearing at each other. The clock-
work movement of multicolored muscles. Feral smile of the
hashishin.

Illusion, he thought. Folly. Maya.

For the first time in his life, shaking and blubbering in the
club, Jonny had a clear mental picture of what the Alpha Rats
looked like. They looked like al-Qawi, like Zamora and Nim-
ble Virtue, the pimps, the politicians, the wheeler-dealers.
The Alpha Rats were the perfect excuse, the ultimate evasion.
It had been that way for a thousand years; Jonny knew that
much of history. The powers that be required enemies as much

as they needed friends, and they could not live without scape-
goats to keep their propaganda machines working. In earlier
centuries it had been the Jews, the blacks, the homosexuals,
the Hispanics. But the closed economic systems of their world
had made old-fashioned bigotry impractical. Like technology,
commerce, and travel: the big lie had expanded outward to
embrace the rest of the galaxy. And why not? Jonny thought.
It's in our blood by now.

He looked at his hand and, to his horror, realized that the
vacuum bottle was no longer there. Sometime after Ice had
been shot, he had let it go. He dropped to his hands and
knees, moving frantically between the gangsters' running feet.
And spotted it across the room—wedged under the skirt of a
Link screen showing Aoki Vega in a Kabuki-porn version of
Casablanca.

Between the shadows and the feet, the angry voices and
breaking glass, Jonny dived for the bottle, and felt his hand
close around it. Then as quickly, it was gone. Shattered in his
grip, a clear sticky liquid dripping onto his lap, gray frag-
ments of industrial glass all around him. In the hills, machines
skipped a beat. Sumi convulsed. Jonny looked up at Easy and
the smoking gun as the one-horned man said "Now nobody
has it" and limped out the door.

Jonny followed him, pushing his way through the thinning
crowd, the German pistol before him. Easy was just turning
the corner at the far end of the pagoda. The Forest's private
security was out. Two men moved through the crowd to inter-
cept Jonny. He waited until they were a few meters away and
calmly blew them to pieces. At the lake's edge, he took a
hovercraft and headed back to shore, ran until his sides ached,
filthy and red-eyed, to La Poupée. In the air recirculation
plant he collapsed beneath two enormous filter cylinders and
retched. Outside, he found a motorcycle in the employees'
parking lot. A lithium-battery-powered BMW. The owner had
hooked an air compressor to the exhaust outlet; the bike roared
and sputtered like an old-style piston-engine model. Jonny
gunned the bike and took off.

12

DEATH AND REVELATION IN A DARK BAR
ON A BAD NIGHT
AT THE END OF THE WORLD

SAND WAS BLOWING in from the desert, flaking paint from parked cars, filling the bottoms of drained swimming pools. Death owned the streets. Two A.M., November second, two hours into the Day of the Dead: *Dia de los Muertos*. Processions filled the thoroughfares of Hollywood like some graveyard Mardi Gras. Lepers danced together in papier-maché skulls behind white-robed bishops carrying enormous chrome crucifixes, hologram Christs floating a few centimeters above the crossbars, writhing in agony for all their sins. Behind the hills, orange flared and lit the sky from the burn-off towers at the German synth-fuel plant to the north. Jonny licked sand from his lips. He had never seen so many people in one place. Zombie Analytics flashed the crowd images of dead pop stars, superimposing the outlines of their own bones on the famous faces. Even the Piranhas were there, so far untouched by the plague, but now drawn from the safety of their internal exile by the docks to the more inviting lights of the boulevard.

When he first saw Death lingering at the back of the parade, skull molded from old newsrags and clutching a crude sickle of pounded metal, Jonny charged, gunning the big BMW up onto the sidewalk. But he never connected. Never killed Death. It always saw him coming or Jonny had to turn the bike at the last minute when he heard human voices screaming from inside the paper skulls. And each time he rode away, he grew more desperate, more furious, knowing that Death had fooled him again.

Somehow, he ended up at Carnaby's Pit. The parade was

moving quickly down the boulevard. Jonny stood alone before
the chained entrance, reading a notice printed in six languages
that was plastered across the rusted and pockmarked metal
doors:

WARNING

Public buildings, except those constructed exclusively
for the use of religious expression, are OFF-LIMITS to
gatherings of three persons or more.
Emergency Ordinance #9354A—By authority of:
The Committee for Public Health

The parade was blocks away now, the sound of music and
voices fading fast. Everything was dying. He looked around
for the mercado. (No way those people would miss a night
like this.) But all he could find were glassy scars in the asphalt
where the grills had sat, an ancient scratch-pattern indicating
the placement of tent poles. Jonny pulled the SIG Sauer from
his jacket pocket and blew the doors to Carnaby's Pit off their
hinges. The pistol's breech remained open this time, meaning
he had run out of bullets. He tossed the gun away. Clouds of
green, metallic flies buzzed loudly into the night through the
the Pit's ruined doors.

Inside, the game room stood silent, all dust-shadows and
hints of greasy fingerprints where light from the street struck
glass. Jonny had never seen the club like this before. In the
weak mercury-vapor light, without the sound and the colors of
the games to distract him, the place seemed small, pathetic
even. Lengths of frayed copper wires covered the walls, broke
up the ceiling into a water-stained grid behind the dead holo-
projectors.

In the main room, a stack of St. Peter's Krupp-Verwand-
lungsinhalt amps had fallen over. To Jonny's exteroceptors,
the Freon leaking from around the speaker cones appeared to
shimmer in turquoise pools. The air was damp and stale, close
around him. Jonny shivered, looked back the way he had
come in, and watched sand sift in through the open doors.
Death was in the club with him. Jonny could feel its presence.
He pulled Nimble Virtue's Derringer from his pocket and went
into a crouch, stalking Death through the jungle of abandoned
chairs and broken glasses, finally spotting it behind the bar.

Jonny recognized Death from his dreams. The mirror shades gave it away.

The kick from the little Derringer, when he fired, nearly broke his wrist, but Death was gone. The sound of the mirror shattering behind the hollow-point shell caught him off guard. By the time he scrambled behind the bar and understood what he had done, he was shivering again, realizing he had wanted to do it for a long time.

If death was an illusion, as the roshis had told him, then, Jonny reasoned, he had just proved the lie of his own existence. He kicked at shards of the broken mirror with the toe of his boot and decided he needed a drink to celebrate the discovery of his true nature.

Shelves behind him held all manner of liquor: domestic, imported, and bootleg. Jonny selected an unopened bottle of Burmese tequila and drank deeply. Gin, he reflected, would have served him better at this point, but he could not stand the taste of the stuff neat. He laughed at the idea of taste.

What is taste when you don't exist?

"There's this old man, comes to a Buddhist priest, see," Jonny said to the empty room. "Turns out he's the ghost of another Buddhist priest who's been reincarnated five hundred times as a fox." He took another pull from the bottle. "In life, he'd argued that the laws of cause and effect do not apply to enlightened beings. So here the poor fucker is, you know, five hundred times—pissing in the woods, freezing in the winter and eating raw squirrel. And the other priest says: 'Schmuck, of course cause and effect applies to enlightened beings.' And the ghost disappears, suddenly enlightened. He doesn't have to be a fox any more." Jonny moved around to the front of the bar, dropped onto a stool and propped the bottle on his knee, the tequila already half gone.

"I have swallowed every kind of shit," he said.

Across the room, near the pile of fallen German amplifiers, a swarm of flies was moving over the carcass of some dead animal. Massed together like that in the dark bar, the insects looked to Jonny something like waves kicked up on the shore of some crazy-quilt ocean. He giggled and lurched to his feet, threading his way drunkenly through the club, deliberately kicking over some chairs and tables as he went.

Jonny approached the body slowly. From the bar it had looked pretty big for a rat, but that it could be human had not occurred to him until he was right up on it. Batting at flies that buzzed around his face, Jonny edged around the corpse, noting the discolored tumors on its arms, the leonine welling of the face, all the obvious symptoms of the virus's mock-leprosy. The corpse's limbs were twisted, back arched until the body was bent almost double, fingers splayed, hands turned back on themselves at the wrists in the spastic posture of advanced neuro-syphilis. Jonny forced himself to lean closer and look into the half-open mouth. Standing up, he momentarily fingered the edge of the soiled apron, thinking that the body did not look much like Random any more.

Jonny did not turn when he heard the footsteps, expecting it to be Zamora or some Committee boy come to take him away. When the steps came to a stop a few meters off, he turned and saw Groucho brushing sand from his English schoolboy jacket. "He swallowed his tongue," Jonny told the anarchist.

"I'm sorry," Groucho said. "I've seen a lot like this these last few weeks. Gonna be a lot more, too."

"You come looking for me?"

Groucho nodded. "Yeah. I figure I've got a vested interest in you."

Jonny took a drink from his bottle. "How'd you know I'd be here?"

"Isn't this where you always end up?"

"Yeah. I guess." Jonny shrugged. "Kind of shabby little place to run and hide, huh?" He took another drink and threw the empty bottle back toward the bar, listening to it shatter. "Ice is dead," he said quickly.

"I heard. I'm sorry, man," said Groucho. "So what are you going to do now?"

"I don't know," Jonny mumbled, crouching down near Random's body. "Lotta bottles to work through," he said, gesturing back toward the bar.

"Yeah, always the clear thinker. I knew we could count on you."

"Save that shit for your own people, okay?"

Groucho leaned under a nearby table and picked up a small silver bell from the floor; he rang it softly as he spoke. "What were you doing at the Forest of Incandescent Bliss tonight?"

"There's a cure for the virus. I was supposed to pick it up, only Easy Money blew away the container it was in and now it's gone," said Jonny. Bending, he touched one of Random's arms, disturbing the flies that rose, droning, into the air. "Sumi's infected, you know. Gonna die just like Random. Pretty surreal way to go, huh?" Turning, he swung a drunken fist at Groucho, but the anarchist danced out of the way. "What would your fucking surrealists say about that?" Jonny shouted.

"So you're just going to let her die like that?" Groucho asked. He bent again and came up with a toy switchblade, about the length of his thumb.

"What are you talking about?"

"I'm saying that if you love her, you're going to take some responsibility." With his long fingers, Groucho *snicked* the tiny knife open-closed a couple of times. "Ever since we left the fish farm, I've been thinking how all these little bits, how all the shit that's been floating around you is possibly related. I heard from some people that Conover was the one that was moving that layered virus that got loose. Then, when Zamora picked you up, he starts talking about spacemen and how he wants you to turn Conover for him. All the time, though, he's planning a raid to take out all the lords and the gangs with them. And this is happening at the same time the city's going balls-up from this plague."

"You think Zamora might have planned all this?"

"I don't know yet," said the anarchist. "Doesn't really sound like him, though. A bit subtle."

Jonny stood, brushed away some flies that had landed on his aviators. "There was this Arab at the Forest tonight, he was talking about the Alpha Rats. Said something about a war."

"Well, man, we got our own war right here," Groucho told him. When he leaned over this time, he was holding a key ring with a plastic Ganesha on top; cheap paste rhinestones glittered in the elephant-god's eyes. He dropped the key ring and switchblade into his jacket pocket. "I wanted to tell you —Zamora's moving on the lords tonight. Guess he figures it's a holiday, so half the city'll be blasted. We're moving, too. All the gangs."

"Jesus," Jonny said. "Are you guys ready?"

"Vyctor Vector's waiting out in the van with Man Ray, so we've got the Naginata Sisters and the Funky Gurus, también.

We're stronger than Zamora realizes." Groucho smiled. "Besides, amantadine supplies're running pretty thin around here. If the Committee doesn't get you, seems like the virus will. Nobody's got much to lose anymore."

"What about going to the lords for help?"

"The lords?" Groucho said. "Are you really that naive? The lords protect themselves. Period. They're no better than Zamora."

"What are you talking about? Not all the lords are sell-outs like Nimble Virtue."

"Sure they are. This is big business, Jack. The big fix. The algebra of need." The anarchist gestured as he spoke, his hands open wide. "I mean, if you're in the desert, you sell the natives ice water, right? Nimble Virtue, Conover, and the rest have a captive market here, and they like it that way. This underground market drives the prices of their goods right through the roof. The lords aren't dealers, they're vampires. They live on pain. And you're as much a part of it as they are."

Jonny frowned. "I sold medicine. People needed me."

"You're just afraid to face the real issue," Groucho said. "By selling Conover's shit you are just another part of the dope organism. People don't need you. They need to be free of this ridiculous cycle of drugs and pain. Free from the Committee and the lords, because they're two sides of the same coin. One can't exist without the other. This whole city is built on bones. And you've helped them do it, Jonny. That's what I mean about taking responsibility."

Jonny walked back to the bar and started sorting through the various bottles. At the back of the bottom shelf he found a half-empty quart of mescal and set it on the bar. The small hallucinogenic worm inside bobbed momentarily to the top of the golden liquor. Dead fetuses. He saw Nimble Virtue's children floating in alcohol. Pushing the bottle aside, Jonny said to Groucho, "If I'm such puke, what the hell are you doing here?"

"I'm here because, in the end, I don't think you are one of them," said Groucho. He came to the bar, still ringing the silver bell in his left hand. "You're what those old warriors used to call Dragon-head-Snake-body. You're intelligent; you've got courage and integrity, but you keep sabotaging yourself through fear and stupidity." The anarchist picked up something the size of a playing card from the bar. When he touched it, the card flashed a series of animated views of Japanese casinos and resorts, spewing a prerecorded sales-pitch in a tinny female voice. "Also, I thought you might be able to help the revolution. Ice liked you and I wanted to keep her happy. Zamora was interested in you and so was Conover. I thought maybe we could make use of that somewhere along the way." He looked up at Jonny. "Revolution's a hard nut. See what happens to us? I guess I was using you, too."

"If I go back to Conover's, will you go with me?" Jonny asked.

Groucho shook his head. "There's no time. We've got a lot to set up if we're gonna take on the Committee tonight."

"Sorry. A silly question."

"I know where Conover's place is," Groucho said. "I'll meet you there later if I can."

Jonny nodded. He took the mescal bottle and set it back on the shelf behind the bar. Removing his mirror shades, he turned to Groucho, making sure the man got a good look at his new eyes. The anarchist raised his eyebrows a fraction of a centimeter, but that was all. "These exteroceptors are funny," Jonny said. "It's like watching a movie or something. Kind of a detached feeling. I don't know what to do anymore."

"Here," Groucho said, and handed him the little silver bell. "For luck. And remember: thought is an illusion." He touched his chest. "This is an illusion. Fear, confusion, dread—the worst elements of your life can lead to enlightenment as easily as the best. When the time comes to act, you'll do all right."

The silhouette of a tall woman was framed in the door of the club. She wore tight leather pants and boots, a racing top crossed by studded leather straps; in her hand was some kind of heavy wooden staff that was almost as tall as she. Her skin shone silver in the street light, a heavy layer of metal-based makeup covering all her exposed skin, except for a band around her eyes. Naginata war paint. "Groucho, we gotta hit it," said the woman. "Hiya, Jonny."

"How're you doing, Vyctor?" he called.

The woman shrugged. "Getting ready to die right. Heard about Ice. Sorry, man. I gotta tell you, though, I was kinda jealous when she moved in with you and Sumi. I really went for her."

"You got good taste, Vyctor."

"You know it. Groucho, I'll see you outside." She went out then, her shadow curving over the small drifts of sand that were collecting around the fallen doors.

Jonny left the mirror shades on the bar and followed Groucho out of the club. In the game parlor, he said to the anarchist, "So what are you, anyway? You really an anarquista or just some loco with a bodhisattva complex?"

They continued out under the awning, through the falling sand to the van parked across the street. Finally, Groucho grinned. "Tell you the truth," he said, "I spend most of my time feeling like everybody's mother." Man Ray nodded as Jonny came over. The Funky Guru's new van was as big as his old one, with the same ugly-beautiful lines. Something like a mechanical claw protruded from one side, hydraulic digits tense against the body of the vehicle. Groucho pointed to Jonny's motorcycle. "You have fuel?" Jonny nodded, walked over to the bike and climbed aboard. "You take care, Jonny," called Vyctor. Jonny waved and kicked the bike awake. Then he and the van moved off in opposite directions.

From the desert, the wind was picking up, hard-blown grit biting into the backs of his hands, grinding between his teeth. The heat of the night and the tequila came down hard on him. Jonny felt himself moving through a dream-time, no longer trusting or quite believing in anything he saw. Heading north out of Hollywood, he watched bands of junkies roaming the streets eating piles of sugar-candy skulls they had stolen from merchants below. Monks hiding their tumors behind things like fencing masks took the confessions of lepers squatting in Griffith Park, while nearby, Neo-Mayanists cut the beating hearts out of captured Committee boys, offering them up to gods whose names they had forgotten, begging for forgiveness and an end to the plague. Writers had been busy with their canisters of compressed acid, turning the walls outside the park into a fair representation of the skull walls at Chichen Itza. They had left messages behind, too:

BOMB TOKYO NOW
BOMB L.A. NOW
BOMB EVERYTHING

Jonny swerved to avoid some animal in the road and al-
most flipped the bike before he realized that there was nothing
there. He kept flashing on recordings of Ice's face: the mo-
ment she saw his cat eyes, when she kissed him in the Forest,
as she lay dying. He had not yet accepted that she could really
be dead and he knew that that was good. Barely functional as
he was now, Jonny understood that some animal survival
mechanism in his brain had cut in during the course of the last
few hours, pumping him full of specific neural inhibitors, pre-
venting him from accepting the true nature of his loss. He
knew it was there, though. The loss. He imagined that he
could feel it, like a sac of poison lodged at the back of his
skull, ready to burst when all this was over.

He throttled up on the bike and skidded around a section of
asphalt that was jutting at an angle from the narrow roadbed.
The air compressors attached to the BMW's exhaust obliter-
ated all sound but their own, while the thermographic display
in Jonny's exteroceptors glazed the park into a series of slick
surfaces like the ones he had seen in a Dali landscape.

Nearing the top of the hill, Jonny began to consider the
notion of payback. It seemed to him that if he was to take the
responsibility he had been avoiding all this time, others ought
to do the same. There was blame here to be laid at somebody's
feet. But whose? Ice was dead, and Skid and Raquin before
her. Soon Sumi would be gone, too. Because of his failure to
salvage her cure? Because Easy Money had stolen Conover's
virus? Or was it because he had left Sumi alone for so long
while running from Zamora?

Yes, to all those questions. But was that enough? Jonny
sensed it went deeper than any of that, but the chain of respon-
sibility and blame, when he tried to trace it back to its source,
seemed endless, extending beyond any of their lifetimes.

How many will die tonight? he wondered.

How many have died already?

Jonny tried to count up the bodies, the friends and acquain-
tances that had snuffed it or disappeared over the years. He
could not remember them all. Again the chain—one face
always leading to another. For a few he could remember no
name, just the movement of a hand, the tilt of a head or a
panther-tattooed shoulder.

Jonny thought of Ice, in many ways just another one-per-
center, living the same foolish life as any of them, dying the

same senseless death, and all the while being unaware that it had all been laid for her in advance. Like a ship's course computed, entered, and executed, she had lived according to the strange process that seemed to take them all in the end, Random, Skid, and the rest. They were the dead wandering the streets on Dia de los Muertos. Drifting their whole lives through the city, living by rules they never really understood. The cops had been part of it. The Committee. And yeah, Jonny thought, the dealers, too. He had been a part of it as much as anyone, supplying the medicine and the dope that kept the people docile. Groucho's city of bones became more real, more palpable each time he considered it.

Lights on the hill above startled him. Jonny swung the BMW onto the driveway leading to Conover's mansion, wondering why the hologram dome was down. Sand whispered through the trees. He left the bike in the drive and made his way to the house through the bamboo grove, hoping that the billowing sand was dense enough to confound the smuggler lord's surveillance equipment.

The front door of the Japanese wing was open. Sprawled face-down in the walkway was one of the smuggler lord's medical techs, a hole from what looked like a Futukoro shell burned in the man's back. Inside the house there were more bodies, techs and security staff, some lying in groups, others meters away where they had been gunned down trying to run. In the art-glutted dining room in the Victorian wing, soft Elizabethan music was coming from the hidden speakers; the sound chip on the stereo read, "William Williams: Sonata in Imitation of Birds." He found the African staff dead, scattered through the kitchen and service corridors.

Working his way back through the house, Jonny located the elevator he had used the day they had given him his new eyes. Not certain of exactly where he was going, he punched in the code for the lowest level. He pulled the Derringer from his pocket, turned it over in his hand once, and put it away. It would not do him a hell of a lot of good against a Futukoro.

In the clinic area were more dead techs. The hall was littered with overturned drug carts, Pyrex culture dishes, and leaking drug vials. Jonny saw Yukiko's body, recognized a couple of the Russians who had assisted on his eye surgery. A security man lay dead on his back; most of one shoulder and his lower jaw had been shot away. He was holding a small cardboard box. Scattered around the guard's head like a plastic numbus were dozens of interferon inhalors similar to the one Easy had been using. Jonny knelt by the guard's body and stole his Futukoro. The man had not even gotten it out of the holster.

It did not take Jonny long to find Sumi's room.

At the bend in the garbage-strewn corridor was a door marked with diamond-shaped warning signs: orange biohazard marker, color-coded symbols for flammable liquids and cryo-protectants.

The door was locked, and when he could not kick it open, he shot the lock off. Inside, he passed through a short retrofit airlock, ignoring neat piles of sterile paper gowns and caps, to a dust-free clean room beyond. Inside, the sterile chamber echoed with the steady whining of malfunctioning life-support units and the gurgling of protein vats. Near the circular vats, four nude male bodies were laid out on what looked like stain-less-steel autopsy tables. From the sour smell of the place, Jonny guessed that it had been at least twenty-four hours since the life-support had shut down.

Looking into the protein vats, Jonny found what at first he took to be several dead eels, drifting limply in the swirling solution like individual strands of seaweed. The animals had been dissected bilaterally, exposing the entire length of each spinal column. When he saw the delicate Toshiba micromani-pulators poised over each open back, Jonny realized that the animals were lampreys. He remembered Conover telling him that the nerve tissue his techs had spliced into Jonny's injured shoulder had been grown in a specially bred variety of the animal. Seeing them now, Jonny was glad the poor fuckers were dead.

He touched one of the manipulators, running his fingers along the rows of microscopic lasers that sliced intact tissue from the lampreys' backs. A bundle of mil-thin wires ran from the base of each manipulator and was secured to node points along the exposed spines. He touched one of the bundles. A tail twitched. Jawless mouth gaped. "Shit," Jonny said and re-leased the manipulator, realizing (and the realization turned his stomach) that the animals were still alive, swimming in their absent way against the whirling current of the protein solution, alien tissues taking root in their backs.

That's when he found Conover, chest neatly lasered open,

lying on one of the autopsy tables. Jonny had turned in disgust
from the lamprey tank and froze, staring down at the body of
the smuggler lord lying under ten centimeters of clear liquid.
But it was not the Conover Jonny knew. It was the Conover he
had seen in photos in the storage room that earlier night. The
Conover from Central America in the nineteen eighties:
healthier, before the Greenies addiction had set in. Jonny
checked the other tables and found Conovers lying on each of
them, sunk in the same fluid, torsos neatly split from crotch to
chin. All the bodies were wired into a complex array of life-
support units. They were all missing certain organs—livers,
stomachs, hearts, and pancreases mostly. Jonny knew that
what he was looking at was essentially a farm.

Conover had become a parasite, feeding on himself. Some-
where in his drug-ruined body, his techs must have found
some cells that the Greenies had not yet invaded. They had
used these to clone copies of the smuggler lord to use for
patch jobs. The liquid in which they floated would be some
kind of perfluorocarbon, Jonny guessed, to keep the bodies
oxygenated. He just stared. It was amazing; suicide and
murder all rolled into one package. The taste of tequila and
bile was strong in his throat. Jonny fled through a door
beyond the tables, away from the butchered young men.

The room he entered was still and very cold. The thermo-
graphic readout in his eyes showed it to him as an almost
seamless blue surface, broken here and there by neon-red
patches of warmer electronic equipment. Some kind of gas
vapor was crusting on cryogenic pipe inlets, drifting in white
clouds to the floor. A dozen gray laminated tanks—(he
thought of coffins or sealed specimen cases)—stood against
the walls. Jonny spotted her in the only tank that was occu-
pied, near the far end. When he tried to wipe a layer of frost
from the Lexan faceplate, his fingers froze to it instantly. He
jerked his hand away, stifling a small cry of pain as he left
some skin behind. Using his jacket sleeve, he rubbed at the
port until he could see her face clearly.

Sumi appeared to be asleep in the cryogenic tank. A VDT
inset at chest level in the gray laminate displayed her life
readings as a series of slow-moving horizontal lines, hills and
valleys indicating her body's various autonomic functions.
The top of the screen was dominated by an animated 3D dis-
play of some growing crystal. For some reason, it reminded

Jonny of a cocoon; he kept expecting to see some new form of plant or animal life burst suddenly from the fragile eggshell facets that the crystal kept unfolding from within itself. Someone had written "L VIRUS" on a strip of surgical tape and stuck it to the VDT just below the crystal display. Jonny nodded, recognizing the animation as a growth sequence. He had a pretty good idea of just what the programmers had been modeling when they created the display. The lesions around Sumi's mouth confirmed this.

Jonny backed away from the cylinder, spun and kicked savagely at the door to the clean room, his face hot. All the half-conscious illusions of a daring rescue he had been nursing up the hill were dying fast. He prowled the edges of the frigid room, cursing to himself, punched a Sony monitor off a work station and kicked it into a wall, shattering the screen.

A minute later, he was standing in front of the tank in which Sumi slept. "They never told us how it worked," he explained. "So naturally it got all fucked up." It was an apology of sorts.

The concussion from the first Futukoro round cracked the Lexan plate above Sumi's face. Steam from the super-cooled liquid inside screamed through the broken plastic, condensing in the air as a miniature whirlwind of ice. Jonny kept on firing, pumping round after hot round through the walls of the cylinder until the room was full of freezing white vapor and the life readings on the tank registered as a series of flat, unwavering lines.

When some of the vapor had cleared and he could see again, Jonny peered through the cracked Lexan to find that Sumi's face had remained unchanged. He was aware, on some wordless level, that from that moment on he would be utterly alone. But he found himself comforted by Sumi's face, the lines of her cheeks, the set of her lips. There was no hint at all of pain or betrayal in her smooth features. Jonny stepped back. Calmly, grateful, he placed the barrel of the Futukoro between his teeth and aimed for the back of his head. Closing his eyes, he was filled with an odd sense of euphoria, thinking: from now on, we make our own rules.

He pulled the trigger.

The gun clicked once.

Jonny shouted and threw the thing across the room. Behind

him, the door to the clean room slid open and Conover came in. Not one of the pretty boys on the autopsy slabs, Jonny saw, but the red-eyed death's head he knew. He was sure the smuggler lord had been watching him. "Listen, son—" Conover began.

"You pig!" Jonny shouted. "How could you do that to her? Treat her like a piece of meat!"

"I never intended for you to see this," Conover said. He opened his hands in a gesture of sympathy. "Really, we had no choice. She could have infected everybody here."

Jonny looked back at Sumi in the cryogenic tank. Most of the fluid had evaporated, leaving a few feeble streams of vapor trailing from holes where the Futukoro shells had breached the plating. "Did you kill all those people upstairs?" Jonny asked.

"I'm afraid so," Conover said. He moved to sit on the edge of a disconnected Hitachi CT scanner. Jonny noticed that the smuggler lord was holding a Futukoro loosely at his side. "In a sense, though, they were already dead. Between the virus and Zamora, if they didn't die now, they would be gone very soon." He shrugged. "Besides, I'm leaving. The life's gone out of it. L.A.'s no place for me anymore."

"What are you talking about? You're leaving Last Ass?"

Conover lit one of his brightly colored Shermans and nodded. "Yes, my ride ought to be here in a few hours. You interested in coming?"

"Where are you going?"

Conover smiled. "New Hope."

"What?"

"I think you should come," the smuggler lord said. "In fact, I insist on it." Conover had moved the Futukoro so that it was lying across his legs, pointing casually in the direction of Jonny's midsection.

Jonny felt his brain frosting over, as if he were asleep and dreaming in one of the cases next to Sumi. "Mister Conover, what the fuck is going on here?"

"It's the end of the world, son."

"Great. Think anyone'll notice?" Jonny asked. He looked at Sumi and shook his head, thinking that, once again, he had failed her.

Conover got up, dropped an avuncular arm around Jonny's

shoulders, and said, "Don't sweat it, son. We've got big plans for you." He steered Jonny out of the clean room, upstairs and through the Victorian wing toward the roof. "There's so much to say before our ride gets here, but if we hurry, I think we might just have time to give you the fifty-cent tour of the universe."

— 13 —————————

THE FIFTY-CENT TOUR
OF THE UNIVERSE ————————

"YES, THE END of the world, son, can't you smell it? No finer time to be alive." Conover chuckled reflectively, moving Jonny along a dark and narrow service staircase, idly jabbing him in the back with the barrel of the Futukoro.

"It's the war, isn't it?" asked Jonny. "The Tokyo Alliance and New Palestine. They're finally going to do it."

Conover nodded sleepily. "What else?" he answered, shivered. He mumbled "Need a shot." Then, louder: "Yes, the war. Don't look so surprised, son. Historically speaking, it's long overdue."

Jonny shook his head. "Christ, then that Arab was telling the truth."

"Arab?"

"There was this Arab at the Forest of Incandescent Bliss. Said that Tokyo and Washington were getting ready to launch a sneak attack on New Palestine," said Jonny. "When he said the Alpha Rats were involved, I thought he was just spaceman-happy, like Zamora."

Conover laughed heartily at that. "Oh, that's delightful; they must have partially decoded one of the transmissions. The poor bastards don't have a clue."

"To what?" asked Jonny.

"That we are the Alpha Rats," said the smuggler lord.

Jonny turned on Conover, who casually flicked his gun up at Jonny's face. Jonny just ignored it. "I knew it," he told the lord. "It's all a ruse, isn't it? There never were any extraterrestrials. It's been the government all along using the

Alpha Rats as an excuse for the rationing programs and the damned war preparations."

"Bravo!" yelled Conover, clapping his left hand against the one holding the Futukoro. "Well done, Jonny. What remarkable deductive powers." He smiled apologetically. "Of course, you're wrong on most of it. But it was a good try. Keep moving and I'll straighten you out." Before they continued, Conover lit another Sherman, the flame on his lighter briefly illuminating the wreckage of his face. He had developed a slight tic in the cracked skin under one eye. His lips were moist and slack. Getting thin, thought Jonny as the smuggler lord nudged him up the stairs.

"Of course there are Alpha Rats," Conover told him. "Do you really think the Tokyo Alliance would put itself in such a dangerous economic position intentionally? The extraterrestrials' ship crashed on the moon fifteen years ago. Yes, crashed. They're dead, you see. All the Alpha Rats on board. It was a plague ship, son, on auto-pilot, packed full of dead Alpha Rats.

"Think about it, Jonny. The odds are staggering. The Alpha Rats drifting through empty space for god knows how long, getting caught in the moon's gravity and crashing there. I don't think that it would be far-fetched to think that in some way they were sent there for us to find. We're just lucky a Canadian team got to the site first. If the Arabs had made it, they would have discovered what we did; eventually, they would have analyzed it and figured out how it worked."

"The layered virus," Jonny said. He stumbled on loose carpet, felt Conover's gun in his back before he found his footing.

"See? Your history's not so bad," said Conover. "Of course, what killed the Alpha Rats had very little resemblance to NATO's layered virus, but it was during the early research we did on the bodies of the Alpha Rats, breaking down the genetic structure of the plague that killed them, that we finally found the key on how to make the damned thing work."

"Funny," said Jonny. "I thought for a while that maybe you'd gotten some surplus virus juice from somebody and decided to let it loose in L.A. so you could peddle the cure through us dealers."

"You think too small, Jonny. I keep telling you: You're in

business, but you're not a businessman. This is government work, boy. Multinational dollars."

"But all the rationing for all these years, that was a put-on, wasn't it? Keep the Pentagon fat and happy."

"Yes and no. After the Alpha ship was loaded, we couldn't very well have people trampling all over the moon. The local military authorities took the opportunity to burn the Arab bases and mining operations. Naturally, we had to take out a few of our own to make it look good, but the circumlunar labs are still operating. You didn't know that, did you? Yes, that's where the Alpha Virus was synthesized. All we did was blow up a few non-essential orbiters and dress the ones we needed with debris from the surface."

"So the government's got their virus and their war. What do you get out of this?"

"Freedom. From this," said Conover, touching his chest. "They're going to give me a new body, Jonny. With the government's bankroll I can leave this place and not have to worry about territory disputes or watered-down drugs or the rabid dogs that run this city breathing down my neck."

"They must have given you a bundle for releasing that virus," said Jonny.

"Not at all. Raquin, as the Colonel no doubt told you, was working for the Committee. He stole the virus from me to turn over to the Colonel, but before he had the chance, Easy stole it from Raquin. No, son, I'm afraid what Washington is paying me for has nothing to do with releasing the Alpha Virus. I'm being paid to deliver you." Conover sighed. "I was hoping you might figure this part out on your own. That's why I set up that little game with *Blue Boy* and the cases of Mad Love. I thought maybe if you knew who I was, you'd see some of this coming. Maybe I'm getting eccentric in my old age. Playing too many games. After a century or so it's easy to forget how ordinary people think. And it was probably too much to expect of you with all you've had on your mind lately." They came around a sharp turn and started up another flight of stairs. Along one wall was a stained-glass fresco depicting men in armor carrying Christian banners into battle. Why would you put that in a stairway with no lights? Jonny wondered. "You going to tell me why the Federales want me, or should I just assume it's my magnetic personality?" he asked the smuggler lord.

"Actually, they'd prefer your grandmother, but she disappeared years ago. Then, when your mother OD'd in Mexico City, it left you as heir-apparent to the throne," explained Conover. "See, your grandmother was a child of the streets, much like you and your friends. She sold blood, breathed polluted air for pay in university experiments, you know the routine. Then, in 1995, she volunteered for a series of injections at UCLA. Of course, she didn't know it was one of the Defense Department's genetic warfare projects. The school told her they were testing a new hepatitis vaccine.

"Tokyo and Washington were still thinking of war strictly in terms of atomic weapons back then. Some Pentagon bright-boy had the idea that through bio-engineering he could increase the general population's tolerance to certain wavelengths of radiation. Like the rest of the Pentagon's programs, it eventually ran out of money, but not before your grandmother and a few other volunteers had been doped with an experimental retrovirus.

"The actual synthesis of the bug was done at a Navy lab in the Philippines. Essentially, the virus is just a simple chain of single-function molecular assemblers, microscopic factories, really. The retrovirus went for your grandmother's bone marrow like a kid to candy, releasing the nanoassemblers. In the end, they produced what amounted to a radiation-proof antibody bonded right to her red blood cells.

"But, as I said, the project went broke. The subjects were paid off with whatever money was left and dismissed. Having come from the streets, your grandmother and the others returned to the streets. The government had no way to keep track of any of them."

"And now the Federales think because my *abuela* had lead in her veins that something in my blood is the cure for the layered virus?" Jonny asked.

"Apparently so."

"Then if there is no cure, why the hell did you let me go to Little Tokyo after Easy Money?" Jonny shouted. "What were you setting me up for?"

"Oh yes, Easy," said Conover. He looked tired; the junk flesh around his eyes was drawn and brittle. "Well, I couldn't take a chance on Nimble Virtue finding out what she had. It was a second batch of the virus, of course. Ricos had orders to kill her and Easy when she turned it over."

"Beautiful. Fucking beautiful," Jonny mumbled. "Then I'm it as far as this cure goes? I mean, with all of the government's resources, they couldn't come up with one other person connected with those tests?"

"It's been a long time, Jonny. Records get lost; disks get erased. When you ran away from the state school as a boy, they were sure they'd lost contact with the program for good. Then you turned up on the Committee. You couldn't hide that blood from them for long."

Jonny laughed mirthlessly. "Serves me right."

At the top of the stairs, they came out into an immense geodesic solarium. Through the bulletproof glass, Jonny could make out the tattered edge of the HOLLYWOOD sign, and the crawling neon of the movie district below. Overhead, the moon was obscured by billowing waves of sand, like hordes of locusts moving across the sky.

"You know, Mister Conover, you really piss me off," Jonny said. "I mean, I expect this kind of chickenshit behavior from Nimble Virtue, but I thought you were my friend."

"I am your friend, Jonny. Understand, there's nothing personal in any of this."

"Right, I know. Don't tell me. It's business. Economics— it always is."

"You're looking for someone to blame again," Conover said. "I told you once: life's more complicated than cowboy and Indian movies. You think the Arabs wouldn't use the virus if they had the opportunity? Or your friends the Croakers? What if Groucho had a weapon like this?"

"You know what's funny?" Jonny asked. "What's really funny is even though you're telling me all this now, I keep thinking that maybe I'm hearing it wrong. I keep thinking, 'Maybe Mister Conover got sucked into this deal by mistake, just like everybody else.' But that's not how it is, is it?" Outside the solarium was a sculpture garden. Jonny could make out smooth Greek marbles and Indian bronzes laid out along the severe geometry of Victorian flower beds. "When we were driving out to Santa Monica to pick up your dope from those Gobernación boys, I asked you about the new leprosy. You just laughed and told me you hadn't had a cold in forty years. But it wasn't until a few days ago that the Croakers found out that the layered virus was attached to a cold bug. That means you knew all along exactly what this virus was, which means you've been lying to me ever since this mess got started. Or was it just another clue in your game? Am I supposed to be flattered that you decided to fuck with my head all this time?" His voice was growing shrill; he took a step toward the lord.

Conover nodded toward the statues. "Come outside. I want you to see the garden before we leave."

"Fuck you, old man."

Conover casually raised the Futukoro a few centimeters. "Jonny, consider that, from my point of view, the simplest thing for me would be to shoot you and put your body on ice until my ride arrives. But I'm giving you a chance to stay alive. These people don't want to hurt you, they just need your blood."

"How are you going to get us to the desert, man? The roads between here and New Hope are gonna be full of Committee boys and gangs. You can't fly over it; a hovercar can't make it that far."

"There's no reason to go to the desert," said Conover tiredly. "There's nothing out there. New Hope is on the moon, safe and out of harm's way. That structure in the desert is little more than a grandiose movie set. This is Hollywood, boy. A crew from CineMex put it together for us. It might have blown the Alpha Rats' image if the general public knew about all that old money sitting right next door."

Jonny took a deep breath. Between the tequila and the bombs Conover kept dropping on him, he could hardly see straight. "Ever since Zamora asked me to turn you, I've been trying to figure out who was lying to me and who was telling the truth. Now I find out that you're the only one who was lying. Everybody else, including Nimble Virtue and that sheik, was telling me whatever part of the truth they knew. That situation never even crossed my mind."

"Don't be such a pussy, Gordon," said a gravelly voice from the garden. "Come outside and have a drink."

Jonny looked at Conover. "That makes the evening perfect," he said. The smuggler lord shrugged.

"I couldn't realistically keep the Colonel out of it forever," said Conover apologetically.

"Of course he couldn't," said Colonel Zamora from the doorway to the sculpture garden. "I've got contacts in government circles, too, you know. I put enough of it together to see what Conover was up to."

Jonny followed Zamora out to the garden. Conover fol-
lowed. A light scrim supported by a network of poles sheathed
in some light-absorbing material kept out most of the blowing
sand; the scrim fluttered in the storm, beating like the wings
of grounded birds. "You're an asshole, Colonel," Jonny said.

"And you got funny eyes, kid." Zamora set down his
drink. Jonny tensed, ready to intercept the blow he knew
would come—but the Colonel just smiled at him. "You
should be nice to me, Gordon. We're partners now."

"Did you have your brains surgically removed or some-
thing?" Jonny asked. "Don't you know this guy's talking
about war?"

"You think I don't know about war, Gordon?" The Colonel
went to a portable teak bar, poured amber liquid into a glass
and brought it back to Jonny. "After tonight, with Conover
gone and the gangs squashed, I'll own this city. Take a look
down there," the Colonel said, steering Jonny to the edge of
the roof.

The Hollywood Hills fell away sharply from Conover's
mansion, forming a featureless black lake whose shore was a
million burning lights. Straight ahead was Hollywood and the
translucent tent where Jonny had once lived. Off to the right
was the business district, Lockheed's glowing torus and the all
but invisible silicon sphere of Sony International. Jonny
glanced back at Conover and caught him tying off with a
length of green surgical tubing, a loaded syringe in his other
shaky hand.

"Listen," said Colonel Zamora.

Jonny turned back to the lights. He could not hear it at first
above the hissing of the falling sand, and when he did hear it,
it was as an echo. Faint backslap of an explosion from below.
His ears, having found the sound, could identify other explo-
sions, the garbled reverberations of amplified voices barking
stern warnings in several languages.

Zamora was resting his elbows on the top of the low garden
wall. "You think I don't know about war?" he asked. "I've
lived in this city all my life. I eat, drink, sleep, and shit war."
Jonny looked at the man and would have laughed, had he not
been so sure the Colonel was absolutely serious.

Jonny walked to the bar and set down his drink, un-
touched. Conover was resting against the base of a bronze of
Shiva (face lost in the Destroyer's shadow), green surgical

tubing dangling from one hand, the Futukoro from the other, breathing deeply as the Greenies came on. Something moved by a ripped section of scrim at the far end of the roof. Jonny moved back to the garden wall, not wanting to be in the open if it was one of Conover's sentry robots.

"It's the end of your world down there, Gordon."

"That's what Conover keeps telling me," Jonny said.

"Don't get me wrong, the gangs were ballsy bastards, especially the Croakers," Zamora said. "But they're a bunch of romantic idiots. Junkies with zip guns and rocks cannot stand up to a well-organized fighting unit like the Committee."

"Really, Pere Ubu, if you keep talking like that I'm going to think you're an idiot, and what fun is it beating an idiot?" There was a crackle of Futukoro fire from down below, as from the top of the scrim a crystal geko fell and burst into a fountain of flame, spewing a stream of fish, flowers, birds, and all five of the Platonic solids straight up into the air. Sections of the netting burst into guttering flame where the fountain touched it, the wind and sand blowing down on the garden through widening holes.

"What would you say if I told you your boys were going to lose tonight?" The voice came from right behind them, low on the garden wall. Crouching there all in black, Futukoro in hand, Groucho flashed Jonny a quick smile. "Told you I'd come if I could. Besides, I thought you might have run off again. Glad to see you didn't."

"Me too," said Jonny.

Zamora half-turned in Groucho's grip, gazing up at the anarchist good-humoredly. "Nice stunt, kid, but you aren't going to win this thing with card tricks."

"I'm not worried about the Committee right now, Ubu," said Groucho, hopping lightly off the wall. "I'm here for you."

"I see. And this is the part where I fall apart and see the error of my evil wasted life?" Zamora laughed. "Come on, kid, wise up. In the morning I'm going to be running this town. You want to make a deal?"

"You guys are just full of deals, aren't you?" Groucho said.

"Come on, Groucho, figure it out. Everybody does exactly what they have to to get the job done. Now what do you want? A piece of the city for the Croakers? A cut of the drug action? You can have it."

"It's not enough," said the anarchist. "We are the revolt of the spirit humiliated by your works. We live on our dreams. We can't settle for anything less than everything."

Zamora shrugged and leaned against the garden wall. "Then you're dead."

"Admit it, Colonel: It's over," said Groucho.

"Boy, it's never over."

Zamora's old lizard flesh was fast. He moved to the right, feinting a back knuckle to the head, and drove a knee up at the anarchist's midsection. Groucho, however, was faster. He slipped the Colonel's kick and swept his foot, knocking Zamora onto his back. Jonny saw Conover then, emerging from Shiva's gloom. "Down!" he yelled, but the anarchist was already falling, Conover's Futukoro still smoking as he emerged into the light.

By the time Jonny got there, Zamora was on his feet, rubbing at one uniformed shoulder. Groucho's eyes were wide, bubbles fringing an exit wound in his chest, matching his breathing. Groucho gripped Zamora's trouser leg, not recognizing the man. "I am here by the will of the people," he said, "and I will not leave until I get my raincoat back." The bubbles on his chest were smaller and fewer each time they appeared. Gradually, they disappeared altogether.

He stopped moving. Zamora bent and pried the anarchist's hand from his trouser leg. "Nickel and dime asshole," the Colonel mumbled. "Didn't have a clue."

Zamora started back to the bar. Jonny calmly took Nimble Virtue's Derringer from his pocket and blew off the back of the Colonel's head. Zamora stiffened as the hollow point hit. Then he collapsed, a solid reptilian waterfall of flesh, joints loosening from the ankles up.

Conover was on Jonny before he had a chance to move. "That's all, son. It's over," the smuggler lord said, and touched his gun to the base of Jonny's spine. "It's time to go." Conover pulled him away from the bodies, directing him to the far edge of the garden where a set of wrought-iron stairs wound down to the bare hillside. At the top of the stairs, Jonny looked back. The scrim was no longer burning, but large black-rimmed holes allowed the sand through. It was

squalling in great gusts all over the garden, already beginning
to cover the bodies of the dead anarchist and Colonel Zamora.
Jonny walked down the metal stairs and started off across the
pale scrub grass, Conover right behind him.

They walked with the storm to their backs. To their left,
part of the city was on fire.

Jonny's ears became quickly accustomed to the steady rat-
tle of far-off gunfire. The explosions seemed to take on a
strange rhythm of their own, playing counterpoint to his foot-
steps. Black smoke from the burning buildings was whipped
up by the Santa Ana winds; mixing with the blowing sand, the
smoke closed over the city, taking on the appearance of a solid
structure, as if Jonny were seeing the lights through the walls
of a dirty terrarium. Hovercars cut back and forth through the
mist like glowing wasps.

They walked for some time without speaking. Then Con-
over said: "Down the hill here." Scrambling through the net-
tles and fallen branches, they eventually hit a rise and Jonny
saw the rusted skeleton of the dome, the grimy white walls.
He knew then that they were headed for Griffith Observatory.
Years before, after a seven-point quake that had dropped most
of Malibu below sea level, the observatory's corroded dome
had fallen in on itself like the shell of a rotten egg. Since then,
various religious groups had claimed the place, performing
secret rites in the husk of the old building under the full moon.

Scattered through the courtyard of the old observatory in
rough concentric circles were shrines to dead technology, use-
less mementos of the collective unconscious of the city. The
gear box from a gasoline-powered vehicle; a German food
processor; a Nautilus exercise machine; pelvic X-rays of for-
gotten movie stars; piles of pornographic video cassettes,
dressing dummies, and primitive Japanese tube televisions.

Jonny left Conover's side and touched the yellowed keys of
an ancient upright piano. It had been outside for so long that
the lacquer was coming off it in great chocolate ribbons, re-
vealing the weathered grain of some badly warped wood be-
neath. Jonny hit a chord, and to his surprise, the thing still
worked. He picked out a one-fingered melody, his off-key
singing masked by the sour notes of the out-of-tune piano.

"I went down to Saint James Infirmary
Saw my sweetheart there
Stretched out on a long white table,
so pale, so cold, so fair
I went down to Saint James Infirmary—"

"Come on," called Conover, "let's get out of this storm." He gestured at the open doors of the observatory with the Futukoro.

A few steps inside the high-vaulted chamber, Jonny was swallowed up by absolute darkness. It was like walking down the gullet of some enormous animal, he thought. He breathed the hot air (sour with the reek of oxidizing metal) deeply, relaxing in his sudden blindness. Since leaving Sumi, Jonny had refused to let his exteroceptors see for him in any but the most ordinary way. He felt comfortable in the darkness of the observatory because he had been waiting for it; it or something just like it. He had not felt the same since the gun had failed to kill him in the clinic. He understood then that he was still waiting for the bullet he had been denied. Each time he turned around, Jonny expected to see Conover raising the Futukoro to firing position. But it did not happen.

There were things hanging from the ceiling of the observatory. They rang softly, like the tinkling of small bells or wind chimes. Occasionally, a tiny flash would catch his eye. Something cool touched Jonny's face. He batted it with the back of his hand, and it swung away in the darkness. A few steps further, he bumped into a narrow railing that circled a sunken section of the floor, and waited there for Conover.

The smuggler lord came into the observatory, his head cocked to one side as if listening for something. It occurred to Jonny for the first time that Conover might be insane. What proof had the lord offered him of rich people slumming on the moon, or dead extraterrestrials? Just some fairy tale about his grandmother renting out her blood. Not having contracted the layered virus meant nothing. Luck or natural resistance could account for that, Jonny told himself. There were a lot of people left in the city who were not infected.

However, if Conover were insane, he might insist that they wait in the observatory for his spaceship all night. It seemed pretty likely to Jonny that a structure this size would eventually attract fire from below.

And if Conover is insane, he thought, what will he do when his spaceship doesn't arrive?

Outside, the sandstorm was slacking off. Through gaps in the twisted metal of the dome, Jonny could see the pale curve of the moon. He thought of the celebration in the city, disrupted now by gunfire. The Day of the Dead. Illuminated in the weak moonlight, Jonny finally saw the room in which he was standing, and decided that if Conover was not crazy, whoever had rebuilt the observatory was.

A bank of ultra-sensitive photo-cells ringed the ceiling above a parabolic mirror cradled in a steel lattice nest; the structure supporting the mirror had been bolted beneath a section of dome open to the sky. When the pale lunar light came down through the fallen girders, the walls began to flicker; gears shifted ponderously underground and a dozen blurry moons suddenly circumscribed the room. Video images, three meters tall; old NASA footage Jonny remembered from his childhood. Car mirrors suspended from the ceiling on nylon lines picked up the pale images, flashing them back and forth like cratered stars. Narrow rows of low-voltage track lights shone through prisms and beam-splitters, bathing the highest parts of the room in tentative rainbows.

"It's wonderful, isn't it? Absolute madness," Conover said. A brightly painted Virgin Mary, part plaster of Paris and part ancient electronic gear, revolved on a creaking turntable—a technocratic moon goddess.

"You've been here before?" asked Jonny.

"Many times. I come here to think." In the wasted gray video light, Jonny thought Conover looked like one of the masked dancers from the procession below. The smuggler lord pointed to a spot in the southern hemisphere of one of the video moons. "In case you're interested, this is where we're headed. A Japanese station a few clicks to the west of Tycho."

Jonny slumped back against the rail. "Mister Conover, there's no spaceship coming here tonight."

"Of course there is. We're going to Seven Rose Base."

"Bullshit. All that's going to happen is we're going to hang around here till somebody decides to put a mortal shell through the wall."

Conover shook his head, smiled indulgently at Jonny.

"Don't go thinking I've lost my mind, dear boy. The fact is, I haven't let you in on all my reasons for wanting to get to the moon."

Jonny opened his eyes in mock surprise. "Oh, gosh, then you haven't been absolutely straight with me? I'm really hurt, Mister Conover."

"What would you say if I told you we have had contact with the Alpha Rats directly?"

"I thought you said they were dead."

"The ones on the ship were, yes. But I mean others."

"Other Alpha Rats? Where?"

"Ah, so now you're interested." The smuggler lord walked along the curving edge of the chamber, passing before each of the twelve grainy moonscapes. Earth's shadow followed him, leaving each video panel dark as he moved beyond it. "They've spoken to us, Jonny. From a ship, maybe an orbital broadcasting station. Three words, clear as day. Three words repeated three times. Once in English, once in Japanese, and once in Arabic."

"Wait, I think I know this joke. They said 'Send more Chuck Berry,' right?"

Conover waited before one of the screens, time-lapse dawn bursting over his shoulder. "They said: 'We are coming.'"

Jonny looked down at his hands, and found dried blood on the backs of his knuckles. His stomach fluttered. He rubbed the knuckles on his jeans. "That's it?" he asked.

"Isn't that enough?"

Jonny shrugged. 'Well, I mean, I don't want to rain on your parade or anything, but so what? They're coming. What does that get you?"

"A chance," Conover said. "One last chance for something new. You can't imagine what it feels like living on pure reflex, half awake, but still functioning. And then something jars you conscious and you realize that another five years have passed but it doesn't mean anything because the next five will be exactly the same as the ones that preceded it."

Jonny nodded. "So basically you're fucking over everybody because you're bored."

The smuggler lord grinned. "Well, if you choose to look at it that way—"

"I do," Jonny said.

"I'm sorry to hear that." Conover stepped away from the videos. "Still, there's not much to be done about it."

"Sure there is," Jonny said, leaping the handrail to the sunken observatory floor. "Kill me now."

"Don't be an ass."

Jonny went to the slowly revolving Virgin Mary, took hold of something by her feet, and came away with a meter-long piece of heavy chrome pipe. He held it before him, testing the balance in his hands, then went to Conover. "Come on, fucker. Kill me."

The smuggler lord held the Futukoro before him, but did not point it at Jonny. "You're being an idiot."

Jonny swung the pipe like a baseball bat, circling the lord on the floor of the dim chamber. "Shoot me. Shoot me or I'll cave your goddam head in."

"I might just have to do it, Jonny."

"Go ahead." He swung the pipe wide, letting the smuggler lord jump out of the way.

"Stop this right now," Conover said. Jonny swung again, forcing the lord back on his heels.

"I knew it!" Jonny yelled. "I'm not worth anything to you dead, am I? They don't want me if I'm dead. All that stuff about giving me a chance to stay alive was just another line. If I'm dead, you haven't got anything to trade for your new skin, have you?" He swung the pipe at the lord's head.

"You're acting like a child—"

"Then shoot me!"

"No!"

This time Jonny connected, snapping his wrists down, driving the end of the pipe into Conover's shoulder. The smuggler lord gasped and dropped to his knees. Jonny threw the pipe, rolled under the circular railing and headed for the door. Futukoro shots hissed past his ear, bringing mirrors and bits of pulverized marble down on his head. He darted to the left, more shots followed him, cutting off his way to the door.

Conover was on his feet, heaving himself over the railing. The smuggler lord kept sweeping the room with the Futukoro as he pressed his back to each of the observatory's doors, grinding them closed over a thin layer of sand.

"Where are you going to go, Jonny?" Conover yelled. "Your friends are gone. It can be a bad place out there when you're all alone."

Jonny kept to the floor behind a gutted exhibit case, barely breathing. He watched the smuggler lord walk back to the sunken center of the chamber, gun in his hand. "Come on out, son. This is insane," Conover said. "We're both going to lose this way." Jonny cut his fingers picking up a wedge of glass from the wrecked case. Moving into a crouch, he waited for the smuggler lord to get into just the right position, and threw the glass edge-first across the room, scrambling for the door at the same time.

He knew it was a lost cause within three steps. The pounding of his heavy boots gave him away. Conover turned away for a fraction of a second when the glass hit, but snapped his gun back the instant Jonny began his run. Jonny heard the smuggler lord's gun go off twice.

"Consider that I don't have to kill you, son. A shot through each kneecap will keep you still until the ship arrives."

Jonny was lying in the shadows, in the dirt, hands crabbed at the edges of worn floor tiles. One side of his face was hot and wet where shrapnel, fragmented marble, or wood from the door had slashed his cheek. His mind was a blank. He watched Conover move about the center of the chamber, keeping to the light. For a moment, when consciousness imposed itself upon him, he felt his will drain away. He did not understand why he was running so hard from death when it was what he had been looking for all along. He pressed his back against the wall.

Clinging is not acceptable, he reminded himself. Clinging to anything, including life (or death), was the sign of a weak mind. One of the floor tiles came loose in his hand.

Anger; greed; folly. Hearing the words in his mind, he almost laughed. They had been the cornerstones of his existence, as had illusion. Before he had left her, Jonny's roshi had told him to picture himself as a man crossing a river, moving from one slippery rock to the next, knowing that each step could send him plunging into the rapids.

Moving from illusion to illusion, he'd assumed he had found himself. Now he was not so sure. Perhaps, he thought, he had just found more illusions.

Conover was moving in slow circles before the video screens. Jonny froze where he was, watched the smuggler lord scanning the room. When Conover's gaze moved over and beyond him, Jonny sat up, throwing the floor tile high, watching it spin and shatter the parabolic mirror at the top of the chamber. The lord covered his head as the glass came down on him, firing wildly, tearing up the ceiling and the edges of the room. The muzzle flash from the Futukoro lit him like a broken strobe as the video moonscapes went dark at his back. When Conover stopped shooting, the room was quiet and very dark. Belly to the floor, Jonny could feel the underground gears winding down. He blinked once. Shapes became solid in the gloom.

Then he was up, his body moving by itself, one foot coming down on the circular rail, the other swinging over, whole body hanging for an instant in midair, unprotected meat, house of illusions, hate, and fear. Conover was below, slow-motion turning, Jonny's new exteroceptors showing the man as a brilliant neon scarecrow with holes in his face.

And then he hit, driving Conover hard into the floor. Jonny hauled him up, holding the wrist that held the gun, so close to the man that when his breath hesitated for a moment, Jonny felt the absence of it on his face.

Something happened then.

Sand whispered down through the roof and the moon emerged from a bank of clouds. Conover looked up. Bathed in the milky light, his face went slack, hung on his cheeks like melting putty. The bird-thin arms fell to his sides, and when the smuggler lord looked at him, for the first time Jonny glimpsed the true face of the man.

It had cost him his eyes to see it. Groucho had had an inkling of it, but had died without a look; Ice and Sumi had been spared it; no junkie or leper would have suspected it. Zamora had recognized its essence immediately, was drawn to it, but had probably never seen the thing itself. Only Jonny, with secondhand eyes stolen from some rich man's gaudy toy, would ever know the smuggler lord's true face.

Blank.

Without expression.

A Halloween spook; a candy skull, dead as the hills when the brush fires claimed them; dead as the sailor in the boiler room of a sunken ship, skull fused to the melted plating of her hull.

There was nothing else he could do. He moved the hand with the gun under Conover's chin. The smuggler lord never took his hand from the weapon, never tried to struggle. Sand fell on their shoulders. When Jonny looked into the other man's eyes and saw his own, he understood their common desire.

Jonny decided to make him a gift of it. And pulled the trigger.

It had not occurred to Jonny that he was not breathing. The kick of the gun triggered a spasm in his lungs and he sucked in a long breath, tasting ozone and the fear smell of his own sweat. Conover's body went down lightly, seemingly without weight, as if, in those last few seconds of life, the smuggler lord had used up everything he was.

Jonny was shaking all over, covered in blood and filth. He crawled under the railing and scraped open the doors. Stepping outside, he stood for some minutes in the falling sand, rubbing it into his face and arms, letting it rasp away the stink of death and illusions.

Later, as he was wandering among the circular shrines in the courtyard of the observatory, Jonny saw something skimming low and fast over the tops of the hills. At first he thought it might be a hovercar flying without its running lights, but as the craft got closer he could tell that it was much too big for that. From what Jonny could see of its outline, it appeared to have the razor-edged fuselage and stubby graphite-composite wings of a Daimyo vacuum shuttle. Something prickled along his spine. There would be a bigger ship up there, he knew, waiting just beyond the cloud layer—

The shuttle came down low over the observatory and leveled off, circling the ruin, a matte-black scavenger. From its belly extended shafts of metallic blue light, sensitive fingers probing the body of the dead building. Jonny hunkered down behind the pile of Sony televisions, listening to the ship's engines whine in the overheated air. It was waiting for something. A signal? he wondered. But the man who would have signaled it was dead on his back, fifty meters away.

After more than a dozen passes, the hum of the shuttle's engines took a sudden jump in frequency, the fingers of light disappearing one by one, leaving the observatory dark. Veering off down the hill, the ship banked sharply to the left and started a rapid climb back the way it had come. Jonny crawled to the edge of the pile of televisions to watch the firing of the shuttle's engines: twin stars. A couple of hovercars detached themselves from formation over Hollywood and buzzed up the hill behind the larger ship, firing their banks of heat-seeking missiles.

The shuttle disappeared from the far side of the hills. The flash of the explosion bleached the sky bone-white before the sound hit him. It rolled like distant thunder, over the hills and on into the city. The hovercars turned off and headed back to Hollywood, merging into the mass of lights that was Los Angeles.

Below, the city was burning. The wind had changed direction; the sand was coming down harder, but behind it was a hint of rain. Jonny wondered if the weather patterns would ever stablize. He removed the bottom panel from the front of the old piano and crawled inside. Something exploded on Sunset Boulevard below. Sizzling fireworks and a choir of hologram angels, enormous lavender lizards, skulls, women's shoes, dice, and playing cards rose from the flames, glowed mad and beautiful, spiraled, screamed, clawed at the buildings, and finally faded into the sky.

The city burned all night.

_ EPILOGUE _____

THE UNCONSCIOUSNESS OF THE LANDSCAPE
BECOMES COMPLETE _____

THE CITY WAS INSIDE HIM, its windblown streets and alleys as much a part of him as the air he breathed, the blood in his veins. What roots he had were sunk deep in its hard soil. It formed the walls and foundation of his soul, a thing of which he possessed little knowledge, but which he had lately begun to consider.

He would never leave the city behind.

Los Angeles lay white and still beneath the sun. The winds that had carried in the sand were now blowing smoke from the smoldering buildings out to sea, leaving the sky a nearly unblemished dome of aquamarine. In the distance, Watts and Silver Lake seemed to still be burning. However, since dawn a crystalline calmness had invaded the city. It happened as the sun rose, shimmering off the centimeters of desert sand that covered every flat surface. The light gave Los Angeles the pure, hard look of a newly minted coin or surgical instrument.

Jonny spotted the first refugees just before daybreak. A small group of them were making their way over the nearby hills, heading for the Ventura Freeway and parts north. Later, he spotted hundreds of people following the highways out of Hollywood. At first he had wondered where they were all going, but as he asked the question, the answer seemed obvious.

Anywhere else.

The revolution was done. From what a young Zombie Analytic girl told him, the Croakers had won. In a sense. "They're not in control of the city, but neither's the Committee, so I guess they won," she said. "They won or they lost in such a way that the Committee can't win. Take your pick."

By noon the hills were full of refugees, winding in ragged lines around the observatory and the HOLLYWOOD sign. Many people were still wearing their costumes from the night before. In the bright sun, newsrag skeletons were hardly more menacing than the flat-footed Meat Boys, hookers, and merchants who followed.

No more fighting, Jonny thought. Let them have it. Let them try to rule an empty city.

"What's so funny, Jonny?"

He had not realized that he was laughing out loud. Easy Money stood a few meters away within the ring of circular shrines, pale and filthy, shielding his eyes from the sun. The arm he had injured at the Forest of Incandescent Bliss was wrapped in tangled layers of dirty gauze.

"That's going to get infected," Jonny said.

"I tanked up on ampicillin in Little Tokyo," Easy replied. There was a subtle irregularity in skin color of the arm he was using to shield his eyes, a burning or mottling. It could be anything, Jonny thought. He looked for other signs of the virus, but under all that dirt there was no way to be sure.

"So, like I said, 'What's so funny?'"

"Everything," Jonny said. "It's over, man. They killed us. We're dead and they can't hurt us anymore."

"You know the Committee's still holding parts of the city? They've sent for the Army."

"Let them. You can't shoot ghosts and that's all that's left down there."

Easy Money lowered his hand and Jonny saw heavy bruising across the man's forehead where one of his horns had broken off. "You going back?"

Jonny shook his head. "Let the rats have it," he said. "You?"

"Where would I go?"

"There's lots of places."

Easy looked over his shoulder at the smoke and the sand. "No."

A dozen Mexican teenagers walked by, nylon athletic bags emblazoned with colorful corporate decals and backpacks full of clothes and food hanging from their shoulders. They were singing together, an ancient melody, low and steady like a hymn, wholly unselfconscious. They were moving against the general flow of traffic, heading south and, Jonny knew, home. When they moved out of earshot, he found himself missing their song.

Easy was pointing at something. "You planning to use that or what?"

Jonny looked down at his hand and found Conover's Futu-koro there. He had a vague memory of having sneaked back into the observatory during the night and taking the thing, though he could not remember why. Jonny looked at Easy. "It's gone a little beyond that, don't you think?" He shrugged. "Besides, I might miss your head and hit something important."

Easy smiled. "You are a classic, you know that? I'd have blown you away on sight."

"Maybe that's the difference between us. I don't have to kill you; you're doing that just fine by yourself."

"But I won't die an asshole."

"I don't know if either of us has much choice in that matter." Jonny laughed. "You know what I can't stop thinking about? Those poor ignorant idiots on the moon. Sitting up there thinking how safe they are from this little war they've dreamed up for us, not knowing about the little green men that are coming to see them. I mean, it's enough to make you think that maybe there is a God and that maybe the fucker has a sense of humor."

"I don't have the slightest idea what you're talking about, but that's okay," said Easy. "Seeing as how you're in such a good mood—you wouldn't happen to be holding, would you?"

"Got a lot of pain?"

"Think I cracked some ribs when I fell."

"That's rough." Jonny pulled one of his pockets inside out. "I seem to be all tapped out." Easy just nodded. "You might check Conover's place. His security's down for good and there's a room there stacked eyeball-high with Mad Love."

Easy shaded his eyes again, frowned at Jonny from under his arm. "Why you telling me about this?"

"'Cause I'm a right guy," said Jonny. "'Cause I'm Dragon-head-Snake-body, and I know that all thought is illusion, that any event in our lives, the worst and the best, can lead us toward enlightenment. Also, I don't really give a fuck."

"You're lost in space, man." Easy shook his head. "They're gonna come after you with nets and needles."

"Goodbye Easy."

"Adios, asshole."

Easy made his way awkwardly up the hill, limping on his clubfoot in the direction of Conover's place. Jonny watched him as the man followed the same squatter's trail Conover had led him down last night. It seemed a long time ago. The sun flashed off Easy's one remaining horn, then he was gone behind a stand of withered madrone.

Jonny stepped off the piano, weighing the Futukoro in his hand, marveling that at any other time in recent memory he would have given anything to have Easy Money and a loaded gun at the same time. The feeling was gone, all echoes now. He had moved on. To where, he was not sure. Jonny took off his jacket and wrapped the gun inside. Just before he dropped the bundle into the piano, something fell from one of the pockets.

He picked it up and rang it gently, remembering that Groucho had given him the small bell for luck in the deserted club. Jonny considered the notion of enlightenment.

Everybody he cared about was gone. Ice and Sumi, Random, Groucho, all dead. Yet he felt their presence strong within him. It was a corny sentiment, something you would read on a greeting card, and he would have dismissed it entirely if the feeling had not been so powerful, so genuine.

Enlightenment.

Jonny still did not know what it really meant, was certain it was not what he was feeling now. All he knew for certain was that although he did not feel good, in some odd way, he felt a hell of a lot better.

He held the bell in his left hand, letting it ring as he walked. The way to Ensenada would be a long one, so he sang himself through the city.

> "I went down to Saint James Infirmary
> saw my sweetheart there,
> Stretched out on a long white table,
> so pale, so cold, so fair.
> I went down to Saint James Infirmary—"

ACE
SCIENCE FICTION
SPECIALS

Under the brilliant editorship of Terry Carr, the award-winning <u>Ace Science Fiction Specials</u> were <u>the</u> imprint for literate, quality sf.

Now, once again under the leadership of Terry Carr, <u>The New Ace SF Specials</u> have been created to seek out the talents and titles that will lead science fiction into the 21st Century.

___ THE WILD SHORE Kim Stanley Robinson	88874-7/$3.50
___ NEUROMANCER William Gibson	56959-5/$2.95
___ IN THE DRIFT Michael Swanwick	35869-1/$2.95
___ THE HERCULES TEXT Jack McDevitt	37367-4/$3.50
___ THE NET Loren J. MacGregor	56941-2/$2.95

SCIENCE FICTION AT ITS BEST!

____ **THE CAT WHO WALKS THROUGH WALLS**
Robert A. Heinlein   0-425-09932-8 — $3.95

____ **TITAN**
John Varley   0-441-81304-6 — $3.95

____ **DUNE**
Frank Herbert   0-441-17266-0 — $4.50

____ **HERETICS OF DUNE**
Frank Herbert   0-425-08732-8 — $4.50

____ **GODS OF RIVERWORLD**
Philip José Farmer   0-425-09170-8 — $3.50

____ **THE MAN IN THE HIGH CASTLE**
Philip K. Dick   0-425-10143-6 — $2.95

____ **HELLICONIA SUMMER**
Brian W. Aldiss   0-425-08650-X — $3.95

____ **THE GREEN PEARL**
Jack Vance   0-441-30316-1 — $3.95

____ **DOLPHIN ISLAND**
Arthur C. Clarke   0-441-15220-1 — $2.95
